Peculiar FAITH

Queer
Theology
for
Christian
Witness

Unless otherwise noted, the Scripture quotations contained herein are from the New Revised Standard Version Bible, copyright © 1989 by the Division of Christian Education of the National Council of Churches of Christ in the U.S.A. Used by permission. All rights reserved.

Library of Congress Cataloging-in-Publication Data

Johnson, Jay Emerson.
  Peculiar faith : queer theology for Christian witness / Jay Emerson Johnson.
    pages cm
  Includes bibliographical references.
  ISBN 978-1-59627-250-7 (pbk.)—ISBN 978-1-59627-251-4 (ebook) 1. Queer theology.
2. Homosexuality--Religious aspects—Christianity. I. Title.
  BT83.65.J64 2014
  230.086'64—dc23
                                    2013047355

Seabury Books
19 East 34th Street
New York, New York 10016
www.churchpublishing.org

An imprint of Church Publishing Incorporated

Printed in the United States of America

Peculiar FAITH

Queer Theology for Christian Witness

JAY EMERSON JOHNSON

Seabury Books
NEW YORK

But ye are a chosen generation, a royal priesthood,
*   an holy nation, a peculiar people;*
*   that ye should shew forth the praises of him who hath*
*   called you*
*   out of darkness into his marvellous light.*

—1 Peter 2:9 (KJV)

I live and love in God's peculiar light.

—Michelangelo

Be who you were meant to be,
*   and you will set the world on fire.*

—Catherine of Siena

CONTENTS

PREFACE

*S*omething rather queer happens toward the end of the Gospel according to Luke. The newly resurrected Jesus joins two of his disciples traveling toward a village called Emmaus. The disciples, however, fail to recognize him until he joins them for an evening meal once they arrive to the village inn. There, sitting at table with his friends, Jesus breaks bread. In that moment the disciples at last realize who he is and, also at that very moment, he disappears (Luke 24:31). This story presents more than one reason for puzzlement, not least the disciples' inability to recognize their beloved companion. Equally peculiar, the abrupt ending short-circuits what we might otherwise expect from such a profound moment of reunion, which ought at the very least to include a joyful embrace. So this story does seem strange and perplexing. But does it qualify as *queer*?

"Queer" rarely appears on anyone's list of aesthetically pleasing words. Its linguistic history began by orbiting around the odd and unusual but eventually served more particularly to demean those whose sexual practices or gender expression deviated from societal expectations. That was in the early twentieth century. By the end of that same century "queer" had been reclaimed by political activists for movements of social change and by social theorists, who appropriated it to dismantle those very same gendered sexual identities that had rendered "queer" such a potent insult.

"Queer" thus poses a cultural riddle. How does a term soaked in derision eventually rally and even inspire those it derided? Helpful analogues for that riddle appear in the history of racial and ethnic epithets. But queer poses yet another puzzle: What does it really mean? Dictionaries tend to point first toward the eccentric and unconventional, or whatever falls outside expected norms and assumptions, as the meaning of queerness. Young children learn that definition with coloring books and the reward they reap for drawing inside the lines. All that queer space outside the lines have led some to use "queer" as shorthand for the many topics, concerns, and sensibilities associated with lesbian, gay, bisexual, and transgender (LGBT) people; others (mostly academic theorists) savor its potential to blur those strictly defined categories for human sexuality and gender. Putting Christian theology in relation to that same word poses more than a riddle. Many Christians would consider that conjunction scandalous and reject any suggestion that something so perverse can have anything to do with something so divine. Others (Christian or not) recoil at the prospect of locating queerness in a tradition that has so often been deployed to condemn LGBT people. I find these multiple meanings, ambiguities, and provocations rife with theological and spiritual insight.

As a white man living rather comfortably in the San Francisco Bay Area with a steady job and good friends, identifying as gay would seem the only thing about my life that others might find even remotely queer, except for something else. I also identify as Christian. Living openly as both gay *and* Christian certainly strikes some as a bit queer. But "gay" and "Christian" sitting comfortably side by side signals something deeper than learning how to reconcile my sexual self with my religious self. My Christian faith and spiritual practice have actually deepened and expanded over the years, not in spite of my gay life but *because* of it. That will strike many more as not only queer but nearly unintelligible.

Coming out as a gay man in my early twenties and in the conservative Christian subculture of the American Midwest proved challenging, not least for the experience of not fitting in where I thought I had belonged, in my hometown and in my own church. Moving to Berkeley, California, for graduate school proved just as challenging when I came out as Christian among my secular, antireligious friends. Both contexts presented the powerful temptation to conform by concealing something important about myself. Resisting that temptation generated life-changing questions: What does it mean to belong? How and why does one "fit in"? Where, finally, does one find or create a home?

Many others have asked similar questions for a variety of reasons over countless centuries, and I take those perennial questions as profoundly theological. When posed in the light of gendered sexual orientation, I take those theological questions still further, as carrying transformative potential for Christian witness in the world today. The transformation extends well beyond whether Christian churches can or should welcome self-identified LGBT people as members and as ordained ministers. To be sure, that remains an open question for some Christian communities, and I am convinced that only a robust theology of sexual intimacy will break the ecclesial stalemate created by that debate. I offered an approach to that theological task in *Divine Communion: A Eucharistic Theology of Sexual Intimacy* (Seabury, 2013). In that book I proposed a way to think biblically and theologically about the role erotic desire can and should play in the mission of the Church. In this book I want to invite reflection more particularly on LGBT-related sensibilities for a similarly broad purpose: to develop a queer theology for Christian witness.

Generally speaking, Christians tend to address sexuality as a matter of ethics, especially behavioral rules and guidelines, and to think about gender as reflecting a given biological feature of the human body. The histories, experiences, and relationships of LGBT people map a much richer terrain for both sexuality and gender, and therefore also for our bodily engagements with race, ethnicity, and class, and still further for our troubled relationships with other animals and with the planetary body of earth, our shared home. Exploring the queerly expansive features of this sexually gendered landscape invites and urges a fresh approach to Christian faith itself, not only for the sake of including LGBT people in Christian congregations but more broadly for the socially transformative witness of the Church. That witness transforms, not by remaining focused on sex and gender but by extending the reach of those bodily insights into all the socio-political and economic quandaries currently vexing the North Atlantic and indeed the whole planet.

Transforming society with Christian faith will seem strange and perhaps even queer to those who have grown accustomed to the interweaving of institutional Christianity and Western culture. More precisely, the legacy of associating mainstream American culture with church membership leads relatively few to look for world-changing resources in the patterns and cadences of Christian practice. Yet both biblical and later theological traditions would invite us to look again. The King James translation of 1 Peter 2:9, for example, refers to Christians as a "peculiar people." That early Christian writer might have recalled a similar declaration about the ancient Israelites, who were delivered from slavery in Egypt to become God's own "peculiar treasure" (Exodus 19:5 and Deuteronomy 14:2). Indeed, nearly every biblical account of divine encounter shimmers with a queerly peculiar character, which then sets the people of that encounter apart as peculiar themselves. As biblical writers likewise insisted, God sets people apart not for the sake of privilege but for service, to live as a "light to the nations," as Isaiah described it (49:6), and as "leaven" in the loaf, as Luke's Jesus urged (13:20–21).

Can Christian faith still qualify as peculiar today? What would it mean and what it would look like to "live and love in God's peculiar light," as Michelangelo once described his own life in the sixteenth century? Do Christians imagine that their faith will set "the world on fire," as Catherine of Siena hoped in the fourteenth century? If so, how might this peculiar faith inspire and inform movements of social transformation for the common good? In 2003 I began experimenting with an approach to these questions in the classes I have been privileged to teach at Pacific School of Religion and the Graduate Theological Union. I am grateful to many insightful students whose questions and observations contributed to the evolution of those classes and the content of this book. I am grateful as well for wide-ranging theological conversations with colleagues and friends, punctuated with more than a little humor and often in hotel bars late into the night during academic conferences. Some of the notes I scribbled on cocktail napkins during those conversations found their way into these pages. My gratitude for these insightful interlocutors should not, of course, imply their endorsement of what I offer here; the conversations will need to continue, just as theological reflection itself never finally ends—or rather, each theological end is to begin anew.

As Luke would have it, what ends with crucifixion does not merely reappear restored. Resurrection declares and presents the unrecognizably new, even as traces of the familiar remain. I read Luke's Emmaus road story that way, not only as a hopeful vision but also as a cautionary tale. Theology, much less God, will not reside comfortably in timeless ideological systems or time-honored institutional structures. In the moment of stable recognition, when what we long for finally appears, it vanishes. Still more, the startled disciples themselves refuse to stay put in Emmaus, not even long enough to finish the meal that had only just begun. They could have stayed right there at the inn. Given the history of religious traditions, we might imagine those disciples not only staying there in Emmaus but declaring that village inn a shrine, erecting a plaque on the very spot where Jesus broke bread, and devising institutional mechanisms for its maintenance and upkeep. Instead, and at "the same hour," as Luke writes, those disciples took to the road again, eager to share life-changing news.

Queer theology for Christian witness finds its animating energy in the search for a place to belong and to fit in, to find a home. That same energy will keep Christians perpetually restless, never fully satisfied with the theological and institutional artifacts created by our hope. Many Christian churches today recognize in this present moment, however, a bit more than institutional dissatisfaction. A rapidly changing world has led many to question the meaning and significance of Christian faith itself. Twenty-first-century circumstances lend novel texture to such questions, but their contours stretch back to the first century. Christians have always lived with post-Emmaus restlessness, and still do. I believe that restless energy of hope can launch a transformative journey once again, just as it has done many times before and among widely diverse communities in far-reaching times and places. No one can say with any certainty where today's road after Emmaus will lead. Like so many who have come before us, we have no detailed map to guide us on the journey; but also like them, we do have something in the wake of the vanishing Jesus—or rather, some*one*.

Luke did not conclude his account of the Gospel with Emmaus. The road on which those disciples embarked from that village led to Jerusalem and eventually to Pentecost, which in turn inspired Luke to write Part Two of his account: the Acts of the Apostles. Luke called the "someone" featured in that biblical book the "Holy Spirit," who appears even queerer than Luke's disappearing Jesus. Strange languages, odd communal configurations, alluring foreigners, riveting confrontations with both civic and religious authorities—these mark just a few of the Spirit-led adventures undertaken by those early post-Emmaus disciples. Luke describes the effect of that Gospel witness by quoting an accusation from the disciples' detractors: they turned the world upside down (Acts 17:6).

LGBT people know something about overturning worlds with unexpected sexualities and unusually gendered bodies. LGBT people of *faith* know something else as well: those world-changing moments can generate profound insights about God and the calling to live as God's own peculiar people. Oddly, and perhaps therefore providentially, decades of ecclesial debates over sexuality and gender have surfaced a treasure trove of resources for the whole Church in the midst of seismic cultural shifts and anxiety concerning the future of institutional Christianity. Those resources contribute to the queer theology in this book, which I offer for a revitalized Christian witness—revitalized, but not entirely new as it draws from the convictions and patterns of an ancient and, thankfully, peculiar faith.

Jay Emerson Johnson
The Feast of All Saints, 2013

INTRODUCTION

Our Own Backyard

he queerness of Christian faith never occurred to me in the Evangelical, nearly fundamentalist subculture of my childhood. Family, friends, and church-going blended seamlessly with the economic and cultural values of an affluent, mostly white suburb of Chicago; nothing seemed particularly queer about that. Rather than odd or unusual, turning daily to the ancient Mediterranean texts of the Bible for guidance felt quite natural. My church youth group discussed those biblical texts frequently yet found nothing unsettling about reading that we belonged to a "peculiar people" (1 Peter 2:9, KJV) or that "here we have no lasting city" (Hebrews 13:14). The greater Chicago metropolitan area certainly seemed built to last, which we celebrated with flag-waving every Fourth of July. It should have seemed a bit strange to suppose that Jesus, a Middle Eastern itinerant preacher from the first century, had anything meaningful to say to an American Midwesterner of the twentieth century. I never wondered why Jesus remained single or why the Apostle Paul advised against marriage entirely (1 Corinthians 7:8). I do not recall ever puzzling over how to hate my mother and father, as Jesus had recommended (Luke 14:26). Both the virgin birth and the divinity of Jesus made perfect sense; such startling claims might as well have been self-evident. I should have found it quite peculiar indeed to anticipate joyfully the imminent appearance of that same virgin-born, divine, unmarried Jesus whose second coming would herald the end of the world.

As the wider world rolled on, my own personal, neatly packaged world unraveled when I came out as a gay man at a private Christian college. Or rather, two worlds collided in that moment, one marked by Evangelical Christian faith and the other by illicit sexual desire. That collision catalyzed years of study, prayer, and conversation with the hope of drawing those two worlds together into one, of turning the crash site into something like

1

a home. Many others have embarked on a similar journey, charting a path of biblical and theological apologetics toward a Christian homeland harmonized with "homosexuality."[1] Rather than finding a "home," that journey surprised me by bringing a strange new world into view.

Delving into the history of Christian thought and practice rendered the once familiar cadences of my childhood faith as something like a foreign language in a faraway land. Sexual desire began to illuminate much more than the romantic rhythms of courtship in a religious history populated by oddly gendered bodies and peculiar social arrangements. This new world at the intersection of religion and sexuality beckoned fresh exploration of ancient texts and spiritual practices that carried me well beyond the question of whether someone like me could be tolerated or even accepted as a member in God's household. Mapping that intersection suggested instead that the Christian household called Church stood on the brink of transformation. This should not have surprised me. When households welcome the formerly excluded, they inevitably undergo change, sometimes dramatically. Just such a moment sits enshrined in the biblical Acts of the Apostles as Jewish disciples of Jesus decided, prayerfully but not without considerable controversy, to embrace Gentile believers in their movement of spiritual and social transformation. That moment prompted a revolutionary shift in the meaning and practice of faith itself (Acts 10–15 and Galatians 2:1–14).[2] The ancient Hebrew prophet Isaiah anticipated that kind of reorientation much earlier by depicting Zion as the mountain of God that draws "all nations" to it rather than remaining the exclusive blessing of Israel alone (Isaiah 2:2–3, 25:6–7).[3] Transformative texts like these prove both troubling and invigorating; they often invigorate precisely for the trouble they cause. Today the Household

---

1. The word "homosexuality" appears in quotation marks for a number of reasons, not least because this medical neologism from the nineteenth century appears nowhere in the original biblical texts and most people ostensibly described by this term actually reject it.

2. Among others, Jack Rogers sees in this text not only a milestone moment in early Christianity concerning Gentiles but also a paradigm case for how and why the Church changes its mind (*Jesus, the Bible, and Homosexuality: Explode the Myths, Heal the Church*, rev. and expanded ed. [Louisville, KY: Westminster John Knox Press, 2009], 86–87).

3. More than a few commentators have noted these unsettling, destabilizing, and therefore insightfully liberating currents running through both Isaiah and the Acts of the Apostles, which will play an important role in the following chapters. See, for example, the approaches taken to these two biblical books by Timothy Koch, Thomas Bohache, Robert E. Goss, Deryn Guest, and Mona West in *The Queer Bible Commentary*, ed. Deryn Guest, Robert E. Goss, Mona West, and Thomas Bohache (London: SCM Press, 2006), 371–85; 566–81.

of God faces a similar moment of troubled invigoration and transformation wrought by the peculiarities of gender and sexual diversity, and perhaps especially the wide-ranging implications of that diversity extending to nearly every other aspect of faithful witness to the Gospel.

Religious transformation begins after apologetic arguments end. There, beyond apology, the queer gifts of diversity begin to materialize in and as the bodies presenting them. These gifts seem queer for their slightly jarring, rather odd, and decidedly peculiar character. They count as gifts when they surface fresh insights from ancient traditions and animate historical practices with renewed energy. Queer gifts emerge in Christian communities when self-identified lesbian, gay, bisexual, and transgender (LGBT) people no longer feel compelled to justify their presence with decades-old biblical arguments. Among these gifts are rich theological approaches to the socially transformative power of Christian faith and practice. These queerly Christian theological ideas challenge the whole Household of God to ponder anew why the Gospel should qualify as genuinely good news and how this peculiar faith shapes Christian witness.

This particular brand of religious transformation has been underway for some time, and especially since the early 1990s when queer people of faith began more explicitly to participate in Christian communities, not in spite of their queerness but *because* of it. After struggling for tolerance and then acceptance, sexually queer and queerly gendered people embarked on the next phase of our explicit inclusion: articulating the meaning and purpose of Christian faith drawn from our own peculiar experiences, sensibilities, and relationships. Much to the surprise of many, not least queer people themselves, these insights carry the potential to transform and revitalize Christian witness and ministry in the twenty-first century—and not a moment too soon.

The seemingly endless institutional machinations and religious wrestling matches over "homosexuality" have all but derailed Christian witness in a world facing severe challenges on multiple fronts, from systemic racism and violent ethnocentrism to economic catastrophes, intractable poverty, and global climate change. Ironically, but perhaps providentially, debating sexual ethics for so long has brought to light a panoply of theological resources for effective and socially transformative forms of Christian ministry that might otherwise have remained neglected, resources that often have little explicit relevance for discerning the moral and ecclesial status of "homosexuals."

Today, a growing number of queer people of faith embrace their queerness as a divine vocation, a way to think and a way to live in the Household of God that calls all Christian people back to the radical roots of the Gospel.[4]

This book draws from the energy of that theological vocation and I hope it will encourage others to offer their own queerly Christian voices in a conversation that has in many ways only just begun. Sadly, the need for biblical apologetics continues in some parts of the United States and even more urgently in other countries, where "homosexuality" can lead to violence and state-sponsored terror, including capital punishment.[5] Legislative and judicial advances for lesbian and gay people (such as the end of the U.S. military's "Don't Ask, Don't Tell" policy) have in some locales fueled a deeper retrenchment of religious intolerance; legislation may shape the course of civil rights but rarely changes hearts. Far too many LGBT people still internalize those hurtful religious messages in suicidal self-loathing (just one would be too many).[6] The apologetic work has addressed, and still does, a critically important need for those yearning to find or reclaim a religious home in Christianity, which for many has seemed impossibly out of reach.

Beyond apologetics, however, rich, life-giving theological resources lie buried in our own religious backyard, in the very traditions that have so often been deployed to alienate and disenfranchise spiritually hungry and theologically gifted queer people. Oddly if not ironically, perhaps even delightfully, Christian communities now stand in need of those same peculiar resources for addressing profound twenty-first-century challenges. The resolute, often intrepid insistence on finding a home in Christianity has led queer people of faith to notice what many modern Christian churches have failed to grasp: the inherent queerness of Christian traditions and why this queerness should

---

4. For an important illustration of this posture, see L. William Countryman and M. R. Ritley, *Gifted by Otherness: Gay and Lesbian Christians in the Church* (Harrisburg, PA: Morehouse Publishing, 2001).

5. A 2013 documentary film, *God Loves Uganda*, chronicles the influence of Evangelical Christians in the United States on the legislative agenda in Uganda to classify "homosexuality" as a capital offense (www.godlovesuganda.com). Jeff Sharlett analyzes the influence of fundamentalist Christianity on contemporary American politics, including the connections between some members of Congress and antigay movements in various African countries (see *C Street: The Fundamentalist Threat to American Democracy* [New York: Back Bay Books, 2011]).

6. Eve Kosofsky Sedgwick analyzed patterns of gender nonconformity as a source of suicidal ideation and cites a study by the U.S. Department of Health and Human Services that found gay and lesbian youth two to three times more likely than other young people to attempt and commit suicide ("How to Bring Your Kids Up Gay," in *Fear of a Queer Planet: Queer Politics and Social Theory*, ed. Michael Warner [Minneapolis: University of Minnesota Press, 1993], 69). For more recent information, see also The Trevor Project that works to prevent LGBT-related suicides (*www.trevorproject.org*).

sound like Gospel. As Elizabeth Stuart rather pointedly notes, "Christianity is a queer thing."[7]

I must confess: this notion of discovering insights in our own backyard inevitably brings to mind the adventures of Dorothy in *The Wizard of Oz*, whose yearning for home punctuated the narrative arc of that classic film. That film still plays a culturally iconic role for American gay men of the baby-boom generation. Some of us wistfully recall that the memorial service for Judy Garland was held on the same day the Stonewall riots began in 1969, which galvanized activists in new ways for a movement of gay liberation.[8] Garland's performance of Dorothy, so far removed from the turbulence and tragedies of her later life and career, contributed to an underground cultural sensibility at a time when "homosexual" visibility carried a wider range of severe consequences. Referring to another man as a "friend of Dorothy" safely identified his sexual orientation in contexts where public knowledge of "homosexuality" could end careers, ruin families, and even lead to violence.

The film depicts a fantastical land beyond the trials and tribulations of Dorothy's hometown in Kansas. To underscore the contrast, Kansas appears in black and white; Oz shimmers in brilliant Technicolor. After World War II, as gay men and lesbians began migrating in larger numbers from the heartland of the American Midwest and the rural south to coastal cities, "Kansas" signified the repressive and secretive lives they left behind to discover a colorful new world in the adventures afforded by urban freedom. In the film, Dorothy travels to Oz by going "over the rainbow," which always comes to mind whenever I see the enormous rainbow flag flying at the corner of Market and Castro Streets in San Francisco, a city many of my friends still refer to as "Oz."

The characters in that film have likewise proved iconic for the process of self-discovery and for coming out, not only culturally but also religiously. As the Scarecrow, the Tin Man, and the Lion journey with Dorothy to see the Wizard, each of them discovers that they possess exactly what they need for the journey, the very things they thought they lacked: a brain, a heart, and courage. This realization proves transformative, especially as the

---

7. Elizabeth Stuart, *Gay and Lesbian Theologies: Repetitions with Critical Difference* (Burlington, VT: Ashgate, 2003); see especially ch. 8, "Christianity Is a Queer Thing," 105–16.

8. I do not mean that Judy Garland's death "caused" the Stonewall Riots, a claim that is rooted more in urban legend than reality. As David Carter has argued, those on the frontlines of those riots—mostly homeless youth—were not of the generation that listened to Garland's music (*Stonewall: The Riots That Sparked the Gay Revolution* [New York: St. Martin's Griffin, 2004], 261).

supposedly all-powerful "Wizard" turns out to be a con artist. Many lesbian and gay Christians can pinpoint a similar moment of epiphany in their own lives, when they realized that the "voice of God" actually came from a priest behind a curtain.

For more than a few lesbian and gay Christians, these familiar points of contact in *The Wizard of Oz* pale in comparison to the primary story line in the film. In contrast to her three companions, Dorothy worries that she will never regain what she lost by traveling over the rainbow—a home. Just like her companions, however, she discovers what she needs, not only with the help of magical ruby slippers but also and especially by searching the depth of her own desire. In doing so, Dorothy travels back to where she belongs, with friends and family. In the final scene we see Dorothy back in Kansas, now filmed again in black and white, where she muses on what she has learned. "If I ever go looking for my heart's desire again," she declares, "I won't go further than my own backyard."[9] That declaration now stands for a truly peculiar moment in Christian history. The yearning for a home among lesbian, gay, bisexual, and transgender people of faith has brought many of us back to our own theological backyard.

The mid-twentieth-century geographical migration of lesbians and gay men to U.S. urban centers mirrors an equally significant spiritual migration. For many it meant leaving organized religion, especially institutional forms of Christianity, and experimenting with new forms of spiritual practice. For some it meant abandoning anything explicitly religious. In the decades that followed, these adventures on the other side of the rainbow reshaped the cultural and political landscape of American society in ways younger generations can scarcely imagine. Police no longer conduct surprise raids on lesbian and gay bars. "Homosexuals" are not routinely hospitalized for their sexual "illness." Openly lesbian and gay people now populate some television shows and movies and are even elected to political office. Equal access to civil marriage for lesbian and gay couples, an unthinkable milestone in the 1970s (and for some lesbian and gay people, even undesirable), now stands within reach.

American society has changed rather dramatically since 1969, yet throughout these adventures, and just like Dorothy, lesbian and gay Christians

---

9. *The Wizard of Oz*, DVD, directed by Victor Fleming, 1939; Los Angeles: Warner Brothers Family Entertainment, 1998.

have never forgotten what they left behind—a place to call their religious and spiritual home. Today the experiences and lessons learned over the rainbow have brought many of us back to the spiritual and theological traditions that we either chose to reject or felt compelled to abandon. Our Oz-like sojourn helped us to draw on our own resources and to learn how to forge powerful bonds with strangers who became our families. Yet for many of us an inscrutable yearning punctuated these moments and beckoned renewed engagement with the same traditions that demanded our exile. Here, however, *The Wizard of Oz* can mislead us. Dorothy's adventures in Oz may have changed her, but it left Kansas untouched. Returning home she finds everything exactly as she left it, in black and white. Queer people know what the producers of that film apparently did not. Going home as a changed person changes the home, even if the journey to Oz was only a dream. The transformative experiences along the Yellow Brick Road and in the Emerald City would surely have added at least a dash of color to Dorothy's familiar farmhouse if not also to the faces of her friends and family and even her own backyard.

Returning to our religious and spiritual home, queer people of faith do not merely recover what we lost. Once taken, the journey uncovers theological insights in our own backyard that can transform the whole household, slowly but surely, from black and white to brilliant Technicolor. That was Dorothy's deep desire and her compelling declaration: What she needed waited right outside her backdoor. Queerly Christian theologies already reside in the Household of God and in Christianity's own backyard. Those theologies are even now reshaping the patterns and practices of Christian witness in socially transformative ways. Giving voice to these queer theologies begins with appreciating some of the key lessons learned over the rainbow.

DISCOVERIES ALONG THE YELLOW BRICK ROAD

In our own backyard we were called fags and dykes, sissies and tomboys. The more polite referred to us as a little odd or a bit "off." In the realm of medical professionals and psychological experts we were "homosexuals," those with a diagnosable and unfortunate condition for which we could, at least potentially, receive curative treatment. In religious circles we were simply sinners, those who violated God's commandments revealed in the Bible. More generally, but still steeped in religious overtones, we were those who committed "crimes against nature" in "unspeakable acts." Beginning as early as the 1950s we began more intentionally to name our own experiences. After referring to ourselves for a short while as a "homophile" movement, the Stonewall riots marked a turn more broadly toward "gay and lesbian." Not long after that we recognized the importance of including bisexual and transgender people in the work of civil and religious inclusion. Today, many of us prefer the acronym "LGBT" to refer to our communities, relationships, and sensibilities.

The act of naming ourselves and creating a communal identity framed a critical strategy for resisting political injustice and religious oppression. Other marginalized communities have relied on similar strategies, which came to broader public awareness in the "identity politics" of the 1980s. Since then, activists and scholars alike have found these strategies a bit troubling. Simply put, to whom exactly do all the instances of the words "we," "us," and "our" in the previous paragraph actually refer? Men dominated the early gay liberation movement, often at the expense of longer-standing feminist commitments and forms of analysis. The later inclusion of bisexual and transgender sensibilities among lesbian and gay people broadened the scope of study and activism but frequently failed to account for the mechanisms of racism perpetuated by predominantly white strategists. William Turner captures these complexities concisely as they emerged in the 1960s and 1970s:

> Activists who originally called themselves "radical feminists" paid relatively little attention to the issue of lesbians, arguing that the question of sexual practice distracted from the real goal of women's liberation. Black lesbian feminists noted the double bind of facing homophobia from black heterosexuals and racism from white lesbian feminists.[10]

In short, the intolerable choice many felt compelled to make among competing movements of solidarity raised critical questions about the notion of identity itself, which seemed clearly to operate in multiple and even conflicting ways all at the same time. Who exactly are "we"?

I count myself among those scholars and activists who prefer the word "queer" to describe all these multiple layers of identity, reflection, and practice. That word does not by any means solve the riddle of identity and solidarity; it actually creates new problems. Calling myself queer might obscure my sexual attraction to other men unless I make that affinity explicitly

---

10. William B. Turner, *A Genealogy of Queer Theory* (Philadelphia: Temple University Press, 2000), 14.

known. Queer might also divert attention away from the gender, racial, and economic privileges I possess and can access as an affluent white man. I may live queerly in some respects, but I can also avoid the more severe social consequences of that queerness in a society constructed for the benefit of white males. Those serious problems notwithstanding, I still believe queer holds significant cultural and religious potential. By troubling notions of mainstream propriety and scrutinizing unexamined assumptions, queerness can tease out fresh insights and energize new modes of action in the broader project of human and planetary flourishing. As Lee Edelman has aptly described it, queerness carves out a "zone of possibilities" in an otherwise static or closed system.[11]

Discerning previously unimagined approaches to time-worn dilemmas can refresh and energize. What Edelman describes as a "zone" has done this by coaxing the word "queer" back into fashion. Ironically, of course, since queer describes the strange and peculiar, that which should remain by definition out of fashion. Today that word can describe people who do not necessarily identify as lesbian, gay, bisexual, or transgender, but who nevertheless resist accommodating to the so-called "mainstream" of Western society, and for a wide range of reasons. Adopting and embracing the word "queer" amounts to an act of defiance and, just as significantly, an act of hope. Queer resists and defies the many cultural and political forces Western society deploys to define the normal and expected. "We are not *that*," queer people say. That same word also fuels the imagination for new visions, the possibility that the standards of what Western society considers normative do not exhaust the possibilities for thriving. "We do not fit in, and that's hopeful," queer people say.

The word "queer" in this book marks that defiant hope and especially the theological significance of that hopeful resistance for Christian witness to the Gospel and socially transforming patterns of ministry. The acronym "LGBT" remains important as well, and can promote a bit more honesty, especially when queer risks covering over and flattening differences, or erasing the specificity of embodied existence. Self-identified gay, lesbian, and bisexual people, for example, all qualify as queer with respect to dominant cultural norms for sexual expression in Western societies but often share little else in common. Even among gay men or among lesbian women,

---

11. Quoted in Annamarie Jagose, *Queer Theory: An Introduction* (Washington Square: New York University Press, 1996), 2.

experiences, sensibilities, and relationships vary, sometimes quite widely. Transgender sensibilities likewise seem queer to many, yet rarely correspond to the issues typically addressed with reference to sexual orientation. Moreover, all of these terms tend to submerge race, ethnicity, and economic class beneath supposedly more significant sexually gendered identifications.

A single acronym like "LGBT" implies commonality, and making common cause has been strategically crucial for political, cultural, and religious reasons. Yet I have come to believe that the theological and spiritual insights of LGBT people emerge not from the experience of commonality but of *shared difference*, which may well stand as the most important lesson learned over the rainbow. LGBT people are different. We differ from the social norms of the North Atlantic and we are also different from each other. In this shared experience of difference we feel queer with respect to cultural and religious expectations but also with respect to each other, not least because of our varied racial, ethnic, and economic histories.

On the other side of the rainbow, Dorothy made common cause with her companions along the Yellow Brick Road. They did this as they navigated the dangers of the Enchanted Forest on their way to the Emerald City. Their companionship provided safety and their adventures created deep bonds of affection. Nevertheless Dorothy remained keenly aware that she did not belong in Oz; her home lay elsewhere. Her journey over the rainbow taught her valuable lessons she could not have learned otherwise, but Oz seemed queer to Dorothy and she felt queer being there. More than anything else, that experience of queerness itself shed new and important light on what "home" really means.

"There's no place like home." Dorothy repeats this three times as she clicks the heels of her ruby slippers. Her declaration can carry at least as many meanings, and not all of them evoke familiar comfort. In the early 1990s some feminist scholars embarked on a decisive renovation project for their professional home of academic theorizing. They did this by using the word "queer" in relation to theory as a verb rather than an adjective. As the standard modes and paradigms of interpretation in modern Western culture had been so thoroughly infused with the assumptions of white, "heterosexual" men, the time had come "to queer" the very idea of theory itself.[12] The linguistic roots of the word "queer" suggest a sense of traversing

---

12. Teresa de Lauretis is often credited with the first use of "queer" as a verb during a 1991 conference at the University of California, Santa Cruz. See William B. Turner, *Genealogy of Queer Theory*, 4–8.

and crossing, which some have adopted in a posture of transgressing generally accepted academic boundaries, or fouling up neat and tidy systems.[13] In that sense, to "queer" theory entails a nearly relentless scrutiny of unexamined assumptions, especially those residing in systems of social or cultural classification designed to benefit some at the expense of the many. Judith Butler, for example, called into question the supposedly natural dichotomy between male and female upon which even many feminist modes of analysis rely. Rather than a distinction rooted in nature or biology, Butler urged us to think of gender as a "performative" quality of being human, something inscribed on our bodies over time by repeating cultural scripts.[14] In similar fashion, Eve Kosofky Sedgwick noted how pervasively modern Western society classifies people as either "homosexual" or "heterosexual" and the extent to which nearly every aspect of our social and cultural engagements turns on that one categorical classification. Sedgwick invited us to see, first, how perfectly natural this classification scheme appears, and second, how odd it is. Given the many, nearly countless ways people differ from each other, why would sexual affinities matter so terribly much?[15]

Some have taken these modes of queer theorizing as an attempt to destabilize or even erase notions of identity itself (not least for all the divisive "identity politics" such notions have generated). Butler, however, understood identities as an important means by which we recognize and interact with each other. More pointedly, "a life for which no categories of identity exist is not a livable life."[16] Butler thus places her emphasis on the *regulatory* character of identity categories, or the various cultural and political forces that demand conformity to allowable forms of identity, the structured norms (whether chosen or not) that constitute the sense of self. "Queer" appears in this kind of analysis, not as yet another identity to adopt but rather as profound resistance to the regulatory regimes that monitor and police our identifications. Michael Warner describes such regimes succinctly:

> The culture has thousands of ways for people to govern the sex of others—and not just harmful or coercive sex, like rape, but the most

---

13. See Susannah Cornwall's tracing of these linguistic roots and their cultural and academic effects in the modern West in *Controversies in Queer Theology* (London: SCM Press, 2011), esp. 10–24.

14. Judith Butler, *Gender Trouble: Feminism and the Subversion of Identity* (New York: Routledge, 1990, 1999); see especially the preface to the 1999 tenth anniversary edition, vii–xxvi.

15. Eve Kosofky Sedgwick, *Epistemology of the Closet* (Berkeley: University of California Press, 1990), 2, 8.

16. Judith Butler, *Undoing Gender* (New York: Routledge, 2004), 8.

personal dimensions of pleasure, identity, and practice. We do this directly, through prohibition and regulation, and indirectly, by embracing one identity or one set of tastes as though they were universally shared, or should be.[17]

Taking queer theory as a mode of resistance frequently renders queer itself as allusive, lacking a determinate character, which for many is precisely the point; queerness derives its cultural traction from its "resistance to definition."[18] Or as David Halperin describes it, queer marks a "positionality vis-à-vis the normative—a positionality that is not restricted to lesbians and gay men but is in fact available to anyone who is or who feels marginalized because of . . . sexual practices."[19]

Most LGBT people would recognize in these academic musings the lessons we learned over the rainbow, and long before theory fell under a queer gaze. Many of us came to see in new ways just how different we are from each other—racially, ethnically, sexually, and culturally—and that no single mode of theorizing or classification scheme will suffice for containing all that diversity. Others learned that gender differences mean much more than checking either "M" or "F" on personal data forms. The discomfort some of us have felt in blurring distinct gender categories helped us to understand better how deeply our perceptions of reality are shaped by dichotomous categorizing, of which the binary gender system constitutes the paradigm case. Over time many of us realized (and with considerable shock) that the debates over "homosexuality" have little to do with love, relationship, and commitment. So-called "same-sex" relationships instead trigger a kind of gender panic among those who cannot imagine a world of multiple gender scripts—a world, that is, without clearly defined spheres of male privilege. We know this from reading newspapers and police reports. While all LGBT people remain vulnerable to harassment and hate crimes, gender conformists (such as "lipstick lesbians" or "butch gay men") are less frequently targeted for violence than the disrupters of gender expectations, the "bull-dykes" and "sissy fags" and increasingly

---

17. Michael Warner, *The Trouble with Normal: Sex, Politics, and the Ethics of Queer Life* (Cambridge, MA: Harvard University Press, 1999), 1.

18. Jagose, *Queer Theory*, 1.

19. David Halperin, *Saint Foucault: Towards a Gay Hagiography* (Oxford: Oxford University Press, 1995), 62. For an extensive overview of differing approaches to queer theory, see Nikki Sullivan, *A Critical Introduction to Queer Theory* (Washington Square: New York University Press, 2003).

transgender people.[20] Sexual behavior and identifications, in other words, invariably entail gender; more pointedly, the urge to monitor and police sexual relationships most frequently appears where the means for patriarchal dominance have lost their cultural traction. More simply: controlling sexual behavior helps to ensure white, male dominance. All of these lessons clearly trouble standard meanings of the words "sex" and "gender," including what precisely one has to do with the other, while also urging a way of speaking that signals their interlaced entanglements. My interactions and relationships with others are always sexually gendered and gendered sexually and, even more, racially coded. Indeed, Laurel Schneider persuasively claims that "sex, gender, and race all constitute each other (suggesting, for example, that whiteness itself has a gender)."[21]

Discoveries along the Yellow Brick Road, in concert with queer modes of theorizing, have urged many of us to take very little for granted. What may seem "natural" or just the "givens" of human life and existence frequently derive from complex patterns of cultural power and institutional ideologies. Whatever it means to live as a man or a woman, or how anyone manifests masculinity and femininity have varied enormously over the course of human history. So also the meaning of sex, of being sexually intimate, which always draws into its orbit the gendered and racialized markers of social value. As William Turner succinctly notes, "definitions of identity, especially gender and sexual identity, vary considerably depending on race, ethnicity, class, geography, and time."[22] Even human desire, what we think we want from our lives and our relationships, springs in large measure from the complex constellations of cultural meaning and social expectations. Corporate sponsors of gay pride parades learned this sooner than the rest of us. Advertising agencies rather quickly capitalized on an emerging market niche to tell gay men what kind of accoutrements, clothing, and toys they should buy to be authentically and attractively "gay."[23]

---

20. The story of transgender woman Gwen Araujo's brutal murder in 2006 seized media attention (and was turned into a made-for-television movie) but is only one of many examples of the gendered character of such violence. See the materials available from the National Center for Transgender Equality (*www.transequality.org*) and the Transgender Law Center (*www.transgenderlawcenter.org*).

21. Laurel C. Schneider, "What Race Is Your Sex?" in *Disrupting White Supremacy from Within: White People on What We Need to Do*, ed. Jennifer Harvey, Karin A. Case, and Robin Hawley Gorsline (Cleveland, OH: Pilgrim Press, 2004), 142.

22. Turner, *Genealogy of Queer Theory*, 7.

23. See Turner's analysis of the relationship between consumer culture and sexual identity, including his caution against conflating the two, in *Genealogy of Queer Theory*, 68.

Our remarkable adventures over the rainbow opened up these wider horizons in ways many of us could not have imagined (or even wanted to) just thirty years ago. A host of quandaries now populates our engagements with politics and social policy, with economics and cultural institutions, and our participation in the constructions of race, ethnicity, and class. Some have objected to these broader questions, perceiving them as a distraction from the movement for mainstream inclusion for lesbian and gay people. Others insist on asking them (even if answers remain elusive) as a way to expose the tenuous if not illusory supposition of a monolithic "mainstream." Michael Warner contrasts these perspectives concisely and rather pointedly. Those seeking accommodation in the mainstream, Warner notes, tend to argue that "gay men and lesbians are virtually normal," while those who question the mainstream suspect that "all creatures gay and straight are virtually queer."[24] Or as William B. Turner wonders, "Could it be that everyone is queer?" After all, "surely all persons at some time or other find themselves discomfited by the bounds of the categories that ostensibly contain their identities."[25]

Religion remained notably absent from the initial impulses toward queer theorizing (for some, religion itself exemplified the intractable problems of theory). Before long, however, a handful of academic theologians and astute clergy began to notice the potential in asking these new, rather queer questions. For them, modern institutional Christianity's standard operating procedure had fallen short of energizing their ministries and shaping vibrant communities of Gospel witness for social transformation. Working tirelessly to create a "place at the table" for LGBT people in faith communities, they began to wonder whether the "table" itself demands further scrutiny. Realizing how often "equality" reduces to "sameness," they started searching out other unexamined assumptions that might reside in Christian congregations, theological projects, and patterns of ministry. They began, in other words, to take Michael Warner's observation with them into their theological and pastoral work:

> Because the logic of the sexual order is so deeply embedded by now in an indescribably wide range of social institutions, and is embedded in the most standard accounts of the world, queer struggles aim not just at toleration or equal status but at challenging those institutions and accounts. The dawning realization that themes of homophobia and heterosexism may be read in

---

24. Warner, *Trouble with Normal*, 142.

25. Turner, *Genealogy of Queer Theory*, 8.

almost any document of our culture means that we are only beginning to have an idea of how widespread those institutions and accounts are.[26]

What would it mean to include theology and the church in Warner's collection of "institutions and accounts"? How have binary modes of thought and reflection, typified by gender, inflected the cadences of theological reflection and spiritual practice? Could the cultural construction of gendered sexuality proposed by queer theorists model a similar posture toward the sexually gendered constructions of theology? What might this mean for our conceptions of God, the person and work of Jesus, and nearly every other doctrinal location that informs the mission of the Church? Where has Christian witness simply adopted the "givens" of modern Western classification schemes rather than critiquing them with a Gospel vision? Is Christian faith really about "fitting in," or does the Gospel instead inspire a hopeful resistance to mainstream values and paradigms? Who defines the "mainstream," anyway?[27]

These questions and many others like them draw from queer modes of analysis, a pastiche of critical social theories rooted in feminist and liberationist commitments. Addressing such questions with those commitments brings the contours of a queer theology for Christian witness into view. To queer Christian theology marks a return of sorts, of coming back home to Christian faith and realizing that Dorothy's backyard cannot remain stubbornly rendered in black and white. Energized by the lessons learned over the rainbow, Christians return to our own religious backyard. There, we discover the tools, resources, and ideas we need to transform the Christian Household of God into a vibrant and colorful foretaste of the home most of us have only just begun to imagine.

CREATING A TECHNICOLOR KANSAS

Human vision relies equally on recognizing differing shapes and discerning the relative distance between objects. Color plays a significant role in these twin tasks. Our visual acuity drops dramatically at night, for example, as

---

26. Michael Warner, ed., *Fear of a Queer Planet: Queer Politics and Social Theory* (Minneapolis: University of Minnesota Press, 1993), xiii.

27. Ken Stone offers a helpful summary of how questions like these have been reshaping biblical studies and Laurel Schneider offers an illustrative theological response to that biblical approach. See Ken Stone, ed., *Queer Commentary and the Hebrew Bible*, Journal for the Study of the Old Testament Supplement Series 334 (New York: Sheffield Academic Press, 2001), 20–32, and in that same volume, Laurel Schneider, "Yahwist Desires: Imagining Divinity Queerly," 210–27.

the absence of vibrant colors shrinks our perception of depth. Photographers and filmmakers have exploited this basic physiology for a variety of artistic and narrative ends, such as the contrast between a Kansas farmhouse and the fantastical Land of Oz.

Dorothy's return to a black-and-white Kansas reinforces the security of the familiar patterns and rhythms of home, but it also lacks the depth of vision that only color can provide. That description of Dorothy's adventure will sound theologically familiar to those who left forms of Christian faith that present only black-and-white answers to complex questions. For me, it meant joining the Episcopal Church during my freshman year in college, a denomination like other self-styled progressive traditions that exhibit a higher tolerance for ambiguity than my childhood tradition. Finding ways to live well with ambiguous grey areas in an otherwise black-and-white world energized me for a time, but only as a first step. Grey, fuzzy edges grew less satisfying as I craved the texture and richness of a full-spectrum world of color. Gay and lesbian theologies set my feet firmly on the road toward such a world, yet brought me only to its threshold. There, on that brink of the peculiar, Christianity's inherent queerness began to map uncharted terrain for a "Technicolor Kansas." Or rather, that terrain seemed uncharted at first but soon resembled neglected fields to explore with faded maps.

Christianity's backyard resources sit untapped due in large measure to modernity's relentless reshaping of Western society to which the institutional church mostly acquiesced. What "modern" means in relation to the West of course varies considerably depending on one's academic discipline; here I mean more than the term's generally popular reference to whatever seems current or up-to-date. I take modernity as shorthand for the potent confluence of several cultural shifts that began emerging roughly three centuries ago: the ascendancy of rationalism and empiricism in the European Enlightenment; rapid advances in both science and technology; the birth of nation-states and liberal democracies; and the industrial revolution, to name just a few. The North Atlantic still lives with the legacy of those tectonic shifts as do many other societies marked by the reach of Western colonialism. How to assess that legacy varies as widely as its definitions. Queer theorists tend to focus their critical gaze on modernity's categorical classification schemes and the divisive identity politics they generated. Under that gaze, the binary gender system stands as a monument to a black-and-white world desperate for the rich nuances of color.

Institutional Christianity lives rather precariously with the traces of modernity's influence on its religious identity. Churches paid a price to retain a sense of relevance in the midst of scientific and sociopolitical advances and equally so when they sought to fend off cultural encroachments. The ongoing anxiety over the decline of mainline Protestantism, underway since at least the 1970s, serves as just one symptom of modern Christianity's malaise. Decline, however, does not signal impending death. Or rather, what has died in Western Christianity has sparked in Phoenix-like fashion some signs of rebirth.

Evidence of revitalization emerging from the detritus of modern institutional religion has gathered under the banner of what some call, appropriately enough, "Emergent Christianity." Phyllis Tickle has been chronicling these multivalent movements springing from the "Great Emergence," or what she believes represents a society-wide awakening in the wake of modernity's failure to make good on its promise of progress. Most though certainly not all of these emergent Christians belong to younger generations who have grown weary of an ever-growing breach on the American religious landscape between liberal Protestants and Christian fundamentalists. The former achieved a great deal since the nineteenth century in bringing Christian faith more directly into movements for social justice while the latter retained a robust emphasis on personal conversion and spiritual practice.[28] Yet neither of these approaches proves satisfying today to Christians who hunger for *both* a deep interior life of communion with God *and* a socially transformative theology to manifest that communion. The widening breach between these two Christianities appears most readily in their divergent views of the Bible and their shared neglect of ancient theological traditions.[29] Both of these sources—biblical texts and historical theology—excite those emerging from the breach with renewed possibilities for Christianity's peculiar faith. A queer theology for Christian witness can lend compelling assistance for that renewal, for all those eager to live as "repairers of the breach," as Isaiah might say in new ways today (Isaiah 58:12).

---

28. See Michael Lerner's analysis of how liberal politics separated itself from spiritual practice in *The Left Hand of God: Taking Back Our Country from the Religious Right* (New York: HarperCollins, 2006).

29. For just one example of an attempt to address this breach from a quasi-Evangelical perspective, see Mark Husbands and Jeffrey P. Greenman, eds., *Ancient Faith for the Church's Future* (Downers Grove, IL: IVP Academic, 2008).

Neither the black-and-white world of fundamentalism nor the grey, fuzzy edges of liberalism will suffice to quench the spiritually hungry people emerging from the breach. Many queer people of faith have tried to occupy either or both sides of this great religious divide and have come to some important realizations. They realize, if only instinctively, that reading the Bible for theological insight begins but cannot end with the kind of historical-critical interpretations championed by liberal Protestants; such reading likewise demands more, not less imagination and creativity than a fundamentalist insistence on the "plain sense" of biblical texts.[30] Queer people of faith also know that no one will create a Technicolor Kansas with boring books about God (and that certainly gives me pause as I write this one). Something has gone terribly awry if theology fails to make us feel like I did as a child whenever my parents talked about summer vacation plans, or if it falls short of exciting our curiosity like the intricately woven plots of a good mystery novel, or if it cannot arouse our bodily passions like the best erotica. I do not mean that God-talk must always generate this kind of anticipation and excitement. Vacation planning, after all, requires tedious logistics. Novelists must carefully set the stage for plausible plot twists. And the most compelling erotica (in my experience) never dwells solely on what people do with their body parts. The history of Christian reflection on all things divine exhibits a similar range of moods and tenses, adopts a variety of methods and postures, some of them quite mundane and pedestrian while others soar with exultations. Still, and in the end, if theology does not expand our horizons, move us inexorably to change our manner of life, and propel us into new patterns of relationship and socially transformative endeavors previously unimagined, then we have not been reflecting on God; Kansas remains resolutely rendered in black and white.

Creating a Technicolor Kansas necessarily involves risk. Embarking on a journey of lifelong conversion, as the Gospel urges, will mean risking mistakes, even colossal ones. It will mean risking the security of how things have always been done for the sake of the new thing God perpetually initiates (Isaiah 42:9, 43:19). At times it will mean starting over entirely when an otherwise promising model for ministry falls flat or a compelling theological

---

30. Both the hope and the particular possibilities of this kind of reclamation in biblical studies—and its application in pastoral settings—are well articulated in a short collection of essays edited by Michael Root and James Buckley, *Sharper than a Two-Edged Sword: Preaching, Teaching, and Living the Bible* (Grand Rapids: William B. Eerdmans, 2008).

idea fails to address how people actually live or the questions that vex us the most. Human thought and human speech and published texts concerning God, just like thinking and speaking and writing on anything else of genuine human significance, rarely if ever achieve perfection; there are always left-overs and blunders. Mark McIntosh reminds us that the mystics in Christian history always stood ready to have their speech stripped away by the mystery of the God they were trying to describe. Mark Jordan insists even further that these "mystics" belong not just to the fringes of otherwise normative Chris-tian witness but stand at its heart. Those traditions, Jordan writes, "remind us that the goal of human life stands beyond human life as it appears to us—beyond the names and rules and institutions that we confect to order lives here."[31]

Mystical cautions of that sort notwithstanding, nothing will short-circuit queerly transformative theology more quickly than the fear of getting it wrong. That fear, whether with reference to orthodox doctrine or to effective political strategizing, has paralyzed queer people of faith for far too long. By the same token, tapping into the infinite well of divine grace and love, which casts out all fear (1 John 4:18), does not grant anyone the license to moral or intellectual laxity. The risks are far too severe, the opportunities too rich for not doing our collective theological homework as God's people—better still, doing our theological "housework" in the Household of God. As any householder knows, managing a home may be a labor of love, but it is labor nonetheless. So too the work of creating a Technicolor Kansas, which will require the sustained and loving labor of committed home economists, and queer ones at that.

QUEER HOME ECONOMISTS

Who are these "queer people of faith" I keep invoking and citing? They cer-tainly appear in a broad array of styles and types and with a wide range of perspectives and histories. Some obvious candidates include self-identified LGBT Christians who insist that forging communities of tolerance for sex-ually gendered diversity aims far too low in a high stakes game of human

---

31. Mark D. Jordan, *Telling Truths in Church: Scandal, Flesh, and Christian Speech* (Boston: Beacon Press, 2003), 64. See also Mark A. McIntosh's description of how spirituality and theology inextricably intertwine in *Mystical Theology*, Challenges in Contemporary Theology series (Malden, MA: Blackwell Publishing, 1998), 9–18.

and planetary thriving. Less obvious candidates would include Christians who may not identify directly with LGBT classifications but who nonetheless resist claiming the privileges of a society built for the benefit of white "heterosexual" men. I would also include "emergent" Christians, LGBT-identified or not, who find Christian faith compelling but its modern expressions and operations sorely lacking if not by now nearly defunct.[32] Queer people of faith also and of course hail from other religious traditions and stand ready to offer a rich panoply of insights to Christian communities.[33] In this book I have in mind a particular subset of "queer people of faith." They feel divinely called and compelled to retrieve the peculiar energy of the Gospel for reshaping Christian faith and witness for the profound challenges of twenty-first-century life. They embrace vocations that bid them remain, even at great cost, within the orbit of historical Christian traditions as they refuse to cede even one iota of those traditions to modern Western cultural distortions. Some of these seek to live their vocations within traditional institutional structures as ordained clergy. Others see opportunities to bear witness to their peculiar faith in a broader range of organizations, social ventures, and communities that may have little explicit connection to institutional Christianity. All of these, however, recognize the indispensably communal character of their passionate commitments. The deep bonds of affection in their shared work resemble in many respects the intimate patterns of a household, much like the networked communities portrayed in the biblical Acts of the Apostles. Freshly inspired by the Holy Spirit at Pentecost, those early Christians expanded their multigenerational households into base camps of spiritual formation for social transformation. Today's queer people of faith take that biblical account not as a blueprint but as inspiration for their own passionately queer callings to live in socially transformative Christian households, both intimately small and congregationally large. I refer to all of these as "queer home economists."

---

32. See, for example, *www.emergentvillage.org*, *www.patheos.com/blogs/emergentvillage/posts/*, and the Wild Goose Festival (*www.wildgoosefestival.org*).

33. See, for example, Daniel Boyarin, Daniel Itzkovitz, and Ann Pellegrini, eds., *Queer Theory and the Jewish Question* (New York: Columbia University Press, 2003); Farhang Rouhani, "Religion, Identity and Activism: Queer Muslim Diasporic Identities," in *Geographies of Sexualities: Theory, Practices and Politics,* ed. Kath Browne, Jason Lim, and Gavin Brown (Aldershot: Ashgate, 2007); Fredierk S. Roden, ed., *Jewish/Christian/Queer: Crossroad and Identities* (Aldershot: Ashgate, 2009); and Susannah Cornwall's helpful summary of some of these intersections in *Controversies in Queer Theology*, 2–4.

The English word "economy" derives from the combination of two Greek words: *oikos*, or house, and *nomos*, or law. Organizing the daily operations of one's personal household, from grocery shopping to meal preparation, and from bill paying to laundry thus describes an economic effort to create a home that functions for the benefit of all who live there. While the orderliness of some households resembles the "rule of law," others rely on something more akin to managed chaos. Depending on the particular household members, both approaches can achieve a thriving home economy; no one model will suffice for all. Economists working on a larger scale, with cities, counties, and nations, likewise turn to a variety of models for understanding and ordering the many types of relational exchanges in a given community or society.

"Economy" sometimes appears in Christian traditions as well, as a way to talk about God. This can sound rather odd and even clunky, as if God were a cosmic banker setting heavenly monetary policy. Far less strange, consider "divine economy" in a more homey sense. Expand and stretch the image of a household to encompass the whole of God's creation. Imagine the creative, redemptive, and sustaining energies of the Divine Home Economist, who longs to see all members of the household thriving and flourishing. To assist in this great work, God-the-Householder calls an astonishing array of people, bestows countless gifts and skills, and inspires ever newer and wider visions of what thriving and flourishing actually entail, not just for some but for all.

This imaginative and expansive vision surely qualifies as peculiar, especially against the backdrop of so much sectarian insularity in Christian history. Separating insiders from outsiders, as the Church has done so frequently, scarcely exhibits the contours of an ever-widening household. More presently and pointedly, a Christian imagination tends to fade against the backdrop of an institutional church that appears indistinguishable from modern Western culture. Few Christians, when pressed, would embrace Western society as the incarnation of heaven. Fewer still actually live as if the Gospel has any critique at all to offer of the modern West. Queer home economists will attend carefully to this potent and mostly unexamined blend of the North Atlantic and Christianity. The confusion of Euro-American culture and Gospel proclamation resides not only in the history of Western colonialism but also lingers in the theological assumptions preached from conservative and liberal pulpits alike.

Queering theology aims toward the transformation of congregational households, yet broader still toward animating a socially transformative Christian witness in a world now unaccustomed to being interrupted by the Church. The urgent need for interruptions, or better still, *disruptions* resounds with heart-breaking clarity from all those whom Jesus called the poor, the blind, the captives, and the oppressed (Luke 4:18). Queerly enough, that means *everyone*—the economically dispossessed, to be sure, but also the emotionally bankrupt; those visually impaired, yes, but also those blinded by cultural biases and systemic roadblocks; those languishing in the prison-industrial complex, absolutely, yet material comfort can create its own jail cell of anxieties. And the oppressed? Queer theorists would have us notice, indeed feel the suffocating weight of Western society's classification schemes bearing down on each of us, even those who reap myriad sociopolitical benefits from categorical classifications.

Queerer still perhaps, theological ideas actually make a difference. Doing our theological housework as Christians, whether lay or ordained, whether unattached to the institutional church or deeply ensconced within it, plays a vital role in queer home economics. Theology makes a difference for many reasons, not least because modern Western distortions of theology have contributed to the very quandaries the whole planet must now confront. Making that critique cogently, constructively, and effectively may well determine the future, not only for the Church but for the viability of life on earth. Critique alone, however, will not sustain queer home economics over the long haul. The great work stretching before us will also draw frequently from the energy Jesus described in the shepherd who leaves ninety-nine sheep behind to find the one that is lost (Luke 15:4). That same energy inspired a man to bury treasure in a field and then sell everything he had to buy that field (Matthew 13:44); likewise a woman to turn her house upside down to find one missing coin (Luke 15:8); and yet another to shed all other possessions for the sake of buying the one pearl of great value (Matthew 13:45).

Each of these gospel parables and many others rely on economic images, and Jesus used them to describe what he called "the Kingdom of God." By most economic standards the energy in each case is foolishly spent. It makes no common sense to put ninety-nine perfectly well-behaved sheep at risk for the sake of just one, or to liquidate one's resources for the sake of buried treasure or a single pearl, no matter how valuable, or to devote so much consternation over recovering one coin. These remarkably *queer* economic strategies sit at the heart of the Gospel, queer enough to interrupt and disrupt any ordinary and recognizable definition of a "kingdom"—or of a household.

Home economists spend considerable time and effort on unremarkable daily chores. Children need to get dressed for school, the pets walked, dinner at least imagined, and the rain gutters cleaned before the coming storm. These quotidian rhythms also oscillate for special occasions—the holidays, birthdays, dinner parties, and anniversaries that punctuate the ordinary arc of household life. These images of homey routine populate more than a few of the parables preserved in the gospel accounts of Jesus's teaching as well as the life he apparently lived in the company of household friends, and still further in the household hubs of the earliest Christian communities on display in the Acts of the Apostles. Like the Gospel *kingdom* with no economically feasible royal realm, these biblical evocations of *home* set a peculiar agenda for our theological housework.

Attending carefully to that agenda, queer home economists will take on familiar theological chores oddly, apparently careless of efficiency and even heedless of propriety. Suspicious of standard narratives, they explore Christianity's backyard in search of buried treasure. This will mean holding previously cherished household goods loosely for the sake of retrieving that one valuable pearl. Otherwise urgent priorities, even ninety-nine of them, might be set aside to attend to that single one, the important one. Inevitably, moments of chaos and disorder will ensue as a woman feverishly sweeping her house in search of a single coin can raise quite a cloud of dust, creating even more work to do when she finally finds that precious coin.

The gospel writers surely knew firsthand the consequences of living in these gospel households they portrayed. A wise householder brings out of the household treasure not only the old and familiar but also the new and thus presumably startling (Matthew 13:52). Delightfully startling perhaps, yet old wineskins filled with new wine eventually burst (Matthew 9:17). Queer home economists do not abandon methods and insights from the past even when they seem at odds with contemporary innovations. Nonetheless, when the household treasure yields both old and new together, side by side, the household itself can fall into disarray, perhaps even unravel at the seams. Why should they, why should any of us risk such chaos? Jesus replies: for the treasure, the pearl, and the coin, yes, but most especially for that one out of a hundred who is lost. Not just "lost," as if temporarily misplaced, but for that one who is pummeled down, trampled, and left for dead; for that one tied to a Wyoming fence post on a lonely stretch of prairie, or dragged until dead and decapitated behind a Texas pickup truck, or beaten and burned on a pile of tires.[34]

Here the queer home economist pauses to remember why theological ideas matter. An actual sheep may simply wander off inadvertently and become lost. The lost ones in human communities, however, and as social theorists remind us, become lost for a reason. The reasons vary, from market mechanisms and corporate profiteering to political gridlock and partisan bickering, as well as the categorical classification schemes critiqued by queer theorists, those social and cultural regimes that render some bodies less valuable than others, if not actually disposable. All of this of course stews in the cauldron of global warming where climatic catastrophes will strike first those already lost to planetary systems of hierarchical stratification.

These socioreligious complexities can remind us of the invaluable assistance theorizing provides. Theory need not sit sequestered in ivory towers, and indeed, it ought not. Critical theory delves to the root of the problems that compel us toward transformative action. The Greek verb from which we derive the word "theory" means rather simply "to view." Theorizing, in other words, need not always refer to academically technical and thick modes of analysis but can mean exactly what most parents urge young children to do: look both ways when crossing the street. We do this to ensure our safety in the midst of traffic and to discern the best way to navigate across a busy street from one side to the other. The objective, of course, is to cross the street and not merely to analyze it; both theory and action remain vitally important and especially as they intertwine. As a form of theorizing, theology likewise offers a way to view the world as clearly as we can, or as I want to propose, as *queerly* as we can.

Queer home economists will not view the world in the same way as other theorists, even as we draw often from a wide range of diverse disciplines for our theological work. Linguistic roots can mislead on this. To recall, "theology" means "words about God" in the same way that "anthropology" means "words about humanity" and "sexology" means "words about sex." But do theologians, anthropologists, and sexologists all speak the same language? Do they define their fields of study in the same way, with the same tools and

---

34. These refer, respectively, to the brutal murders of Matthew Shepard, James Byrd, and Billy Jack Gaither, all of which happened within a year of each other. William B. Turner opens his book on queer theory with their stories (*Genealogy of Queer Theory*, 1).

procedures? *What* do they study? Anthropologists might point to a human being to answer that latter question and sexologists to a physical act of intimacy. To what would a theologian point? Everything?

Dorothee Sölle would have us note carefully that whatever the word "God" actually means and entails, God can never be the *object* of our study; neither microscopes nor telescopes will bring that "object" into view. Theology instead reflects on something far more elusive yet still and always tantalizingly present: the relationship God initiates, nurtures, and sustains with God's creatures.[35] These relationships vary as widely as the creatures themselves do, which will always render our words about God provisional and our speaking potentially hazardous. In a vein similar to Sölle's, Mark Jordan warns against the idolatry of Christian speech, of mistaking our words about God for that divine reality beyond all speech.[36] Clearly, the same cautions apply to the complexities of anthropology, not to mention the delights and perplexities of sexology. All the possible words we may wish to speak and reasonably articulate about these topics will never fully capture or exhaust the profound mysteries of sex, humanity, or God. Nevertheless, we keep on speaking and debating and parsing these topics. Why? Gospel writers and Christian history suggest a reason: deeper participation in the mystery of life itself.

Participating in Divine Life shapes queer home economics with a galvanizing vision. Imagine Dorothy awakened in Kansas to see Auntie Em's face suddenly blush red or the trees in her own backyard beginning to green as the wheat fields shade into an amber gold. Seeing in this way would inevitably change how Dorothy lived, even if others could not see as she did. Dorothy would surely want to explore this transformation further and likely discover yet more tints and saturations exciting her into speech—halting and fumbling speech at first (how does one describe color in a black-and-white world?) yet eventually persuasively. She would persuade not by refuting blackness and whiteness but by inviting spectral depth and breadth into the grey edges and charcoal shallows. Others similarly persuaded would join her speaking, adding what she lacked to a colorizing, colorful process that would never end. For theological rainbows end not in a pot of gold—a fairy-tale fantasy—but always in something new and unexpected.

---

35. Dorothee Sölle, *Thinking About God: An Introduction to Theology*, trans. John Bowden (London: SCM Press, 1990), 1.

36. Jordan, *Telling Truths in Church*, 60.

Rainbows shimmer in and out of view, elusive but present, just like God. Speaking of it remains unfinished, always. Housework, as the old saying has it, is never really done. The unfinished theology in the following chapters mirrors the doctrinal trajectory of historical traditions with which Christian communities have engaged for centuries. The inflection points on that arc will seem plain and obvious: creation, Christ, Spirit, salvation, Trinity, Church, and the "last things" of Christian eschatology. Familiar to many yet also tantalizingly strange as the unpredictable and fluid character of household life rarely fits into neatly arranged systems. Queer home economists know, if only intuitively, how mismatches, slippages, and friction points in the system can offer opportunities for retrieving what system-building necessarily leaves behind. The vocation of queer theological housework relies on those leftover theological pieces as important traces of the God who perpetually disrupts systematic expectations: the prodigal who returns to find welcome rather than punishment (Luke 15:20); the wild branch unnaturally grafted into the tree of promise (Romans 11:24); the baptismal erasure of divisive classification schemes (Galatians 3:28); the lesser member of the body being clothed with greater honor (1 Corinthians 12:23–24); the insistence that in Christ we are a "new creation" (2 Corinthians 5:17) yet having no idea what we will eventually become (1 John 3:2).

Rather than a system, the theological fragments collected in this book resemble a patchwork quilt. Some of the fabrics have enjoyed a cherished place in Christian practice while others have been tossed aside on the ecclesial cutting room floor. Each of them has value on its own, yet stitching them together with the help of queer theorizing can invigorate fresh forms of Christian witness for social transformation. To that end, I invite viewing each theological scrap and fragment through a single lens, through the image of *home*, where quilts often sit, infused with memories and ready to provide comfort.

Unlike quilts, however, I do not mean by "home" all the various places any of us manage to make comfortable and cozy, those familiar habitations of safe haven, important and vital as they are. I mean "home" in all of its dissatisfactions. I mean that ever-elusive space of dwelling and relating that many keep searching to find in so many varied homemaking efforts. I mean to evoke the leftover ache that remains when all has been done that we can do to make a home and yet we still yearn. I mean how our hearts still skip a beat when we read poignant biblical texts: Matthew's Jesus declaring that he "has nowhere to lay his head" (8:20) while John's Jesus insists that in God's house there are many "mansions" (John 14:2, KJV). Queer people of faith can and do find surprisingly fresh resources in their own religious backyard, yet those same resources keep pushing "home" perpetually out of reach, just over the horizon where none of us can see. Even there, in our own backyard, each generation of Christians realizes in new ways what the writer to the Hebrews meant: "Here we have no lasting city" (13:14)—not even Oz. The familiarity of all we find homey as people of faith comes under the perpetual scrutiny of that biblical strangeness.

The familiar made strange, odd, and quite peculiar—queerly enough, this qualifies as "good news" when Christian theology can inspire hope for that home which no one can yet imagine. I offer here an approach to the queerness of theology for Christian witness to that kind of hope, a proposal to defamiliarize what so many Christians believe they already know. To do this, I invite queer home economists to trace the doctrinal arc of Christian faith and theology in some unusual ways. I invite them to reconceive the traditional pattern of Christian ideas as God's own *naturally odd* people follow the *unspeakably divine* Jesus in *perversely Pentecostal* communities, those rich locations where the *erotically social* character of divine life is *ritually aroused* with visions of an *eternally queer* horizon. This reframing of Christian doctrine matters, and not merely for the sake of semantic novelty. Why it matters—and urgently—appears readily enough in the lives and experiences of those queerly called to this divine vocation.

Queerly Called

ECSTASY, HOPE, AND THEOLOGICAL METHOD

he forbidden can prove quite attractive. Augustine had that insight many centuries ago, which I replicated as an undergraduate. The private Christian college I attended required all faculty, staff, and students to sign a statement of belief and its accompanying pledge of behavior. I made sure to engage in one of the items forbidden by the pledge as soon as I graduated: dancing. I relished that moment of feeling rebellious by kicking up my heels, but I had not anticipated stumbling into a theological insight. That happened some years later, at a gay dance club in Provincetown, Massachusetts. Not just the dancing but the venue and the particular clientele all contributed to my delighted surprise.

On a balmy summer night after sipping some beer, my friends and I plowed our way onto an already crowded dance floor and began to dance. I continued to dance for what seemed like hours, long after my friends had pushed their way back to the bar. I danced even as my feet grew tired and sweat poured off my body; it felt euphoric. I had never done that before, not like that. I had certainly enjoyed dancing over the years but not with that kind of abandon and uninhibited delight. Any self-consciousness I usually harbor over my less than gym-sculpted body simply vanished; I felt at home in my own skin. So this was new, this displacement of bodily shyness with joy. Many of the other dancers appeared to feel something similar. With very few exceptions the dance floor carried not couples but all of us. Each of us danced with all the others. The glances and smiles we exchanged did not for the most part signal seduction for a one-night stand but—how to name this?—shared ecstasy, perhaps. Right there and then, in the midst of all that dancing, I caught a glimpse of what it might mean to belong. "I belong here," I remember thinking to myself while dancing and with sweat running down my cheeks. "These are my people; this is my tribe."

Disenfranchised and marginalized populations of all types would recognize that kind of experience and longing. The yearning to belong—somewhere, anywhere—may well describe a universal human experience. As a theologian I recognized something else as well, a possible response to a question that had haunted me for years. In the midst of institutional church contestations over so many things (often quite trivial) and in the long history of complex theological development, what finally is Christian faith all about? Quite remarkably, in the middle of a gay club, I came to this: Christian faith inspires the hope of at long last being at home in our bodies, at home among others, and at home with God *all at the same time*. Augustine penned something similar more than fifteen centuries ago when he tried to imagine heavenly life. The character of that life, he supposed, would be knowing "peace in ourselves, peace among others, and peace with God."[1]

I knew when that insight dawned that it would need considerable refinement, but catching a bodily glimpse of what it might mean mattered a great deal. My memory of that experience (even as I write this) provokes a deep longing, the desire to feel that way again, yet I also find parts of that memory troubling. The vast majority of the men in that club were white. I recall seeing only a few African-American faces, even fewer Latino ones and no Asian-Americans or Pacific Islanders. The only two women there tended bar. Moreover, only a relatively small economic class of people can afford Provincetown in the summer. The men on that dance floor, in other words, may well have been "my tribe," but only a small portion of it, and I have no way to know how I would have felt about any of them after the music stopped. The glimpse I had of being at home was simply that—just a glimpse.

Yearning for what proves troubling marks a rich if vexing combination rife with potential for articulating the dynamics of Christian faith and especially Christian hope. That glimpse of an embodied home has stayed with me, lodging in my bones and muscles. Catching that glimpse in the midst of other gay men, all of us dancing, also provoked some unsettling questions. Why can hearing the rhythms of the kind of music I heard that night so quickly arouse my yearning for home in a way that most "church music" only rarely does? Why would a glimpse of home feel so palpable on a dance

---

1. Augustine, *The City of God*, ed. Philip Schaff, Nicene and Post-Nicene Fathers, Series 1, Vol. 2 (Grand Rapids, MI: Christian Classics Ethereal Library), 1143.

floor and so ephemeral in a church pew? Why did I discover more hope in that one moment among vacationing, anonymous dancers than I often do in moments of liturgical piety?[2]

Some of my friends readily provide answers to these questions, especially those who insist on being "spiritual but not religious." For them, institutional religion belongs to a stultifying history of repression and ought to remain there, in the past. Others see no point in trying to sort through the difference between religion and spirituality; they just want to dance. Perhaps theology begins there, with that unmistakably embodied desire. Perhaps our peculiar faith as Christians draws continually from the sustaining energy of the dance itself, especially as it fuels a home-coming hope. If so, then queer home economists face a particular theological task: accounting for that hope with tools and methods sufficient for home-building. The task begins, though, with pondering why such hope matters before trying to account for it. Only then will a method for doing this theological work find the traction it needs.

DANCERS FROM THE DANCE

Many of my LGBT friends love to dance. The reasons vary, just as they do for everyone. Some dance for joy, others for seduction, and still others for social bonding. Yet a thread of commonality weaves throughout the many reasons LGBT people dance. In a world of oppressive social structures, unwelcoming religious institutions, and constant threats of violence—a world, that is, filled with homeless spaces—we dance for hope.[3]

Dancing has enjoyed a long history of cultural expression and often with religious or spiritual significance. Consider the ancient biblical story of Israel's ruggedly handsome King David, who could barely keep his clothes on in public as he danced before the Ark of the Covenant as it returned to Jerusalem (2 Samuel 6:12–23). Michal, Saul's daughter and David's wife, was scandalized by this display of, well, what exactly? Joy? Eroticism? Perhaps David took his lead from Miriam, who danced on the occasion of her

---

2. Kelly Brown Douglas writes about similar themes in the tension between the historic black church and the development of blues music in *Black Bodies and the Black Church: A Blues Slant* (New York: Palgrave Macmillan, 2012).

3. See my introduction to Christian theological topics and themes with dance as a guiding metaphor in *Dancing with God: Anglican Christianity and the Practice of Hope* (Harrisburg, PA: Morehouse Publishing, 2005).

people's rescue from the Egyptians (Exodus 15:20). Or consider the Shakers, a small communitarian movement among early New England Quakers who established eighteen communities and, by 1850, had grown to 4,000 members. Known best today for their fine woodworking and elegant furniture, they were known at first as the "shaking Quakers" for their elaborate ritualized dances and spirit trances. Separating themselves from the outside world, these spiritual dancers affirmed the absolute equality of men and women and even supposed that God was "bisexual," endowing everyone with both male and female characteristics. Or consider Sufis, "whirling dervishes" in popular parlance, whose Islamic faith in the beauty of the one God with ninety-nine beautiful names rises up in mystical dances. These whirling, ecstatic movements purge the dancers of all desire but the desire for the one God.

To this list I would add the image of sweaty gay men, naked to the waist, stomping their feet to a pounding rhythm in a dance club late into the night. I would also add country-western clubs with lesbian cowgirls twirling their partners around the dance floor at wee hours of the morning, and urban ballroom dance schools as well, where, perhaps one night a month, bisexual and transgender people indulge in the fluid lines of a waltz.

We can quite properly refer to each of these instances of dancing as ecstatic. And that makes them queer. Each falls on the margins of day-to-day routine and each of them occurs among people living on the edges of a given society's dominant culture: ancient Israelites on the borders of powerful empires; the now nearly extinct Shakers, who retreated from the mighty tide of American industrial progress; Muslims, whose medieval civilization rivaled, and in many ways surpassed, that of Christian Europeans and who are now profiled in the West as agitators and terrorists; LGBT people on the borders of gendered sexual conformity, whose clubs and bars still populate the warehouse districts and industrial zones of American cities away from mainstream view. All of these locales vibrate with the queer energy of hope, the odd yet strangely alluring hope of carving out something like a home in otherwise homeless spaces.

Queerly alluring ecstasy resides deep within Christian traditions yet surfaces far too infrequently among today's theologians and pastors. It lures many people into church buildings on a Sunday morning without knowing precisely why; few, if any, venture an answer to that mostly unspoken question. The world of online social media brims with compelling tales of ecstasy of all types, either tapped fully or only glimpsed, and replete with musings on the transcendence of those moments—and nary a word from clergy. Modern institutional Christianity, from its theological formulations to its practice of ministry, has all but forgotten its own queer history in a world eager and at times desperate to hear it, to touch it, to dance to its seductive rhythms late into the night. A second-century Christian believed that "those who do not dance do not know what is coming to pass."[4] Those who *do* dance would likely pose more than a few pointed questions to today's Christian leaders if they had even an inkling of the treasure buried on church grounds.

These dancers from the dance might wonder why so many books on theology seem so dull and lifeless. Have theologians forgotten the endlessly fascinating adventure into the fathomless mystery of the living God, which theology ought to inspire? These dancers might ask whether theology has any room for the kind of whimsical playfulness and childlike awe that can excite our deepest passions and desires. They would ask this not knowing that Christian theology began just there, with that poignant yearning. They would surely want to know why institutional religion turns so often to the policy procedures of bureaucratic machinery when Jesus preferred to speak of God with images of partying at a feast, celebrating with a banquet, and the joy shared by a bride and bridegroom. Why is this? Why do clergy rarely speak about the eroticism percolating in Christian traditions and the peculiar gender identities populating ancient spiritual practices?

If these dancers paused long enough in the dance to read the Bible for themselves (rather than hearing it selectively quoted in movies or in news media), they would likely notice four canonical gospels and not just one. Why, then, do so many insist on only one way to think and speak about Jesus? Reading those gospel texts, they would also likely notice that the gospel writers chose multiple ways to write about Jesus, even within a single gospel account, and that those writers often chose to portray Jesus himself as rather cagey about his own identity. If the Church created that much room for diversity and ambiguity in its own canonical texts, why does it turn so often to doctrinal conformity and split into so many sectarian groups? Indeed, why a canon of institutionally approved texts at all?[5] These dancers

---

4. This comes from the apocryphal *The Acts of John.* See F. Lapham, *Introduction to the New Testament Apocrypha* (London: T&T Clark, 2003), 137.

5. The history of why and how Christians created a "canon," or a set of "official" sacred texts, is rather complex. Elizabeth Stuart offers a helpful overview of that history as well as LGBT-related approaches to reading the Bible in *Religion is a Queer Thing: A Guide to the Christian Faith for Lesbian, Gay, Bisexual, and Transgendered People* (Cleveland, OH: Pilgrim Press, 1997), 37–46.

would doubtless be surprised to realize that the earliest Christians lived for centuries without any officially canonized texts, or that what we mean today by the word "Bible" and "canon" differs from one Christian community to the next. During the Protestant Reformation Martin Luther made proposals for different versions of the canon and many canonical texts themselves underwent significant editorial revision over the centuries to reflect varying theological commitments.[6]

As dancers eager to dance, all these textual questions would likely occur later, if at all. They would wonder first why Christians so often stress the *texts* of Christian theology at the expense of how people actually live with their faith. Might they wonder why a classic text of Augustine in the fifth century attained normative theological status with little if any reference to how fifth-century Christians worshipped and prayed—or even danced?

As the music beckons these dancers back to the dance floor, I imagine them both wistful and resentful: Why did no one tell us how *queer* Christianity really is? Poignant and charged with longing, that question traces the contours of a divine calling. In a world littered with so many homeless spaces, God has something rather peculiar in mind, and always has. God imagines a world where every creature feels perfectly at home, without exception. Few really believe this, but a long history of visionaries and prophets and mystics and the most unremarkable ordinaries have caught glimpses of it, and they still do. As it always has, that glimpse changes lives. Whether the change occurs suddenly or unfolds over a lifetime it nearly always comes with a calling: to work with God on making this world a home, not just for some but for all.

The image of homeless spaces tugs on the heart for more than one reason. Churches might open their buildings for shelter and church members might give money to alternative housing programs and some might make a spare room available to friends during a prolonged spate of unemployment. To these visibly homeless the Church properly reaches out with Christian charity. Less visible yet far more pervasive, modern Western society has left many of us with what Scott Cowdell hauntingly calls "homeless hearts." As modern Westerners create the conditions for comfort, from high-tech gadgets to single-family residences, many live with a lingering discomfort, a

---

6. Bart Ehrman describes well if not also controversially this checkered history in the evolution of the Bible. See *Misquoting Jesus: The Story Behind Who Changed the Bible and Why* (New York: HarperCollins Publishers, 2005).

vague yet ambient sense of rootless dissatisfaction. Modern forms of religion mostly fail to address this dis-ease or even to notice it.[7] Poet and essayist Christian Wiman echoes that analysis with an equally haunting observation about the anxiety that invades even our leisure. Recalling a dinner-party conversation with friends seeking relief from a world of busy-ness, Wiman notes:

> Everyone has some means of relief—tennis, yoga, a massage every Thursday—but the very way in which those activities are framed as apart from regular life suggests the extent to which that relief is temporary (if even that: a couple of us admit that our "recreational" activities partake of the same simmering, near-obsessive panic as the rest of our lives).[8]

Unmitigated restlessness and anxiety turned inward generates ever greater demand for antidepressants; turned outward, it manifests as racial prejudice, misogyny, and violent bullying. More severely still, Western society's inability to diagnose our self-imposed homelessness on this planet only fuels, quite literally, our addiction to earth's natural resources with the vain hope of numbing our collective pain. Most see the result looming large on our smoggy horizon with paralyzing clarity. Contemporary cultural, economic, and geopolitical realities now indicate what has been until recently unthinkable. The last generation to enjoy the benefits of the modern world—such as easy and affordable access to fossil fuels; a temperate, human-friendly climate; manageable disease and preventable epidemics; stable governmental structures—that last generation has already been born.[9]

I believe the peculiar faith of Christians can rise to meet the challenge of homeless spaces, even on a planetary scale. Queerly enough, theology makes a difference. Theological *texts* may contribute to that difference, but I mean more than to aim for the doctrinal acuity that so many assume as theology's substance. Theology takes intimations of home—no matter how fleeting, perhaps intuited only briefly on a dance floor—and makes from

---

7. Scott Cowdell, *Abiding Faith: Christianity Beyond Certainty, Anxiety, and Violence* (Cambridge: James Clarke & Co., 2010), 9.

8. Christian Wiman, *My Bright Abyss: Meditation of a Modern Believer* (New York: Farrar, Strauss, and Giroux, 2013), 85.

9. For more on this admittedly bleak assessment, and in addition to Al Gore's *An Inconvenient Truth: The Planetary Emergency of Global Warming and What We Can Do About It* (Emmaus, PA: Rodale, 2006), see James Gustave Spee, *Red Sky at Morning: America and the Crisis of the Global Environment* (New Haven, CT: Yale University Press, 2004, 2005) and Richard Heinberg, *The Party's Over: Oil, War, and the Fate of Industrial Societies* (Gabriela Island, BC: New Society Publishers, 2003).

them occasions for home-building and invitations for home-coming. LGBT activists for social change know what this means far less abstractly. From eighteenth-century English "molly houses" to twentieth-century dance clubs, "homosexuals" have persistently carved out spaces of safe haven, frequenting these spaces often at the risk of physical harm. Far more than venues for drinking alcohol and finding sexual liaisons (though that happened too), these spaces of homeward longing catalyzed shared reflection, analysis, strategizing, and the deep communal bonds of affection that redrew the cultural and political map of the North Atlantic. The second- and third-century catacombs of ancient Rome bear witness to the same persistence among the earliest Christians.

Catching a glimpse of home in a gay dance club can ignite a divinely queer calling, the passionate urge to bear witness to that glimpse and, even more, to build on it and expand it. Queer home economists need theological tools to translate this calling into sustainable vocations, to channel that hopeful defiance against despair into effective home-building. This daunting challenge facing twenty-first-century churches appears a bit less formidable by noting the lives and sensibilities of so many LGBT people who already occupy Christian pews and preach from pulpits. Their courageous witness frequently humbles me, one of the reasons why I find dancing with other LGBT people so compelling. I know that many of them bring painful personal histories to that dance floor and that some arrive there in the midst of distressing circumstances in their jobs, concerning their physical health, or with their families. And still they dance, and often with abandon, and at times with joy shaking loose from their bodies and gratitude lighting up their faces. Those moments make theological housework not only possible or merely bearable but enlivening and sustaining. More than this, such shared moments of translating musical rhythm into bodily gesture makes visible "the conviction of things not seen," as the biblical writer might remind us about faith itself (Hebrews 11:1).

A wise colleague once cautioned his seminary students about their work. "You cannot do Christian theology from a place of fear," he said. "The only way to do Christian theology is by being open to the possibility of joy." To that insight I would add this: you cannot do Christian theology well if it remains in a book or resides only in the realm of academic contestation. Christian theology forms witnesses, or in the original Greek, "martyrs." The many words employed for theological reflection mean little if others cannot see them lodging in our bones and muscles, etched into the patterns of our bodily relations, creating communities of costly conversion. In a fourth-century treatise on Christian perfection, Gregory of Nyssa declared both boldly and broadly that we ourselves ought to reflect every name and title that expresses the meaning of "Christ." To call ourselves Christian, "we must bear witness to it by our way of living."[10]

Theology matters among and for God's queerly called people to the extent that it helps us bear effective witness, bodily and socially, to our peculiar faith. This peculiar "conviction of things not seen" springs from a deep well of ecstatic hope, the hope—clutched desperately at times—that our hearts will not remain homeless forever. A queer theology thus truly matters when it manages to account for that occasionally elusive yet perpetually galvanizing energy of hope.

ACCOUNTING FOR ECSTATIC HOPE

To speak of an "ecstatic hope" we indulge in a redundancy, and a challenging one for theological accounting. Hopefulness springs inexorably from ecstasy's peculiar energy, which nearly always resists by definition an orderly account. A linguistic reminder may help here. The word "ecstatic" comes from the Greek *ekstatikos*, a word made from the prefix *ek*, meaning "out," and *sta*, meaning "stand." From this latter portion we also derive the word "stasis," referring to the state of standing in equilibrium, or on the mean between extremes. To be *ek–static* means to stand outside oneself, to come out of stasis, or to be jolted to an extreme end of a spectrum and removed from the *status quo*. There, one occupies a queer space indeed, a space that can generate or renew hope for the new and fresh in the patterns and rhythms of the ordinary. A further linguistic note for this theological challenge: the words "order" and "ordinary" come from the same etymological root. The orderly routine of day-to-day life renders it ordinary, especially in contrast to the hope that springs from ecstasy's disruption of all that passes for the quotidian rhythms of daily life.

Here, then, the challenge, in the words of the biblical writer in the first letter of Peter: "Always be ready to make your defense to anyone who demands from you an accounting for the hope that is in you" (3:15). Paul

---

10. Gregory of Nyssa, "Treatise on Christian Perfection," *PG*, 255.

would clarify that task further: "hope that is seen is not hope." After all, "who hopes for what is seen?" (Romans 8:24). Giving an account of the unseen generated by the ecstatic surely poses a challenge, not least when theologians try to replicate the orderly accounting standards set by the modern West.

Few people today would recognize the world or even imagine living comfortably in it apart from the breathtaking advances in modern science over the last three centuries. These advances—from public hygiene and food safety to medical care, transportation, and computing—have all relied on a meticulous ordering of the world around us, a careful parsing and classifying of countless bits of data into explanatory systems and usable applications. The reach of modern scientific method extends well beyond the physical sciences, inspiring philosophers, sociologists, economists, psychologists, and many others to render apparent chaos into manageable categories. Judging the success of these efforts depends almost entirely on where one lands in the classification schemes they produced. Nineteenth-century social Darwinists (mostly from upper economic classes) consigned the poor to the bottom of the evolutionary ladder. Those engaged in "racial science" not surprisingly promoted white people to the top. German sexologists meanwhile created a whole new category of human being called the "homosexual," an attempt to account for those whose lives exhibit characteristics somewhere between recognizably male and female people. Each of these classification schemes and others like them mutually reinforced each other in ways that shape how we perceive the world around us—not perceive as merely suppose but actually seeing the poor failing to thrive, and people of color physically demeaned, and gay teenaged boys bullied for acting like girls. Queer theorists frequently focus their critical gaze there, on the power of social categorization to construct the world we inhabit. And what of theology?

Christian theological ideas and spiritual practices aim quite deliberately to construct a world for Christians to inhabit. The peculiar symbol set, odd social patterns, and stylized rituals of the institutional church, replete with wardrobes of outlandish costumes, have for centuries carved out a space from which Christians see reality in a particular way and then live in a particular way based on that seeing, at least ideally. The question at hand in accounting for ecstatic hope turns not on *whether* Christian faith shapes our perceptions but *what* it invites into our field of vision. Theorizing of any kind, to recall, provides a view of reality to help clarify the path before us and around us for the sake of navigating as best we can. As queer theorists illumine troubling aspects of modern Western society's point of view, institutional Christianity likewise falls under that critical gaze. Feminist theologians have sounded this caution, often with alarm, for decades. The collusion between the institutional church and Western patriarchy constructed a world of male privilege and *therefore* a particular way of seeing God. Rosemary Radford Ruether, for example, describes the evolution of religious symbols in Christian history by noting their original intent, the attempt to shed light on particular experiences. Institutionalizing these symbols, however, created a different effect. "Systems of authority," she writes, "make received symbols dictate what can be experienced as well as the interpretation of that which is experienced. In reality, the relation is the opposite."[11] Mary Daly made the gendered effects of that shift plain: "If God in 'his' heaven is a father ruling 'his' people, then it is in the 'nature' of things and according to divine plan and the order of the universe that society be male-dominated."[12]

Disentangling Christian faith entirely from Western culture, even if this were desirable, remains impossible. Much like the formative effects of family history on our individual personalities and relationships, cultural histories will always imbue religious traditions with a range of quirks, insights, oddities, and joys. Yet Christianity no more remains captive to its cultural history than any us do to our family trees. Queer home economists will turn to theological theorizing like some do to genealogical research and, at times, to psychotherapy as we sort through the formative effects of our families. Viewing as clearly as we can the family dynamics in God's household will equip us better to soothe modernity's homeless hearts, and especially to account for the ecstatic hope for home.

How we tell the story of Christianity's family history matters as much and presents many of the same challenges as telling the story of our own biological families. Do you begin with your parents or reach a bit further back? Did your ancestors arrive to New England colonies on the Mayflower or to southern colonies on slave ships or far western regions by crossing a dangerous border? Perhaps your personal household lives with the unspoken legacy of grandparents interred in Japanese concentration camps on the California coast or great-great-grandparents sequestered in San Francisco's

---

11. Rosemary Radford Ruether, *Sexism and God-Talk: Toward a Feminist Theology* (Boston: Beacon Press, 1983), 12.

12. Mary Daly, *Beyond God the Father: Toward a Philosophy of Women's Liberation* (Boston: Beacon Press, 1973), 13.

Chinatown after building the transcontinental railroad. How we tell these stories is a form of theorizing, a view of the past with an eye on its present influences. Both traumatic and jubilant memories will punctuate these accounts, which demand moments of interpretation in our theorizing and not only narrative recounting. First-century gospel writers did this very thing for their own communities, for their households of faith. They did this, as most biblical scholars would remind us, decades after the death of Jesus and the startling proclamation of his resurrection. Those intervening decades unfolded around the socially transformative practice of table fellowship, of sharing meals inspired by the memory of the cross and the hope of new life. Giving an account of that practice and why it matters energized first-century evangelists while it also proved vexing; the sacking of Jerusalem and the destruction of the Temple by the Romans inflected that early Gospel witness in some profound ways.

Queer home economists share similar vexations with those first-century gospelers. They worry, for example, that Christianity's present entanglement with North Atlantic culture and its perduring imperial inclinations distort the story Christians might otherwise tell of our religious family history.[13] They worry especially about tidying up a messy story for the sake of a respectable account. Orderly accounts do prove useful for organizing a household; they can also stifle creativity and restrict the household's imagination with familiarity. More simply: the sacred character of gospel accounts, signaled by gilt-edged pages bound between leather covers, can easily mask the queerness of the story those accounts preserve. Consider again the bare-bones outline of that story, a story that features a Jewish prophet living in a conquered, backwater province of the Roman Empire; he lived as an unmarried and childless itinerant teacher in a society constructed on marriage and biological family and insisted on the scandalous practice of sharing meals and daily life with the ritually unclean and socially misfit; his manner of life leads to a humiliating, public execution at the hands of an occupying army and shortly thereafter to reports from hysterical women about grave robbers and an empty tomb, reports that no one at first believed. These peculiar features of a familiar story turn especially queer when they generate an ecstatic hope for living in culturally unwarranted, socially unreasonable,

---

13. See Joerg Rieger's analysis of imperial logic as it shapes Christian theology in varying ways over the centuries, including today, in *Christ and Empire: From Paul to Postcolonial Times* (Minneapolis: Fortress Press, 2007).

religiously radical, philosophically suspect, and politically dangerous ways. To that hope and its way of life, the first-century gospel writers devoted their galvanizing accounts.

Something just as queer happened next. A host of political and cultural developments transformed this peculiar hope into mainstream propriety. Early theologians explicated it with philosophical systems. Church leaders defined it with conciliar creeds. Established liturgies confined it to textual rubrics. Clergy employed it for ethical exhortations. In all these ways, ecstatic hope found itself quite literally bound in texts and institutionalized. This eruption of transformative ecstasy from the margins of the ordinary eventually came to define the "stasis" of an orderly society. As hope's queer energy waned, those who did experience something of its ecstatic character found themselves again on the margins, bearing disruptive witness to a peculiar faith.

This historical pattern repeated many times. Consider the early Christian communities described in the biblical Acts of the Apostles, communities networked by charismatic gifts for preaching, healing, interpreting, teaching, and administration. By the time the Pastoral Epistles were written, such as the first and second letters to Timothy, those peculiar gifts had migrated into established "offices." To fill the office of preacher or administrator, of presbyter or deacon, eventually required as much political savvy as charismatic endowment; the two coincided more as fortuitous accident than discerning design. Or a bit later, consider desert ascetics who fled the corruption of urban decadence seeking the refining fires of simplicity. Their insights and experiences gradually intertwined with institutional life and rose to represent the pinnacle of piety in established monastic communities. More broadly, consider some of the earliest Christian communities in the Roman Empire, persecuted by fearful and egomaniacal emperors, meeting in private homes or in underground catacombs. The conversion of the Emperor Constantine in the fourth century brought these outlaws out of their tunnels and into the light of day, where they moved into basilicas for their worship. Those monuments to the power of their former persecutors in turn became monuments for excluding the unbaptized.

These transformations reflect more than the old aphorism that the persecuted, once liberated, run the risk of becoming persecutors themselves. Ecstatic hope always resists containment and control. Hope itself remains perpetually restless and on the move, straining against established patterns and institutional structures, even those it helped to create. Christian hope, with its sweeping and startling claims about divine reality, the destiny it inspires for human life in the cosmos, and the trajectory it portrays of human history, the stories it tells of heroes and martyrs, of saints and visionaries— none of this rests very comfortably in canonized discourses or the stylized gestures of organizational polity. Christian hope always remains dissatisfied with its own artifacts.

Equally curious, the dynamics of Christian hope never fully release it from the sources of its dissatisfaction. Even as theologians write new texts, we still quote from ancient ones; like a bread-crumb trail in a dark forest, those ancient texts can remind us what we might have missed from our past. Even as we revise and sometimes reject misguided policies, we retain the form of the offices that generated them; like a solar panel converting the sun's rays into electricity, institutions can provide a framework for channeling energy constructively. My own life brims over with religious texts and I am deeply ensconced in institutional Christian life. My life of faith would be greatly impoverished without all of these things. As an Episcopal priest and theologian, I admire and rely on the historical development of Christian traditions, but not without significant qualification. The textual and ritual superstructure of Christianity matters only when it inspires the ecstatic, transformative hope that birthed it.

Ecstatic hope and romantic love share something important in common, which makes any coherent account of them difficult to construct. Both ancient Greeks and contemporary psychologists remind us that the dizzying experience of romance resembles a form of madness. We call it "falling in love" for a reason, which can feel like tumbling headlong into the deep end of a pool.[14] Like hope, the disorienting energy of romantic love disrupts the ordinary rhythms of quotidian life, a disruption most people recognize and few try to explain. Poets and musicians strive to capture those moments with verse and melody, yet even the best love sonnet can only gesture toward love itself. Theology exhibits these same limits, always falling short of categorizing and classifying our ecstatic encounters with divine mystery. Why then devote so much effort to theological reflection, to trying to account for what ultimately remains beyond the grasp of even the most carefully constructed

---

14. Some ancient Greeks referred to falling in love as *theia mania* (madness from the gods), and the notion of romantic love as a brand of mental illness has circulated throughout medical literature ever since; see Frank Tallis, "Crazy for You," *The Psychologist* 18, no. 2 (February 2005), 72–74.

accounting systems? Lovers offer at least one possible response: when love's madness abates, we then face all the housework of sustaining a relationship over time. Approaching our theological "housework" as God's peculiar people involves what romantic couples already know; we do this work and we want to do it not for its own sake but for the delectable madness that inspired it.

A METHOD FOR THE MADNESS

How theologians account for ecstatic hope has varied widely over the centuries. The number of approaches to that task nearly equals the number of theologians. The "how" of doing Christian theology belongs to the realm of theological method, which has taken on the contours of its own academic discipline in the modern period. The possibilities for how one might do theology extend widely, ranging from commentary on biblical texts to drawing from popular culture as a source for theological insight. The influence of modern Western sensibilities infused theological method with standards that resembled empirical science, such as systematic coherence and rational articulation. I do not mean that ancient theologians were disorganized or irrational, but in contrast to modern Western sensibilities, they did prefer *contemplatio*—or prayer—as the primary mode of theological reflection. "Contemplation" is the Latin version of the Greek *theoria*, or theory, as both evoke a sense of gazing, viewing, and paying attention, which stands in rather stark contrast to the parsing, dissecting, and classifying that came to be associated with modern science. Blending traditional theological hallmarks with modernity's emerging scientific cadences served an institutional church eager to keep pace with a rapidly changing world. More simply, many Christians in the throes of modernity's breathtaking advances worried that their faith belonged to an old and quickly vanishing world that lacked the sophistication and precision of Western "progress."

Starting in at least the eighteenth century, as the world became less mysterious when placed under a microscope, the realm of religious influence began to shrink rather precipitously. The centuries since then have witnessed both Western and non-Western people alike no longer turning to religion to explain how the world works; science does that. In tandem with scientific discovery, increasing technological expertise placed a previously chaotic and dangerous world of nature ever more firmly under human control, whether in terms of genetics or global communications. Not just the physical world, but also the world of history surfaced with more clarity, emerging from the mists of mythology into the bright light of critical analysis. Applying scientific method to the study of history, however, also came with a price: the reduction of truth to verifiable facts. In the modern West, truth eventually became synonymous with whatever scientists can repeat in a laboratory experiment or what historians can verify as having "actually happened." Today's popular use of "myth" to signal "false" supposedly illustrates humanity's hard-won maturity—to the horror, no doubt, of the ancient Greeks.

Trying to keep pace with the milestones of modernity, many Christian communities felt compelled to tame their own peculiar faith and devise a sufficiently rigorous method for an academically respectable theology. *Modern* Christians believe in God but not in a three-tiered universe with heaven above our heads and hell beneath our feet. *Modern* Christians embrace the Gospel vision of the "Kingdom of God," not mystically but ethically, as a society of equality and justice for all. *Modern* Christians offer their worship decently and orderly with no fear of disturbing the peace, whether intellectually or politically, at least in the North Atlantic. All of this sounds quite reasonable indeed, yet queer home economists pause and wonder: in rushing past Christianity's queerness on the road toward modern respectability, have we left behind a great deal more than unnecessary baggage? Ironically, if not sadly, many people today encounter awe-inspiring mystery, not in religious faith and practice, but in the discoveries and texts of astronomers and quantum physicists. Surely the ecstatic hope of Christian living can spark as much imaginative wonder as peering through a telescope into the Milky Way or pondering the inexplicable behavior of subatomic particles. More than a few modern theologians would agree.

In the nineteenth century, with figures like Soren Kierkegaard and Sojourner Truth, and in the early decades of the twentieth century, with figures like Albert Schweitzer and Dorothy Day, some scholars, pastors, and activists insisted on keeping the strange world of the Bible strange and on finding good news in the disorienting if not apparently unreasonable cadences of theological language.[15] These critics of modernity worried about any project that tries to make Christian faith compatible with contemporary

---

15. Karl Barth is often cited as a champion of this shift in perspective to "keep the Bible strange." See the helpful overview of this shift in James C. Livingston and Francis Schussler Fiorenza, *Modern Christian Thought, Vol. 2, The Twentieth Century*, 2nd ed. (Minneapolis: Fortress Press, 2006), 62–67, 73–75.

culture. The Gospel will sound like good news when it interrupts oppressive systems, especially when those systems appear in the guise of commonsense rationality. As Rowan Williams observes, the Gospel cannot be both palatable and transformative at the same time.[16]

In more traditional language, the Gospel invites conversion, not as a single moment of decision but as a lifelong process of having one's world continually turned upside down in a process of transformation. This invitation to conversion extends to all, including LGBT people whose worlds of unexamined religious and cultural assumptions stand as vulnerable to Gospel overturning as any other. Rather than dismissing the myriad moments of odd encounters, peculiar visions, and outrageous practices in the history of Christianity as simply unreasonable for otherwise sensible people of faith to embrace, God's queerly called people take those moments as sources of divine transformative energy. They do embrace them, not naïvely or uncritically, but faithfully. They recognize in all those queer stories from Christian history the potential, as David Matzko McCarthy puts it, to "disturb the world with God."[17]

Most faith communities likely find little reason to consider their faith disturbing, or why they should. Institutional Christianity has been so tightly woven into the fabric of North Atlantic culture that very few Christians can imagine how their faith would disturb anyone, let alone why the Gospel qualifies as "queer." Developing a method for this theological housework can begin rather modestly, by noting three features of Christian theology that run throughout historical traditions and that carry the potential to queer the expectations of the modern West. These three features in turn set an agenda of retrieval for our collective housework, a reaching back into theological traditions to recalibrate what it means and why it matters to account for an unaccountable hope.

First and at its best, Christian theology *invites* more than it explains. In a society that relies on and even relishes explanations for how things work and why people behave in certain ways, eschewing an explanatory function for theology begins to sound at least a bit queer. Yet even at its most dense and systematic, Christian theology can never capture God in explanatory systems of thought. Theology can only point toward that reality with the hope of inviting

---

16. Rowan Williams, "Postmodern Theology and the Judgment of the World," in *Postmodern Theology: Christian Faith in a Pluralist World*, ed. Frederic B. Burnham (San Francisco: Harper & Row, 1989), 110.

17. David Matzko McCarthy, "Desirous Saints," in *Queer Theology: Rethinking the Western Body*, ed. Gerard Loughlin (Malden, MA: Blackwell Publishing Group, 2007), 307.

others into deeper participation in God's own life. More acutely, anyone trying to speak accurately about God might as well try to catch water with a net.[18] Or as a Buddhist aphorism would have it, "the finger is not the moon." As I excitedly invite you to enjoy the light of a full moon with me, I might point toward the night sky. If you look only at my finger, my pointing has failed. The same can be said of Christian theology; it invites by pointing away from itself.

A second feature sounds nearly self-evident yet carries a queerly disruptive energy. I mean this: Christian theological traditions exhibit a *developmental* character. Or more simply, theological ideas change over time. Or more pointedly, Christian theology contributes to a living tradition rather than a museum collection. Like all human thought and culture, Christian theology undergoes constant evolution. The gospel writer called Matthew may have believed certain things about Jesus in relation to God that have little to do with what Thomas Aquinas believed some twelve centuries later. This does not obviate the past as irrelevant, nor does it compel us to choose which among many historical approaches to God might register as "correct." Instead, and rather queerly, the past is not settled and fixed. History, including theological history, remains fluid and restless, waiting to be refashioned in the hands of contemporary communities. As Oscar Wilde once quipped, "The one duty we owe to history is to rewrite it."[19]

And third, Christian faith and theology are irreducibly social and communal. My own insights will never suffice for pointing adequately or even very well at all to that mystery called God. Christian Wiman ranks this aspect of faith as indispensable:

> I feel a strong need—an imperative, really—to believe something in common; indeed, I feel that any belief I have that is not in some way shared is probably just the workings of my own ego, a common form of modern idolatry.[20]

Building on Wiman's observation, we need not only common but also *un*commonly shared inquiry. More precisely, I need the insights of those

---

18. That phrase comes from the title of a short but compelling book on this very topic by Val Webb, *Catching Water in a Net: Human Attempts to Describe the Divine* (New York: Continuum International Publishing Group, 2007).

19. Oscar Wilde, *The Critic as Artist* (New York: Mondial, 2007), 32. John Henry Newman, another nineteenth-century figure, did not treat history as quite so malleable, but he did argue for the importance of theological *development* over time; see *An Essay on the Development of Christian Doctrine* (London: Longmans, Green, 1885).

20. Wiman, *My Bright Abyss*, 127.

with whom I apparently disagree. Modern Western people, Christian or not, will find this rather odd if not terribly queer. Few of us are taught how to learn from those we perceive as "different," let alone how to relish the idea of building community with them and making families of faith from those peculiar strangers. William Temple, the archbishop of Canterbury during World War II, insisted on this deeply challenging yet vital feature of Christian faith: truth appears slowly, over time, and must *therefore* find expression in a chorus of voices rather than a single one.[21]

These three features of Christian theology begin to trace the outline of a theological method marked by retrieval. I do not mean merely importing material from the past, especially for projects that aim for theological "correctness." To the contrary, queer home economists will turn most often to Christian history for its diverse perspectives rather than for its timeless articulations. An invitational, developmental, and social religious tradition urges that kind of retrieval with respect to the Bible, to theological traditions, and the notion of community itself.

Retrieve the Rich Diversity of Biblical Texts

What does the Bible say? This may well stand as the most frequently asked religious question in both ecclesial and civic arenas throughout modern American history. On the issue of slavery or the role of women in the nineteenth century or regarding sexual ethics in the twentieth, what the Bible "says" has trumped nearly every other source for those debates. Biblical scholar Dale Martin encourages us to remember, however, that inanimate objects like texts do not actually "speak." We use that metaphor often, of course, with all kinds of texts. But when we do so with the Bible we risk implying (and for some, claiming explicitly) that *God* is the one speaking. Martin prefers to shift the focus of that ubiquitous question away from the Bible and toward those who read it. Texts do not speak, in other words, but people do speak with texts.[22] Taking that deceptively simple observation to heart can reorient God's household toward a richer appropriation of biblical traditions. Rather than asking

---

21. While this theological conviction appears in numerous places in Temple's work, it is interesting to note how he develops it for biblical interpretation, including how the gospel writers interpreted each other over time. See the introduction to his *Readings in St. John's Gospel* (London: Macmillan & Co., 1959), ix–xxxiii.

22. Dale Martin, *Sex and the Single Savior: Gender and Sexuality in Biblical Interpretation* (Louisville, KY: Westminster John Knox Press, 2006), 1.

what a text "says," household members can more fruitfully analyze how people use those texts and discern better how they themselves might use them and what they want and need to speak with them.

This retrieval would go a long way toward queering a remarkably pervasive modern assumption: all the many peculiar texts, which have been collected between the two covers of a single book called "The Bible," must always agree with each other and tell but one coherent story. The biblical writers themselves, however, would surely object. The writers of Leviticus and Isaiah, for example, addressed decidedly different questions and presented rather divergent visions for Israel's divine vocation. Or try reading the Gospel of Matthew next to the Gospel of John; even casual readers might wonder whether the very same Jesus inspired those two very different accounts. One might also notice some profound theological differences between the Letter of James and the Letter to the Galatians concerning the effects of divine grace and the role of good works in the life of faith. Protestant reformer Martin Luther actually argued that the Letter of James ought to be removed from the Bible entirely.

The Bible stands as a potent reminder of humanity's constantly evolving understanding and description of God and how divine encounters shape and transform human life. Contrary to popular perceptions, however, "evolution" is not interchangeable with "progress." What comes later chronologically speaking is not necessarily better or worse than what came before. So rather than "making sense" from such textual diversity (or simply covering it over), queer home economists insist instead on "making scripture" from those diverse texts. As Dale Martin has proposed, this will mean spending far less energy (if any) on finding the historically "correct" interpretation of the Bible and discerning instead how to make use of biblical texts for human and planetary flourishing. Martin further urges God's household to restore the Bible as the "church's book" and to think of "scripture" as the process faith communities undertake while reading, interpreting, and making meaning from biblical texts.[23] The Church, in other words, does not serve the text; the Church itself assembled that collection to support its witness to the Gospel.[24]

---

23. Martin proposes a number of images to guide this process in the final chapter of *Sex and the Single Savior* (161–85). See also his *Pedagogy of the Bible: An Analysis and Proposal* (Louisville, KY: Westminster John Knox Press, 2008), especially ch. 4, "Theological Interpretation of Scripture," 71–91.

24. I have proposed a way of doing this today by reading the diversity of biblical texts through the lens of the "one story" of the hope for communion. See *Divine Communion: A Eucharistic Theology of Sexual Intimacy* (New York: Seabury Books, 2013), esp, the introduction, 1–28.

Lesbian and gay Christians accustomed to refuting hurtful biblical interpretations will likely find Martin's approach just as disconcerting as fundamentalists. Modern sensibilities predispose those on all sides of any given
debate to turn to an unchangeable, foundational argument from the text.
This winner-take-all, zero-sum game played with ancient texts now occupies the default position in most religious communities; few can imagine
any other way to make a religious argument. Elizabeth Stuart seeks a much
broader landscape on which to read sacred texts, a contemporary landscape
that has now "shattered" the notion of stable texts with only a single or "correct" meaning. Historical-critical method, she notes, trained many of us to
read biblical texts by focusing on the horizon behind them, or the original
contexts of the writers. That method remains important but more recent
approaches urge reading sacred texts by shifting to the horizon in *front* of
the text, or "the reader and her world."[25] The varying "worlds" of countless
readers will inevitably generate a wide range of meanings from even a single
text. Biblical theologian Hans Frei anticipated this queerer approach as he
described textual interpreters as so "hot in pursuit of the truth" that biblical
texts are left with little if any "breathing space." Frei defined a *good* interpretation not as a trump card to resolve textual disagreements, but rather as
always providing something "left to bother, something that is wrong, something that is not yet interpreted"—breathing space, in other words.[26]

This approach to reading biblical texts not only queers modern notions
of interpretation that rely on "correctness," especially univocal renderings of
meaning; it also queers modern notions of religious authority, which many
Protestants locate in the Bible itself. Queer home economists will insist
instead on embracing the authority of what Martin would call the "scripture
making process," or Frei, the "breathing-space community." Even better than
"authority," we might more modestly seek guidance from the Holy Spirit,
the "breath of God," who Jesus promised would lead further into truth
(John 16:13). Creating breathing space for our Scripture-making will entail

---

25. Elizabeth Stuart, "Camping Around the Canon: Humor as a Hermeneutical Tool in Queer Readings
of Biblical Texts," in *Take Back the Word: A Queer Reading of the Bible*, ed. Robert E. Goss and Mona West
(Cleveland, OH: The Pilgrim Press, 2000), 29. See also Ken Stone's treatment of "interpretive communities"
in *Practicing Safer Texts: Food, Sex, and Bible in Queer Perspective* (London: T&T Clark, 2005), 25.

26. Hans Frei, *Theology and Narrative: Selected Essays*, ed. George Hunsinger and William C. Placher
(Oxford: Oxford University Press, 1993), 162. See also Daniel Boyarin's description of Talmudic culture
in which multiple interpretations and disagreements concerning textual traditions were not merely tolerated but "canonized" for the sake of a living tradition (*Carnal Israel: Reading Sex in Talmudic Culture*
[Berkeley: University of California Press, 1993], 27–29).

a variety of techniques and not a little courage. The outcomes will likely surprise everyone to varying degrees—occasionally playful, sometimes evocative and perplexing, and always inviting deeper conversion. Queerly enough, the goal in this textual housework will not turn on "getting it right" but instead on "getting it better," where we judge "better" based on how much thriving and abundant life a particular reading generates for all of the household's members. After all, biblical texts exist for those who read them, not the other way around, just as God created the Sabbath for humanity, not humanity for the Sabbath (Mark 2:27).

Retrieve the Rich Diversity of Historical Traditions

Augustine's fifth-century texts on the Trinity differed in some respects from the eighth-century views of John of Damascus, which differed even more from those of Thomas Aquinas in the thirteenth. Anselm and Abelard, both writing in the eleventh century, differed on what "atonement" means in relation to Christ and the hope of salvation. So which of these theologians, each considered a "saint" in Christian traditions, articulated the correct theological position? Remarkably, institutional Christianity refuses to say, and those figures occupy only the tip of a large, complex historical iceberg.

Perhaps even more remarkable than canonizing divergent theologians, the so-called "religious right" in the United States has managed to dominate American public discourse by presenting their approach to Christian faith and practice as the only genuine and authentic expression of it. This makes perfectly modern sense, as modern Western sensibilities rely on consistency and coherence as bottom-line markers for truth. Christian history, however, resists those reductionist impulses, even when considering the earliest Christian communities portrayed in biblical texts. The long history of Christian theological traditions discloses far more diversity and thus far more richness than most people realize today. Those traditions exhibit quite a breadth of opinion, even on such fundamental questions as the identity of Jesus, what salvation means, and how to structure the Church and its ministry. Most Christians likely realize that the doctrine of the Trinity did not suddenly emerge whole and complete in the minds of the first disciples. Yet even the later development of Christian "orthodoxy" over the first five or six centuries of Christian history incorporated a fairly wide range of views on how to think and how to speak a Trinitarian faith.

Much like biblical texts, the history of Christian ideas evolves slowly, punctuated by as many moments of contested ambiguity as insightful clarity. Rather than "making sense" from that wide-ranging diversity, queer home economists approach historical traditions with multiple lenses, strategies, and ways of reading. If, for example, Augustine's critique of Christian empire in his now classic *The City of God* still proves useful today, we need not reject it just because his texts on human sexuality might vex and trouble us. Better still, we might read the latter texts in light of the former one and find surprisingly fresh insights about both, even if we cannot be sure that Augustine himself intended those insights. Or consider the provocative fourteenth-century meditations of Julian of Norwich, who imagined Jesus as our mother and his pierced side flowing with both blood and water as the "womb" from which we are born anew.[27] Julian could serve nicely as a frame of reference in which to read Gregory of Nyssa's fifth-century reflections on the fluidity of gender, even though centuries divide these two figures and neither would likely understand the other if we put them together in the same room.

Actually, Christians throughout most of Christian history would insist that Julian and Gregory and a host of others already reside in the same "room," and the rest of us enjoy their company even now. Christian traditions refer to that room as the "Communion of Saints." Queer Christian housework will always root itself there, in that room of lively conversation transpiring with myriad opinions and perspectives. To be sure, treating each of these saintly theologians and each biblical writer with the integrity they deserve demands historically and contextually appropriate readings of their texts. Even so, respect for the integrity of each does not require sealing them off from each other in historical silos; we can read them in concert even when their historical insights resist tidy translation into contemporary communities. Rather than detailed blueprints or agendas for conformity, ancient traditions often serve best as historical provocateurs, spurring us to expand our imaginations, question our assumptions, and remain open to the possibility of conversion. Just as Dale Martin urges us to "make scripture" from diverse biblical texts, so also queer home economists can weave compelling proposals from even divergent theological traditions and with the same goal perpetually in view: to enhance the thriving and flourishing of all.

27. See Veronica Mary Rolf's biographical sketches of Julian and commentary on her "revelations" in *Julian's Gospel: Illuminating the Life and Revelations of Julian of Norwich* (Maryknoll, NY: Orbis Books, 2013), esp. ch. 21, "The Motherhood of God," 512–37.

Retrieve Human Diversity as a Gift

Modern Western sensibilities extol the virtues of community in the midst
of a history punctuated by segregation. Americans can trace the origins of
this discomfiting conjunction to New England colonists, including Puritan
settlers who believed English reformers had not sufficiently "purified" the
Church of England of Roman Catholic influences. They were not alone or
unique in that belief, yet the Massachusetts Bay Colony represents in par-
adigmatic fashion a much longer history of conceiving "community" as a
homogenous collection of like-minded individuals who conform to shared
doctrine, to "genuine" and "authentic" belief. This perception of what constitutes human community has cut along racial and ethnic lines, economic
and class strata, and of course gender and sexuality.

Christians can reach much farther back in our history for the same
dynamic. Paul's letters to the Galatians, the Corinthians, and the Romans
all address communities that apparently struggled mightily with their own
diversity. The church in Corinth, for example, seemed to devolve into a
host of varying factions, each with its own charismatic leader (1 Corinthians 3:1–9). At the same time, Paul stubbornly insists on referring to all
of these communities as the "body of Christ." Just like the human body
needs diverse members to function and thrive, so also the ecclesial body
(Romans 12:3–8). This claim certainly does not render Paul an ancient
version of a modern libertine. Paul proposed and often insisted on some
fairly rigorous standards for Christian faith and life. Yet modern Christian churches have mostly overlooked or have failed to notice Paul's more
radical claim that spiritually thriving communities need not, and in fact
cannot, rely on rote conformity in order to flourish (see 1 Corinthians
9:20–23 and 10:23–32 for an indication of Paul's own vexations about
this question).

As Anglican Christians witnessed and some participated in schismatic
rhetoric over the 2003 election of openly gay priest Gene Robinson as the
bishop of New Hampshire, a gospel opportunity fell tragically by the way-
side. Modern Western society knows perfectly well what it looks like for communities to fracture over disagreements. The history of Christianity since
the Protestant Reformation lurches from one moment of fragmentation to
the next; a Christian denomination splitting over conflict hardly qualifies as
news. Communities that choose instead to learn from those with whom they
disagree remain notably absent from historical portrayals and contemporary

media reports. Is such learning even possible? Are such communities imaginable? How much diversity is tolerable?

Queer home economists do not have ready-made answers to these questions, but they insist on asking them. If both the Bible and theological traditions evolve over time and bear witness to strikingly divergent points of view, then God's household would likely benefit from a good deal more humility in our theological invitations. Queer householders committed to humility need not, however, shy away from boldness. They can articulate firm positions, adopt postures with confidence, and offer urgent proposals and all the while reserve the right to be mistaken, to practice above all the kind of hospitality that admits differing points of view as potential sources of new insight. This would surely seem quite queer indeed for both those who stake out progressive spaces and fundamentalist ones alike, and probably everyone in between. Joerg Rieger manages to evoke succinctly that queer discomfort by citing a statement from a self-professed liberal congregation: "We are a radically inclusive church: everyone who walks through this door is welcome." But as Rieger notes, "those who submit to the community (symbolized by walking through a very specific door) and thus promise not to create trouble are always welcome."[28]

Retrieving diversity in biblical texts, from historical traditions, and among communities marks only the beginning of a queer theological method, but a good one nonetheless. Rather than trying to "manage" diversity, or more severely to "solve" it, like a problem, diverse texts, traditions, and communities can instead rise up as the divine gifts of a startling if not disconcerting grace. These queer gifts can nudge or even shock us out of complacent assumptions, confront us with unimagined horizons, or potentially soothe the anxiety bred from the restrictions of one-dimensional approaches to Christian faith. Even this modest beginning for a theological method can elicit both delighted surprise and a good deal of relief in many faith communities. This can happen without once using the word "queer" or even mentioning LGBT people. Surprise, because so many Christians today have never been exposed to anything other than modern forms of religious belief and practice. Relief (if not at first delight), because here the unspoken queerness of so many people's lives begins to resonate with their own queerly diverse faith traditions, which they had assumed would always remain out of synch if not actually in conflict.

---

28. Joerg Rieger, *God and the Excluded: Visions and Blind Spots in Contemporary Theology* (Minneapolis: Fortress Press, 2001), 37.

Recalling William Turner's musing, perhaps everyone really is in some sense "queer." Perhaps everyone at some point or another has experienced a sense of not fitting in, of falling through the cracks, of wondering whether any place can feel like home. Far more than just a few people likely feel "homeless" in their own faith tradition, the very location where they expected or at least hoped to find themselves at home. The queerness of Christianity launches faith communities on a journey in which "belonging" and "fitting in" mean something quite different than meeting standard cultural expectations of conforming to social norms. Belonging among others who have caught a vision of the queerly good news of the Gospel skews what usually passes for "normal" and shapes a common life that feels oddly but compellingly out of synch with the wider social order. Paul seemed to nudge Christians in Rome along a similar path. "Do not be conformed to this world," he wrote, "but be transformed by the renewing of your minds, so that you may discern what is the will of God—what is good and acceptable and perfect" (Romans 12:2). Perhaps the observation attributed to novelist Flannery O'Connor says it best: "You shall know the truth and the truth shall make you odd."[29] God's queerly called people know exactly what that means. God assembles a household of peculiar faith from all those who feel culturally, spiritually, theologically and, quite naturally, odd.

---

29. Ralph C. Wood, *Flannery O'Connor and the Christ-Haunted South* (Grand Rapids: William B. Eerdmans, 2004), 160.

2

Naturally Odd

IDENTITY POLITICS, DESIGNER BODIES, AND BAPTISMAL MINISTRIES

ategorizing human beings on the basis of gender seems perfectly natural. Many if not most people greet the announcement of a newborn baby with the same initial question: Is it a boy or a girl? But wait—are they asking about *gender* or the child's *sex*? Relegating what we mean by sex to biology or anatomy and gender to culture or society creates a good deal of gender trouble, as Judith Butler would remind us. William Turner explains why this can prove so contentious: "Butler argued that feminists lose the possibility for thinking about subversive ways to convey gendered meanings when they insist that gendered identities depend on sexed bodies as the loci of agency."[1] No matter your gendered behavior, in other words, you cannot fool "mother nature." Still more trouble emerges whenever we try to discern what makes something seem or feel or look *natural*. What exactly is "nature"? Today even savvy grocery shoppers treat "nature" with suspicion and read food labels carefully. More often than not, less than 10 percent of something called a "fruit juice drink" with "natural flavors" will come from the juice of harvested fruits. It may taste natural, but those flavors resulted mostly from an ingenious chemical process designed to mimic the flavor of, say, apples or blackberries. Whatever might be natural about fruit juice drinks comes to us through various processes of human intervention. Even fruits and vegetables in the produce section of a grocery store have been processed and packaged through a long chain of human intermediaries. Does that process render all of those supermarket products unnatural? Would this mean that the degree

---

1. Turner, *Genealogy of Queer Theory*, 110.

of naturalness decreases as human contact with something increases? Why would human activity make something more unnatural?

My backyard garden demands my regular attention. Benign neglect would soon lead to unwanted encroachment from my neighbor's ivy, eventually choking my young camellia bush. Without yearly pruning, my two fruit trees would grow much taller but produce less fruit. Left to its own devices, in other words, the natural evolution of my garden would look quite different than it does today. What then can be considered natural about my own backyard? Does human intervention make that space unnatural?

What comes naturally to human beings? Answering that question by comparing ourselves to other animals poses some interesting quandaries. Human beings clearly differ from birds as flight does not come naturally to us. Yet with the help of winged machines we have quite remarkably managed to fly. Similar skills have made it possible to spend extended periods of time under water with fish, where we do not naturally belong. If nature makes us flightless and air-breathing, should we consider airplanes and submarines unnatural? Should we go further and declare those machines "wrong" or "bad" or even "sinful"?

Together with hunger and eating, erotic desire and sexual intimacy surely meet the standard for natural features of human life. Firmly rooted in biological drives and hormonal impulses, finding food and having sex ensure the survival of the species. The procreation of children is not, of course, the only thing natural about sex. It can also feel naturally painful as well as pleasurable and the difference between these two sensations can sometimes blur. At the same time, human beings have assigned a good deal more meaning to both eating and having sex than merely staying alive or ensuring the survival of the human race.

A wide range of customs and even elaborate rituals accompany the otherwise simple and natural act of gathering and preparing food. In some societies, food preparation and with whom one shares it carry both cultural and religious significance. Setting my dining room table with fine china, linen napkins, and silver candle holders seems quite natural to me yet has little to do with the natural need to eat. Frequent sexual relations can at times indicate virility or social dominance; abundant fertility might also signal divine blessing. Some ancient cultures treated procreation as but one among several important functions of sex, including securing one's rank in a social hierarchy of value (especially the socially superior male over the female as well as any other person lower on that ladder of cultural power).[2] In contemporary Western societies sex can consummate relational intimacy or seal a commitment to exclusive pair bonding. For others, it serves as recreational activity or the means for financial gain. Setting my dining room table with a bouquet of roses in addition to candles may mean more than preparing to enjoy a fine meal. It could be read as a romantic prelude to sexual intimacy.

How do we distinguish the natural from the cultural elements in both food and sex? If the otherwise simple and natural act of genital contact among humans can carry widely divergent meanings derived from historical expectations, social significance, and religious sensibilities, where does nature end and culture begin? Should we consider all these many and diverse layers of cultural meaning somehow unnatural human interventions into simple natural acts? What's the difference between nature and culture if culture comes naturally to human beings?

Historically, religion has intervened into this perplexing line of questioning with a deceptively simple claim: nature means whatever God intends. Deviating from that divine intent constitutes an unnatural act, and religion provides not only the means to know what God intends but also to ensure the manifestation of that intent in practice. Not surprisingly, the two most basic and apparently natural human activities—eating food and having sex—have also been the most frequently regulated human activities in nearly every society, and religion has most often been the means to regulate them.[3] For centuries Christian traditions have portrayed sex between a man and a woman, and more particularly in monogamous marriage as a baseline of divine intent for human beings. That arrangement rises to the surface of the many other cultural configurations of human relationship as the most natural thing we can find in nature, tied directly to the perfectly natural division of humanity into two "genders." A man having sex with another man and a woman having sex with another woman violate God's own laws of nature on both counts—the purpose of sex and the binary division of gender. Eventually, not only those sexual acts but also the people who commit them qualify as deviant, aberrant, or simply and self-evidently *un*natural.

---

2. Martti Nissinen, *Homoeroticism in the Biblical World: A Historical Perspective* (Minneapolis: Fortress Press, 1998), 45–52.

3. See Ken Stone, *Practicing Safer Texts*, especially ch. 2, "Border Anxiety: Food, Sex, and the Boundaries of Identity," 46–67.

The powerful bond between religion and nature—the naturalizing of religion and the spiritualizing of nature—resides deep in the collective consciousness of Western culture. This bond received most of its
power from Christian traditions, especially the doctrine of creation. The
first line of the Nicene Creed, for example, which many Christians recite
in worship services each week, reinforces the bond between religion and
nature in subtle but significant ways: "We believe in one God, the Father
Almighty . . . maker of heaven and earth." The familiarity of that creedal
statement tends to occlude its socioreligious significance. The rest of the
creed, and by extension the whole of Christian faith itself and its wide-
ranging social effects all derive from the implications of that one claim
about the Creator God.

LGBT people have learned particularly well how these religious discourses on nature shape our sense of self and place in the world—in our
families, among friends and coworkers, and with our own bodies. What
feels natural to lesbian, gay, and bisexual people translates as unnatural in
religious speech; gender transition stands for some as a rejection of God-
given nature, which transgender people often embrace quite naturally.[4]
To alleviate the distress that so often accompanies nature, the latter third
of the twentieth century witnessed a number of both scientific and religious projects depicting "homosexuality" as no less natural than "hetero-
sexuality."[5] Significantly, those projects rarely considered what bisexual
and transgender sensibilities might mean for arguments rooted in "nature."
Queer theorists, by contrast, relentlessly question any appeal to supposedly
natural identities, especially those that turn on "self-evident" truths about
human beings and human relationships. The more we learn from biologists, geneticists, and anthropologists, very little seems self-evident about
the endless mystery called humanity (not to mention the mystery of planetary life in the work of geologists, quantum physicists, and astronomers).
Indeed, Eve Kosofsky Sedgwick alerts us to how little seems to qualify as
self-evident about human beings and our relationships by providing just a

---

4. See Jakob Here's account of trying to navigate a medical system that required a diagnosis of mental
illness before providing the medical care he needed in his gender transition ("Toward a Queer Theology of Flourishing: Transsexual Embodiment, Subjectivity, and Moral Agency," in *Queer Religion, Vol. 2:
LGBT Movements and Queering Religion*, ed. Donald L. Boisvert and Jay Emerson Johnson [Santa Barbara, CA: Praeger Publishing, 2012], 143–66).

5. For a good overview of this posture and its implications, see Daniel T. Spencer, *Gay and Gaia: Ethics, Ecology, and the Erotic* (Cleveland, OH: Pilgrim Press, 1996), 63–75.

short list of the many possible ways we differ in our sexual desires, practices, and sensibilities.[6]

Queer home economists affirm the traditional belief in God as Creator yet remain deeply suspicious of "nature." Modern theologies remain especially vulnerable to static conceptions of nature, or an "intelligent design" in contemporary popular parlance, that God completed in the distant past (or for some, only relatively recently, between 5,000 and 10,000 years ago).[7] Reifying nature in a closed system generates a host of unexamined assumptions, not only about divine creation but also about the Creator; those assumptions draw much more into their orbit than religious arguments about Darwinism or questions about sexual ethics. Socioreligious postures toward nature carry profound consequences for the lives of women in patriarchal cultures, for racial and ethnic minorities in white supremacist societies, and even for the constructions of economic class and privilege. Many gay and lesbian theologies made considerable progress in exposing these deeply problematic religious discourses on nature, yet these attempts too often relied uncritically on arguments for "natural" sexualities.[8] Ancient approaches to the doctrine of creation, by contrast, present a tantalizing alternative in this highly charged religious mix of nature and culture. Some of the earliest Christian apologists, for example, proposed the notion of creation *ex nihilo*, of God creating out of nothing. By doing this they sought in part to relativize Greco-Roman cultural institutions and dethrone the supposedly divine stability associated with their sociopolitical effects.[9] In short, destabilizing the "natural order of things" can bring some surprisingly good news to light. Good news not just for LGBT people but for all those who have ever wanted to feel more at home in their own bodies. This might actually include everyone.

---

6. Sedgwick, *Epistemology of the Closet*, 22–27.

7. James Usher, the archbishop of the Church of Ireland in the seventeenth century, promulgated a "young earth" argument, dating the actual moment of creation to the year 4004 BCE. Today's young earth creationists (who generally try to refute Darwin's theory of evolution) offer varying opinions concerning the actual age of the planet, but usually no more than 10,000 years. See Ronald L. Numbers, *The Creationists: From Scientific Creationism to Intelligent Design*, expanded ed. (Cambridge, MA: Harvard University Press, 2006).

8. For an overview and critique of some of these approaches, see Elizabeth Stuart, *Gay and Lesbian Theologies*, especially ch. 2, "Gay Is Good," 15–32.

9. A distinctly Christian doctrine of creation was used in early Christianity to respond to a number of overlapping concerns, including a refutation of Aristotle's claim that earth was eternal. Insisting on divine creation "out of nothing" thus helped to secure a theological claim about God's sovereignty over not only "nature" but "culture" as well; see Gerhard May, *Creatio Ex Nihilo: The Doctrine of 'Creation Out of Nothing' in Early Christian Thought* (London: T&T Clark, 1994, 2004).

In a world where nature grows ever queerer with each newly proffered scientific theory, the queerly good news of Christian faith will turn less on an "intelligent designer" than on a wildly creative God, the God who not only makes the sea "great and wide," but also the Leviathan just to play and frolic in it (Psalm 104:25–26). A queer theology for Christian witness can begin quite fruitfully there, with a Creator who more often resembles an avant-garde artist. To recall Hans Frei's image, Christian communities have lived for too long without adequate "breathing space" in the biblical accounts of creation. Or to recall Dale Martin's approach, those well-worn texts in Genesis deserve a more intentional "scripture making" endeavor. Sifting through the many layers of translation, interpretation, and cultural appropriations that have accrued around Genesis will require a wide range of tools and strategies for critically constructive approaches. Even so, queer home economists can achieve a great deal by turning to three interrelated tasks.

First, expose the gendered character of classifying "homosexuality" as a "crime against nature." The criminals in question commit their crime against the gendered order of things, especially against the male privilege that attends the binary gender system and from which so much of the contestation in modern identity politics springs. The level of panic and even violence that can attach to openly transgender sensibilities, for example, urges a careful analysis of Western society's obsession with natural classification schemes.

Second, reject the religious controversy over Darwinian biology and recast the doctrine of creation in robustly evolutionary terms. Whoever we are is not yet finished and our wildly creative God yearns to work with us on the unfolding project called "humanity." Today, that project necessarily and gratefully incorporates other animals in whatever meaning we construct for humanity, as well as the many ecosystems on which all life relies and that now face unthinkable collapse. More simply, the "others" with whom any of us hope to find ourselves at home include more than *homo sapiens*. Or as James William Gibson has argued, the modern West yearns for a "re-enchanted world," for a new sense of "kinship" with the world of nature.[10]

---

10. The industrialization of Western society, Gibson argues, rendered the world of nature as merely a warehouse of resources to be exploited. The next phase of ecological work invites a much deeper engagement and relationship with the other-than-human world (*A Reenchanted World: The Quest for a New Kinship with Nature* [New York: Henry Holt & Co., 2009]).

And third, take these cultural and theological points of contact into the practice of ministry to address pastorally the mostly unspoken sense of homelessness with which so many in our pews presently live, especially around our own bodies. Among the various ways to do this, the queer home economist can consider turning again, and perhaps surprisingly, to the traditional rite of baptism for shaping a compelling, countercultural witness to the hope of making a home out of our queerly human and naturally odd bodily life.

GENDERED CRIMES AGAINST NATURE

An otherwise unremarkable bodily posture as a teenager, punctuated by a brief comment from a friend, jolted me into a new and disorienting awareness of my own gendered body. Gathering in our high school auditorium for a school-wide assembly, I found a seat next to a friend from my youth group at church; I'll call him Steve. After sitting down and saying hello, I settled in by crossing my legs, by folding my right knee over the left knee, rather than resting my ankle there. This posture prompted Steve's remark: "The least you could do is sit like a man."

This shocked me, like a punch in the gut. I suddenly felt alienated from my own body, even more than a typical adolescent male might. What did crossing my legs have to do with being a man? I chose to sit that way for comfort yet found myself making a statement. More troubling still, why did Steve use the word "least" in his comment? If the least I could do is to sit like a man, what else about me failed to conform to manliness? Did Steve know something about me that I only vaguely intuited about myself? Back then I sat on the edge of realizing my sexual attraction to men; perhaps the way I sat disclosed more than I myself fully knew. But why would gender conformity have anything to do with whether I (as I actually did) found someone like Steve attractive?

People speak volumes when they want to know, first and foremost, the "sex" of a newborn baby. Some mothers and fathers want to know this before their child is born. Others like to be surprised but even then insist on knowing at the very moment of birth. Some newborn babies make this determination difficult, with genitalia that appear ambiguous. Rushing to determine which side of the gender divide the child will occupy, physicians or parents or both simply assign these ambiguously sexed babies to one sex or the other. Until recently, the physician often made that decision unilaterally, usually with surgery.[11] Discomfort with gender ambiguity appears between adults as well. Countless habits of social interaction, from bodily postures to eye contact and manners of speaking, depend on the perceived gender dynamics of a given encounter. No one knows precisely how to relate to a generic, ungendered human being.[12]

Human socializing relies on specificity, including all the myriad ways a given culture trains us to vary the style of our interactions with each other depending on a particular person's gendered sexuality, race, ethnicity, and socioeconomic class. My high school friend Steve provoked that particular insight for me. Living in modern Western society means being identified and based on that identity to occupy one's proper social place. By not sitting "like a man" I transgressed the boundaries of my social place long before engaging in sexual intimacy with other men. Premodern societies certainly structured their interactions with an equally defined sense of a cultural propriety. People who engaged in "sodomy," for instance, belonged among the "sodomites"; women who challenged male authority found themselves labeled as "witches." In the modern period, however, these social classification schemes calcified in the rapid advances of biology and medical science, where they evolved into categorical identities rooted in nature itself. Jane Shaw alerts us to this profound shift. Only in the modern period, as she describes it, did scientists begin to think of men and women as naturally different kinds of human being.[13] She cites Thomas Laqueur's work on this and his analysis of an emerging "two-sex model" for humanity in the eighteenth and nineteenth centuries, a model in which men and women differed in *kind* rather than only by degree or *type*.[14] This certainly seems rather queer indeed if nature supposedly makes sexual difference perfectly plain and self-evident. To suppose otherwise, as some have feared, would plunge the world into social chaos without a gendered compass to guide our sexual behavior. In such a world as that, might everyone fall prey to sodomy's temptation and

---

11. The Intersex Society of North America provides research data, publications, and videos on these complex topics (*www.isna.org*). See also Susannah Cornwall's introduction to and theological analysis of intersex and other "queerly" gendered realities in *Sex and Uncertainty in the Body of Christ: Intersex Conditions and Christian Theology* (Sheffield: Equinox, 2010).

12. This may reflect a particularly modern discomfort as ancient rabbinic sources on Genesis, for example, actually seemed to carve out space in those texts for those whose gender was indeterminate. See Michael Carden, "Genesis/Bereshit," in Guest, Goss, West, and Bohache, *Queer Bible Commentary*, 26–27.

13. Jane Shaw, "Reformed and Enlightened Church," in Loughlin, *Queer Theology*, 226.

14. Thomas Laqueur, *Making Sex: Body and Gender from the Greeks to Freud* (Cambridge, MA: Harvard University Press, 1990), see especially ch. 5, "Discovery of the Sexes," 149–92).

not just "homosexuals"? Oddly enough, that very anxiety simmered in Euro-American culture prior to the nineteenth century.[15]

The modern confluence of inherited cultural norms, the ascendancy of rationalism, and remarkable advances in scientific method provided new ways to speak and to enact social distinctions, or the categorical classifications of human identity. As Michel Foucault once famously observed, the late nineteenth-century medical profession invented "homosexuality." He did not mean that same-sex sexual behavior did not exist prior to that date. Foucault instead wanted to highlight the emergence of a distinct categorical identity—the "homosexual"—as one of the many products of modern medical and psychiatric science. In his words, "the homosexual was now a species."[16] Significantly, the medical construction of a "homosexual" identity emerged in tandem with similarly scientific categorizations of both gender and race. While the uterus naturally predisposes women toward domesticity, thus supporting the cultural practice of separate spheres for men and women, differently shaped skulls and varying metabolisms predisposed people of color to particular kinds of labor and social locations.[17] In this matrix of social-scientific discourse, gender, race, and sexuality mark mutually informing modes of categorical classification. These classification schemes, furthermore, never remain value neutral but always serve to bolster particular dynamics of cultural and political power. Laurel Schneider quotes Robert Young's observation about that key link between nature and social dominance: "The 'natural' gender relations of European society," Young notes, "establish the authority of the natural laws that determine the relations between the races." This move among nineteenth-century racial theorists, as Schneider describes it, "made explicit the association between the gender dominance of males and the claims that they were attempting to establish scientifically about whiteness" and further associated race and sex with economic class position.[18]

---

15. Mark D. Jordan has shown the extent to which "sodomy" could describe a range of objectionable acts in Christian history until its near reduction in the eleventh century to anal intercourse between men. It was this categorical religious definition that crossed the Atlantic with the European colonizers of America, where virtually everyone needed to guard against the temptation presented by "sodomitical vices" (*The Invention of Sodomy in Christian Theology* [Chicago: University of Chicago Press, 1997], 43–44, 110–11).

16. Michel Foucault, *The History of Sexuality, Volume 1: An Introduction*, trans. Robert Hurley (New York: Vintage Books, 1980), 43.

17. See Nikki Sullivan's overview of the social constructions of race and ethnicity in *A Critical Introduction to Queer Theory*, 57–80.

18. Schneider, "What Race Is Your Sex?" in *Disrupting White Supremacy from Within*, 154.

The notion of a "homosexual" identity emerged from these same overlapping spheres of identity construction, an identity that emerged first as a type of gender inversion (a man's compulsion to take on the role of a woman), and later as analogous to ethnicity in the emerging identity politics of the 1970s and 1980s. As Melissa Wilcox observes, religious institutions and faith communities were woefully unprepared to address any of these modern social-scientific notions of distinct sexual orientations.[19] The theological doctrine of creation, however, easily and quickly lent a helping hand. The natural order of things, both self-evident and confirmed by science, simply reflects God's own order of creation, to which the Bible clearly bears witness: "God created humankind. . . . [M]ale and female he created them" (Genesis 1:27).

These modern social-science complexities creep into nearly every aspect of Christian ministry and congregational life, often in subtle but at times explicit ways. Profound gender anxieties can infect both conservative and progressive communities alike. Recognizing not merely anxiety but also a type of gender panic at the root of ecclesial debates over "homosexuality" (frequently tapping into unacknowledged traces of misogyny) can set an important theological agenda for queer home economists. George Chauncey's study of early twentieth-century American society provides a particularly trenchant example.

Chauncey analyzed the 1919 U.S. Navy investigation of "homosexuality" in Newport, Rhode Island, which had quickly spread to the local ministerial association. Some of the sailors staying at the Newport YMCA accused a prominent Episcopal priest of making sexual advances in the course of his pastoral care. The ministerial association, including the Episcopal bishop of Rhode Island, vigorously defended the accused, hoping to prevent the accusations from spreading to other ministers. The concern here, however, had little if anything to do with a potential epidemic of "sodomy." Instead, as Chauncey argues, the ministerial association worried mostly about their own gendered performance of ministry. As upper-class clergy offered compassionate care to working-class sailors, the sailors perceived this care as effeminate, tantamount to a solicitation of sexual intimacy. These clergy defended themselves by insisting that acts of compassion did not compromise their masculinity.[20] The

---

19. Melissa Wilcox, *Coming Out in Christianity: Religion, Identity, and Community* (Indianapolis: University of Indiana Press, 2003), 39–46.

20. George Chauncey, "Christian Brotherhood or Sexual Perversion? Homosexual Identities and the Construction of Sexual Boundaries in the World War I Era," in *Hidden from History: Reclaiming the Gay and Lesbian Past*, ed. Martin Duberman (New York: New American Library, 1989), 308.

need to make this argument startles as much as the argument itself: religious piety and pastoral care do not make a man more like a woman.

More recently, the sense of crisis that began roiling the worldwide Anglican Communion in 2002 and 2003 underscores the relentlessly gendered arc of modern Christianity. In 2002 the Canadian diocese of New Westminster agreed to bless same-sex unions, and a year later, the diocese of New Hampshire elected Gene Robinson—an openly gay and partnered priest—as their bishop. The objections made to these decisions turned more explicitly than in previous decades to the supposed violation of God's own gendered order of creation manifested by same-sex unions. Andrew Carey, son of a former archbishop of Canterbury, clarified quite succinctly the gendered character of these objections. Rather than a selective reading of a few biblical passages, Carey argued, the prohibition against "homosexuality" derives from "an entire theology and anthropology arising from the creation narrative." The relatively few passages dealing explicitly with "homosexuality," he continued, "only make sense in the light of the bias of scripture towards the complementarity of men and women as the ideal of God's created order."[21] New Testament scholar Edith Humphrey repeated this gendered horizon in her analysis, which she insists rests at the very core of Christian faith and doctrine. "The difference in gender of husband and wife, united in marriage," she writes, "points to the wonder of the Trinity, our ultimate pattern of 'other-but-same in relationship.' Homoerotic relations reject the gift of sexual otherness and cannot echo the nature of the Trinity."[22] More than merely immoral, in other words, same-sex unions qualify as heretical.

Order itself infuses this theological paradigm as the proper ordering of gendered relations testifies to the divine order of the Creator. In this view, violating that order would plunge human society into frightful chaos. I imagine many gay and lesbian people find this kind of theological reasoning absurdly funny. We look at ourselves—at our intimate relationships, how we shop, have brunch, do the laundry—and marvel at the power we apparently possess to unravel the fabric of historic Christian theology. Beyond the parodic and humorous, the U.S. Supreme Court demonstrated the chilling effects of alarmist theologies ensconced in the binary gender system. In its

---

21. Quoted in Stephen Bates, *A Church at War: Anglicans and Homosexuality* (New York: I. B. Tauris, 2004), 39.

22. Edith Humphrey, "What God Hath Not Joined: Why Marriage Was Designed for Male and Female," *Christianity Today* 48, no. 9 (2006): 36.

2003 landmark decision concerning *Lawrence v. Texas*, the court overturned state sodomy statutes, but not unanimously. In his dissenting opinion, Justice Antonin Scalia argued that society has a right to reject "homosexuality." To do otherwise would result in a "massive disruption of the current social order."[23] Edith Humphrey would concur as she identifies "homoerotic activity" with humanity's "primal rebellion against God," a view echoed in a 2003 statement by Peter Akinola, the Anglican archbishop of Nigeria. Marriage between one man and one woman constitutes, for Akinola, the "divine arrangement" in creation, the rejection of which amounts to nothing less than an "assault on the sovereignty of God." This "assault," furthermore, rises in Akinola's view to the level of environmental catastrophe on par with the depletion of the ozone layer. "Homosexuality," he claims, marks a "terrible violation of the harmony of the eco-system of which mankind is a part."[24]

Queer home economists will for good reason find these socioreligious claims excessive if not preposterous. Yet Scalia, Humphrey, and Akinola did not simply invent this reading of theological traditions. The ancient Mediterranean societies that produced biblical texts understood the natural order of things in strictly hierarchical terms: God over man, man over woman, humans over animals. In those societies, ideally speaking at least, with whom one eats and how one has sex should reflect that natural (read "divine") order. Stephen D. Moore paints this picture a bit more severely. For ancient communities, "absolute inequality is intrinsic to both good worship and good sex." So rather than dismissing the thinly veiled gender panic of religious figures like Peter Akinola, queer home economists could push biblical scholars like Edith Humphrey toward more historical honesty. The natural world of biblical writers did not promote "other-but-same" relationships, as Humphrey would have us believe. Their world of nature reflected instead "dominant-and-submissive" hierarchies of value. Sex in that symbolic economy, Moore insists, depended on "eroticized inequality."[25]

---

23. Quoted in William Stacy Johnson, *A Time to Embrace: Same-Gender Relationships in Religion, Law, and Politics* (Grand Rapids, MI: William B. Eerdmans, 2006), 162.

24. Quoted in Stephen Bates, *Church at War*, 39. See my analysis of the gendered character of the debate over "homosexuality" among Anglican Christians in "Sodomy and Gendered Love: Reading Genesis 19 in the Anglican Communion," in *The Oxford Handbook of the Reception History of the Bible*, ed. Michael Lieb, Emma Mason, and Jonathan Roberts (Oxford: Oxford University Press, 2011), 413–32.

25. Stephen D. Moore, *God's Beauty Parlor and Other Queer Spaces in and around the Bible* (Stanford: Stanford University Press, 2001), 153. For a good introduction to the complexities and confusions around sex and gender, both in ancient societies and our own, see Martti Nissinen, *Homoeroticism in the Biblical World*, 1–18.

Historically honest appraisals of Christian traditions set a proactive agenda for our theological housework. The mechanisms of social inequality prove resilient for theological and not only cultural reasons, or rather those reasons intertwine with a stubborn potency. Reading Genesis as the divine blueprint for social, not to mention ecological hierarchies resides deeply in Western society's cultural DNA, even for those who may not even own a Bible. Reading differently, sufficiently different to modify that gendered code, will mean reading queerly. If the natural order of things appears to favor a scant few at the expense of all others, perhaps God would have us commit "crimes against nature" as a gospel imperative. Queer home economists believe so, and more—God actually shows us how to do that.

SHAMELESSLY CREATIVE

Crimes against the gendered order of things take many forms. The way I sit and cross my legs certainly resembles a misdemeanor more than a felony. Still, my high school friend's quick and stinging objection to my bodily comportment triggered a rather powerful sensation: public shaming. His comment lodges in my memory with remarkable clarity all these years later, testifying to the insidious effects of shame, which differs significantly from guilt. If I do something wrong—run a red light while driving, overdraw my bank account—I can make restitution, seek forgiveness, and move on. If, however, my crime consists in how I interact bodily with the world around me, guilt passes rather quickly into shame and attaches to my sense of self. In those moments I see myself through the eyes of others as fundamentally flawed. Human beings respond instinctively to those moments with the urge to hide, perhaps retreating entirely from public view or more modestly veiling the flaw itself.[26]

Most people keep secrets quite regularly, whether a pedestrian quirk of personality or a deeper inclination of will. We do this most often for the sake of belonging among others and fitting in, or perhaps more negatively, to avoid harassment or shunning. Many LGBT people learn from an early age, if only intuitively, how to avoid the risk of exposure, the risk of being known as "different." Concealing sexual or gender difference may help us navigate a

---

26. See Gershen Kaufman and Lev Raphael, *Coming Out of Shame: Transforming Gay and Lesbian Lives* (New York: Doubleday, 1996), 15–16; and Brené Brown, *Women and Shame: Reaching Out, Speaking Truths and Building Connection* (Austin, TX: 3C Press, 2004).

world of conformity, at least for a time, but it does nothing to stave off a lingering sense of internal shame.[27] The relief so many experience in revealing these secrets carries the additional risk of public branding, of displaying one's own "scarlet letter." Michael Warner captures this dynamic well:

> Stigma, like its etymological kin *stigmata*, refers to a mark on the body, like a brand or a tattoo or a severed ear, identifying a person permanently with his or her disgrace. . . . It marked the person, not the deed, as tainted. . . . The shame of a true pervert—stigma—is . . . a social identity that befalls one like fate. Like the related stigmas of racial identity or disabilities, it may have nothing to do with acts one has committed. It attaches not to doing, but to being; not to conduct, but to status.[28]

Stigmata—an unmistakable recalling, at least for Christians, of the bodily wounds Jesus carried from his publicly humiliating execution. Religious for yet another reason as the dynamics Warner describes surface quickly in the iconic biblical story of Adam and Eve in the Garden of Eden. That story saturates Western cultural sensibilities, even for those who have never opened a Bible or attended a Christian worship service. Cultural references to the "forbidden fruit" stand quite happily on their own without any need to cite the third chapter of Genesis. Many imagine an apple when hearing that reference; still more take it euphemistically for an illicit and therefore desirable sexual encounter. Few, however, credit that sexual imagery to its proper source—not the Bible, but the theological musings of Augustine more than fifteen centuries ago.

Blame for Christianity's reputed disdain for sexual pleasure or even desire falls rather easily on that Augustinian legacy, and a bit too quickly. The biblical story itself provokes consternation but for reasons Augustine only partially articulated. Tracing humanity's distress and the need for salvation to the guilt over Adam and Eve's disobedience bypasses the story's more poignant feature: heartbreaking shame. Poignant for its portrayal of broken intimacy and heartbreaking in the range of its effects.[29]

---

27. Andrew Tobias wrote about this in his pseudonymous *The Best Little Boy in the World* (New York: Ballantine Books, 1993) in which his sense of living with a "fatal flaw" while growing up shaped the course of his entire life.

28. Warner, *Trouble with Normal*, 27–28.

29. For a helpful summary of the odd and compelling readings of this story, see David M. Carr, *The Erotic Word: Sexuality, Spirituality, and the Bible* (Oxford: Oxford University Press, 2003), especially ch. 4, "The Eden Garden, Part 2: The Tragic Loss of Connectedness," 39–48.

This ancient storyteller focuses less on the act of disobedience than the fear it triggers and the readily familiar response to such fearfulness—the urge to hide. As Adam and Eve hide themselves from each other with fig leaves and then more, from their Creator behind a tree, God searches them out to ask a profound question: "Who told you that you were naked?" (Genesis 3:11). Here this biblical writer so far removed from the modern West both historically and geographically nonetheless pinpoints the source of so much of our distress: not guilt, but shame. God wants to know, not with anger but with tender sadness, who told us to cover our nakedness, to veil God's own handiwork. Who told you, God asks, to be ashamed of my creation?[30]

James Alison has linked this iconic story with yet another, the biblical story of Jonah and the whale. He draws the two together by recalling patterns typically found in the coming out stories so often told by LGBT people. After all, being expelled from Eden and being vomited up on a beach by a mighty fish surely count as rather dramatic accounts of "coming out." In Alison's reading, Jonah repeats the dynamics of Eden, not by disobeying a law, but by fleeing from God's call, by trying to hide from God (Jonah 1:1–3). Jonah, Alison believes, can help us read the story of Eden with hope, a theological rereading to loosen the grip of shame. The effects of this rereading extend from theology to sexual ethics and into the repetitious contestations over identity politics still roiling public debates.

Religious and secular activists alike will recognize this terrain from the argument most commonly if not exclusively made to secure religious tolerance and civil rights: lesbian and gay people are born lesbian and gay. The argument seduces with its simplicity—no society should penalize unchosen accidents of birth—and the seduction proves risky, as queer theorists would urge us to notice. Africans were not enslaved by Europeans because they *chose* to be African. Women were not relegated to the domestic sphere because they *chose* to be women. Arguing from biology, genetics, or even theology ("God made me this way!") guarantees nothing. A controversial and quickly modified statement from Albert Mohler, the president of the Southern Baptist Convention in 2007, rendered this queer caution in bold relief. Acknowledging the possibility of a genetic "cause" for "homosexuality," Mohler indicated his support for developing a treatment to reverse that sexual orientation in utero.[31]

---

30. For more on the effects of shame and their implications for a Eucharistic theology, see my *Divine Communion: A Eucharistic Theology of Sexual Intimacy* (New York: Seabury Books, 2013).

31. "Mohler Would Favor Altering 'Gay' Fetus," *The Christian Century* 124, no. 7 (April 3, 2007), 15.

Alison wants to interrupt this conversation by posing an entirely different kind of theological question. Seeking an essential self either to affirm or deny overlooks poor Jonah in the belly of a whale. The only "self" one finds there is the self whom God is in the process of making, a process Alison notes, that requires Jonah's cooperation.[32] Perhaps only transgender or bisexual sensibilities will suffice to shift a more typically lesbian and gay reliance on nature, or as Alison might urge, to make more room in our rhetoric for God's own creativity.

How much room that might require can astonish when we complement biblical texts with research from evolutionary biologists. Joan Roughgarden, for example, offers compelling depictions of the nearly limitless variations in sexuality and gender exhibited by earth's creatures (including humans). She critiques Darwin in that regard, not for his evolutionary framework but for how he understood evolution to function based on rather crude sexual mechanisms. Gender binaries do sometimes occur in nature, Roughgarden admits, but often with only subtle differences. Animal life often relies on "more than two genders, with multiple types of males and females. This real-life diversity in gender expression and sexuality challenges basic evolutionary theory."[33] Writing not only as a practicing scientist but also as a transgender woman, Roughgarden's work opens up fresh and often astonishing ways of reading and thinking divine creation. Christine Gudorf makes similar observations and urges more attention in faith communities to the work of biologists and geneticists, many of whom today question the dimorphic "two sex" model for human beings. Divvying up the human species into two neat categories based solely on visible bodily markers, like genitalia, ignores many other factors (including brain chemistry) that contribute to the complex matrix of gendered sexuality.[34] Roughgarden maps this out even further by citing recent studies of the human brain that propose roughly eight types. When correlated with two body types (though there could be more),

---

32. For Allison's extended argument on Jonah and theological anthropology, including the role played by the natural law tradition in Roman Catholicism, see *Faith Beyond Resentment: Fragments Catholic and Gay* (New York: Crossroad, 2001), especially ch. 4, "Sputtering up the Beach to Nineveh," 86–104.

33. Joan Roughgarden, *Evolution's Rainbow: Diversity, Gender, and Sexuality in Nature and People* (Berkeley: University of California Press, 2004), 5–6. For a good introduction to Roughgarden's work and perspectives, see the interview with her, "Nature Abhors a Category," *The Gay and Lesbian Review* 15 (January-February 2008): 14–16.

34. Christine Gudorf, "A New Moral Discourse on Sexuality," in *Human Sexuality and the Catholic Tradition*, ed. Kieran Scott and Harold Daly Horell (New York: Rowman and Littlefield, 2007), 51–69.

this would yield "sixteen people types."[35] In the realm of biological science, in other words, binary constructions of the human species fall far short of describing reality. Does this make a theological difference?

Considering all the many factors contributing to any given human person—multiple body types, varying brain chemistries, diverse chromosomal patterns—queer home economists eagerly wish to add another to that list. But what should we call it? Soul, perhaps? Or maybe Spirit? Psyche? A less highly charged word than any of these likely works better, a word like *vocation*. Justin Tanis agrees, and movingly describes his own journey as a transgender man by referring to gender as a "calling." Like any other vocational call, gender may take time to discern or it may appear quite early in one's life. Tanis had "a sense of being called into gender," a call from God. "I was called to trust God," he writes, "and step out into uncharted territory to learn about myself and about who and what God has called me to be. Calling is about what we are to do and about who we are to be, as well as who we will become."[36] Judith Butler encouraged a similar approach by proposing that "gender is something that one becomes—but can never be" so that gender itself is "a kind of becoming or activity."[37]

This fluid and open-ended posture toward identity may sound odd if not terribly queer to modern Western ears, yet perhaps less so to the Johannine biblical writer. That ancient Christian witness assured his readers that we are indeed God's children, then quickly added that "what we will be has not yet been revealed" (1 John 3:2). Here theologians and evolutionary biologists might share a peculiar posture in common: Whatever it means to be human is still in process and unfolding. Human nature, just like the wider world called "nature," resists any reduction to static categories of classification. In more traditional theological language, rather than conceiving of divine creation as an event of the distant past, think and speak about it eschatologically, with a view toward a horizon over which we cannot presently see.

As Justin Tanis' work illustrates, transgender sensibilities disrupt a good many cultural assumptions while they likewise propose a subtle but significant shift in theological rhetoric. Regardless of sexuality, gender, race, ethnicity, intelligence, or any other marker in social classification schemes,

---

35. Roughgarden, *Evolution's Rainbow*, 240.

36. Justin Tanis, *Transgendered: Theology, Ministry, and Communities of Faith* (Cleveland, OH: Pilgrim Press, 2003), 146.

37. Butler, *Gender Trouble*, 143.

"God made me this way" fails as a good theological claim. The past tense in that claim demands revision in our theological reflection for a more lively and dynamic insight: "God *is making* me in a particular way," and not only with my help but also in concert with a community of others for a project currently underway and far from over. That "project" is you, me, all of us together.

A queer theology for Christian witness could easily take root there, by embracing our God-given freedom to live in ways as shamelessly creative as the handiwork of the Creator. That sounds risky, perhaps excessive, yet not without precedent in historical traditions. The nexus of free will and divine prerogative has always vexed yet also inspired theologians to ponder an unfinished creation. Gregory of Nyssa even imagined human beings "birthing ourselves" in ways of our own choosing.[38] Cautionary notes will of course accompany these exultations of human freedom. We have good reasons to worry about "designer bodies" just as we worry about genetically modified foods. Should we set limits on genetic manipulation or cosmetic surgeries or chemical realignments? Do we seize technological power without restraint to do whatever we please with our own bodies, with other bodies, with other animals, with the planet? Who decides?

Queer home economists will affirm the vital importance of such questions yet also worry about asking them too quickly, which tends to dampen creative energies before they even spark. On matters such as these, God's household will want to resist the temptation to store up prepackaged answers to questions that have not yet been asked and setting limits to human creativity in advance. This will mean cultivating a theological and spiritual culture of shared discernment where a range of disciplines—whether biology, psychology, medicine, or ethics, to name a few—contributes to the evolving project of human flourishing. Each of these fields of inquiry offers key insights the others lack, including theology. Offering queerly biblical and theological resources in such a culture of shared discernment matters, especially in a society where so many still perceive "religion" as standing opposed to "science."

Imagining a world where religious faith and scientific investigation cooperate for the sake of planetary thriving should seem far less queer than it does to so many today. The Bible might actually help. Long before religious

---

38. See Virginia Burrus, "Queer Father: Gregory of Nyssa and the Subversion of Identity," in Loughlin, *Queer Theology*, 147–62.

institutions treated modern science as a threat, the biblical writer of Genesis portrayed a creative God making human creatures in God's own image, the *imago Dei*. This claim has posed a puzzle ever since: In what exactly does that "image" consist? Proposals have ranged from the capacity for rational discourse to dimorphic sexuality. Rather than choosing just one, the image of an infinitely creative God likely appears with countless facets and aspects. Queer home economists will find two of those possibilities particularly fruitful, especially as they intersect.

First, a creative God makes creative creatures. The long history of the arts, from music to poetry, painting and sculpture, certainly bears witness to that divine creativity, but so also the physical sciences and technological innovation. Viewing the world not only as God's household but a divine multimedia studio invites sustained reflection on what we make and why. Help for that reflection can come from another feature of the *imago Dei*—the primacy of relationship. The biblical writer proposes such primacy not only for humanity but also for God. It is not good, God says, that the human creature should be alone (Genesis 2:18), the very creature created in the divine image.

Taken together, these two modes of the *imago Dei* launch human beings on a creative quest for communion, a quest animated by the hope of being at home in our own bodies, to be sure, but also at home among others as we long to find our home in God. The tragedy that unfolds in the third chapter of Genesis disrupts that quest, not only with the guilt of disobedience but even more severely with shame. Fig leaves testify to intimacy interrupted, yet shame's effects extend much more widely. Exiled from Eden, the first humans no longer enjoyed a harmonious intimacy with the world of God's creation (3:16-19), and that surely understates the tragedy today in a world of factory farming, fossil fuel depletion, disappearing ecosystems, and the stunning specter of hundreds of species vanishing into extinction every year because of human activities.

Forgiveness may stand as a hallmark of Christian salvation, yet the *imago Dei* vibrates among us with hope for still more: renewed intimacy, with each other and also with the planet. Read that way, Genesis portrays a wildly creative God eager to work with us in the ongoing project of creating a fully unashamed humanity. Only those in the process of stripping away their barnacled layers of shame can find the courage to make a home in their own bodies. Only shameless bodies fully recognize the contrivance of categorical classification schemes that prevent us from finding a home among others—not only human others but with all our planetary kin. Only an unashamed humanity can stand naked before God and find in God our true home.

Making that kind of scripture from ancient texts suggests that Christian theology needs little prompting from "queer theory" to destabilize the static classification schemes of modern society, the ones that segregate races, isolate economic classes, and objectify nature as mere resources to eat or burn. A queer theology for Christian witness suggests something still further: it makes the long religious argument over Darwinism all the more pointless. Darwin's brilliant theorizing could have been hailed by theologians as a way to appropriate in fresh ways what our own traditions have struggled (with varying degrees of success) to articulate from the beginning about the ongoing creative intent of God. Paul highlights this in his letter to the Romans where he describes the whole creation groaning for the fulfillment of that divine purpose, and he does so with language teetering on the edge of erotic desire (Romans 8:22–23).

Speaking of creation in both erotic and evolutionary terms undermines static conceptions of *nature* with an image of God's own *creation* infused with dynamic desire.[39] A queer approach to theology, perhaps, but how does this shape Christian witness? I mean not only our witness to God's naturally odd creation but also our witness to living in shamelessly creative and socially transformative ways. Queerly enough, the traditional rite of Christian baptism can help.

CALLED OUT AND SWEPT AWAY

I was baptized as a young adult—and nearly drowned. At least, that's how I remember it. Rather than infant baptism, the Christian tradition of my youth encouraged waiting until adolescence to baptize children born and raised in Christian families. A study-abroad trip to Israel after my sophomore year in college seemed like the perfect occasion. Planning ahead, I made arrangements for the rite during an excursion to the eastern shore of the Sea of Galilee, not far from the mouth of the Jordan River. What could be more iconic (if not romantic) than that?

An ordained minister on that trip agreed to perform the rite, a man who was a good deal shorter than I was; this turned out to be more significant

---

39. For a concise and carefully crafted articulation of the theological felicity in distinguishing "nature" and "creation," see Martti Nissinen's appendix in *Homoeroticism in the Biblical World*, 135–40.

than I imagined. We reached our sea-side destination late in the afternoon on my baptismal day, and that too mattered. As often happens on that inland sea, the wind grows stronger by day's end. Rather formidable waves rolled on to the beach where we gathered while surfers dotted the coastline just north of us. After offering a short testimony to my faith in Christ, the minister and I waded out from shore. On my body the water reached to my waist and the waves tugged at my ankles with a surprisingly strong undertow. Still, we were committed to three distinct moments of submersion, one for each person of the Holy Trinity. Performing the "Father" and "Son" went smoothly, but as the much shorter minister put me under for the "Spirit," the sea knocked me off my feet and swept me several yards further out from shore, where the seabed dropped away dramatically. I surfaced sputtering and gasping for air, a newly baptized Christian.

I remember that experience with a profound sense of gratitude, not for its sentimental locale but for the vivid recollection of a dangerous sea. Paul insisted in his letter to the Christians in Rome that baptism performs death as a prerequisite for rising to new life (Romans 6:3–11). The peculiar faith of Christians roots itself precisely there—dying with Christ. The ritual performance of that death in baptism has been scrutinized and analyzed in countless theological texts over the centuries, a fundamental marker of what makes Christians "Church." Far fewer have analyzed the ritualized character of those moments in the lives of LGBT people when we "come out."

These religious and secular moments intertwine. The experiences and rituals of "coming out" as LGBT people and the linguistic roots of the word "ecclesiology" share a great deal in common. The Greek *ekklesia* roughly translates as "the called out ones" and poses a crucial question. From what are Christians called out in order to be Church, to order ourselves as Church? A pioneer in queer theologizing, Marcella Althaus-Reid recalls the story of a man in her South American church who decided, finally, to come out as gay. He had been "dead for too long," as she describes it. He also decided to do this with his faith community and to change his name on that day to "Renato," which in Spanish means "reborn." This moment marked a passage from death to life as Renato emerged from the tombs, as Althaus-Reid puts it, of "heterosexual systematic theology."[40]

---

40. Marcella Althaus-Reid, *Indecent Theology: Theological Perversions in Sex, Gender and Politics* (New York: Routledge, 2000), 123.

Queer home economists want to ask something more of such stories and consider how these multivalent images of coming out shape and reshape Christian witness more broadly. Beyond questions of whether the sexually marginalized can find room in institutional religion, coming out interrogates the Church's own vision of itself as a "peculiar people" (1 Peter 2:9, KJV). What does such peculiarity portend for North Atlantic societies where Christianity has long since blended rather seamlessly with its Western cultural environment? Anita Fast asks that question of her own Mennonite tradition, which traces its roots to sixteenth-century Anabaptists and their understanding of a divine call to live counterculturally. As Fast notes, this call was frequently perceived as threatening by the wider culture and occasionally fueled brutal persecution.[41] Can a queer theology animate a disruptive Christian witness today?

As naturally odd creatures of a wildly creative God, Christians bear witness to the hope of Communion in a world suffering from a host of anticommunion forces. The litany of those forces has grown despairingly familiar: epidemic loneliness and alienation; families reeling from domestic misery in both physical and emotional abuse; deep wounds inflicted by racially and ethnically fractured neighborhoods; and the weight of death-dealing militarism and unrepentant environmental degradation of our collective planetary home. "Called out" from that kind of world would make church membership costly and even sacrificial in a society thoroughly mapped by categorical classification schemes that divide, fracture, and isolate human beings from each other, from other animals, even from earth itself. In such a world it must surely sound queer to suppose that not only the doctrine of creation but also the rite of baptism could make any difference. Elizabeth Stuart identifies her own queer theological turn there, in baptismal ministries, where all the thorny issues of identity bubble up in bold relief.[42] Can Stuart really mean to do this? Can baptism perform sufficiently a radical coming out from all the anticommunion commitments riddling the modern West? Surely not in the simple sprinkling of water over wailing babies or even the near-drowning of a young adult in the Sea of Galilee; but Renato would have us think again.

If nowhere else than here, on the questions that percolate in the complex stew of identity, nature, creativity, and community, queer home

---

41. Anita Fast, "A Peculiar People: Queer Christianity and the Foolishness of God," *Outspoken* 1, no. 3 (Winter 2007): 5.

42. Stuart, *Gay and Lesbian Theologies*, 106–8.

economists turn to the insights of queer theorists for help in (re)claiming the queerness of theological traditions. On the issue of identity alone, on just the word itself, Daniel Mendelsohn has offered a helpful insight. The word "identity," he reminds us, comes from the Latin *identidem*. This word resulted from the repetitive joining of the words in the Latin phrase *idem et idem*, or "same and same." Buried there, in the linguistic history of this one deceptively simple word, one finds the notion of identity as a process of repetitive performance.[43] What precisely one repeats in that process and the role played in it by learning, adopting, adapting, changing, and realigning remain open questions. Yet the insight remains and, as Judith Butler proposes, this process applies paradigmatically to gender, which is inscribed on our bodies in exactly the same way, through the repetitive performance of a cultural script.[44]

More than a few will find these musings discomfiting. Coming out as lesbian or gay has been for some a rite of passage in cultural as well as religious arenas. Most approach this rite as a liberating disruption of the heteronormative script that modern Western society trains each of us to perform. Queer theorists, however, want to add an important nuance to that claim: the disruption performed by coming out does not disrupt the social reliance on performance itself. Rather, it interrupts or discontinues the performance of one script in favor of another; in this case, the script called either "lesbian" or "gay." Without such a script, coming out signifies virtually nothing.

While no one comes out in a sexually gendered way just once, doing so the first time can linger as a milestone moment. In the early 1980s, ensconced in a conservative Christian college, a friend I had known since childhood came out to me as a gay man. I returned the favor, both of us in tears. Significantly, Peter and I sought the company of other gay men as the first thing to do in our newly out lives. In some instinctive way, we recognized a need to learn how to be what we had just declared about ourselves. This followed a fairly typical pattern for gay and lesbian people of the baby-boom generation. We found it difficult and disorienting not to have any language—whether grammatical or conceptual—for the experience of feeling out of place in

---

43. Daniel Mendelsohn, *The Elusive Embrace: Desire and the Riddle of Identity* (New York: Vintage Books, 2000), 39, 90.

44. See Eugene F. Rogers's analysis of Butler in relation to Thomas Aquinas and natural law, especially the importance of performance for self-knowledge ("Bodies Demand Language," in Loughlin, *Queer Theology*, 176–87).

a "heterosexual" world. Many of my gay male friends from that era went through the motions of dating girls in high school, as I did, wondering somewhat vaguely why it felt rather odd. It astonished many of us to find even one other person with whom to hash out the language for our experience, not just in words but also in how we comported ourselves while interacting with others and reading the signs and gestures of what amounted to a tribal language. We needed, in other words, to become oriented to this emerging reality, to have an "orientation."

Today, the language of gay and lesbian desire visibly punctuates American culture in ways neither Peter nor I could have imagined back in the 1980s; a mark of progress, yes, but not without qualification. Many people in their late teens and early twenties now prefer to handle their sexual and gender identities a bit more lightly, resisting the cultural mechanism of identity labels. They seem to know, perhaps only intuitively, what I realized in a very different way at that age. Coming out as gay or lesbian depends on a performative script, and younger generations today tend to resist scripted lives, especially as those scripts now come prepackaged with the commercial market mechanisms of global capitalism.

If coming out demands finding a language and a communal practice to render an identity intelligible, then LGBT people face a rather vexing quandary as coming out falls short of declaring a uniquely individual identity. Instead, one comes out into something already there—a social script—even if that script disrupts the one constructed as normative. Queer theorists insist on this point. Living in modern Western society means being identified and to occupy a particular cultural space based on that identity. Coming out as L, G, B, or T does not disrupt that identity-placement system. To the contrary, it reinforces it by performing a different script, one that comes ready-made with its own social place to occupy, usually that of an "outcast" or a "rebel" or a theological "dissident," but also more recently as a lucrative "market niche" for corporate advertisers.

Similar notions of adopting a social script punctuate early Christian history when those seeking baptism underwent a rigorous process of catechesis. One did not just appear at the local church office to arrange for a nephew's baptism that coming weekend when family members would be visiting from out of town. Baptism required an intensive period of instruction leading to vows of commitment for leading a particular way of life. The ritual itself enacted a moment of coming out, of being *called out* from one worldview and into another. This baptismal coming out did not disrupt the process of scripted performance. It did, however, exchange one type of social performance for another, urging the adoption of a particular communal script. In that way the newly baptized became with all the other baptized an "ecclesial person," one of the *called out ones*. "Called out," as John D. Zizioulas would urge us to notice, not as a unique individual but rather as body member. The Eucharist, he notes, is the most "anti-individualistic act of the Church" as the "human ceases to be an individual and becomes a person," that is, one who, along with others, strips away the old self to put on Christ.[45]

Noticing how coming out as gay or lesbian reinforces the categorical identity mechanisms of a heterosexist society surfaces a similar dynamic in the *modern* practice of baptism. More than a few mainline Protestant and Roman Catholic Christians now approach baptism as a familial and cultural rite of passage. Few seem to perceive in that moment the disruption it invites of Western cultural sensibilities, the disruption especially of the categorical classification schemes that fuel our distressing divisions. Or as Elizabeth Stuart argues, those systems of sexually gendered classifications "grate against the sign of baptism."[46] "Grate" actually understates Stuart's much deeper anxiety: the cultural captivity of baptism stands as a significant betrayal of the Church's own theological traditions, which certainly recalls for me the experience of nearly drowning in the Sea of Galilee, of being called out and swept away by the tides of that rite.

Perhaps Paul's insistence on performing our death with Christ can urge us to abandon the stone "birdbaths" that sit as baptismal fonts in so many churches and gather again at the river—preferably a swiftly moving one with dangerous rapids. Absent that opportunity, to distribute water guns and hook up fire hoses in our sanctuaries. Nearly anything, really, that will alert us to the power of water to wash, cleanse, scrub, and sweep away.[47] Queer home economists will need to cultivate their ritual imaginations for this, an imagination sufficient to the task of enacting Paul's still radical claim that

---

45. John D. Zizioulas, *The Eucharistic Communion and the World* (London: T&T Clark, 2011), 128–29.

46. Stuart, *Gay and Lesbian Theologies*, 108.

47. One of my students, J. Matthew Smith, proposed at the very least that baptismal liturgies should evoke that sense of a "river" or other large, running bodies of water that can help bring to mind the power (and sometimes danger) of water itself ("A Queer Baptism," unpublished paper submitted to Pacific School of Religion, Berkeley, CA, 2006).

in Christ there is no longer Jew or Greek, slave or free, male and female (Galations 3:28).[48] There is no longer, in other words, any categorical classification that can thwart our longing for communion, our yearning to free ourselves from shame as we make a home in our own bodies, among others, and with God.

Living as ecclesial people shifts the priorities in God's household rather significantly. Asking whether LGBT people can find a home in Christian churches, for example, misses the queerly good news of the Gospel entirely. The question turns rather on how the Church will live as God's own "called-out ones"—called out, certainly, from all the seemingly natural divisions that make human enmity appear self-evident; yet called out as well to enact gracious "crimes against nature" as Gospel imperatives; and still more, called out to live as God's own naturally odd people in a creation that remains unfinished. In these and other ways, living as called-out ones often comes with considerable risk. The privilege and benefits that attend categorical classification schemes will not dissolve quietly or quickly. A queer theology for Christian witness will speak of this risk honestly: our peculiar faith comes with a cost. That cost remains high, to which the unspeakably divine life of Jesus amply attests.

---

48. See Dale Martin's compelling retrieval of this Pauline passage in *Sex and the Single Savior*, ch. 6, "The Queer History of Galatians 3:28," 77–90.

3

Unspeakably Divine
Eros, Incarnation, and the Body of Jesus

*I*n the mid-1990s a friend from seminary ripped a page out of a glossy fashion magazine and sent it to me in the mail. The full-page photograph featured a rail-thin model, scantily clothed, and lying on piles of trash. She lay there with her eyes closed, lips colored slightly purple, and a man's foot pressing down on her arm, planted there as if in triumph. It was an advertisement for the sneaker that man was wearing.

My friend included a post-it note on the photograph: "Here's an icon for Epiphany." This confused me at first. I found that photo spread disturbing for more than one reason: for objectifying women as disposable play things; for perpetuating masculinity as inherently domineering and violent; and for commodifying human bodies to sell other commodities, to name just a few. Pondering my friend's note and that image, those disturbing qualities soon began to coalesce into an icon of human flesh, its denigration, humiliation, and abuse standing in desperate need of redemption. An ideal icon, in other words, for Epiphany.

The twelve days of Christmas on the Christian liturgical calendar begin when gift-giving on the secular calendar ends, on Christmas Day itself. Those twelve liturgical days in turn end with still more gifts on the feast of the Epiphany. According to Matthew's gospel account, magi from the East, perhaps astrologers or magicians from the region of Persia, present Jesus with gold, frankincense, and myrrh (Matthew 2:11). Ancient Mediterranean societies sometimes used those latter two gifts for embalming, as burial spices. Matthew thus offers a literary foreshadowing of events to come. The child receiving those gifts shall not escape the fate of all mortal flesh. Indeed, he will suffer the kind of indignity no human deserves, but which continues to this day, even in the glossy pages of what passes for the latest fashion.

Icons serve as windows into an unseen or perhaps forgotten reality. The flesh portrayed in that disturbing "fashion" spread opens a window on Western culture and can help to strip away the sentimentality that so often drenches the Christmas/Epiphany holiday cycle. The original story behind those holidays actually startles, or it should. Matthew describes the magi's gift-bearing journey as a quest, yet they search not for insight or an institution or even a place, but for a person, a flesh-and-blood child. This child does not bear ideal flesh, the kind suitable for Greek or Roman statuary or for today's cult of youth and beauty. The child eventually found and adored by the magi bears entirely unremarkable, ordinary flesh. Flesh ordinary enough to trade like a commodity on Wall Street, or to disrobe on Hollywood's silver screen for quick titillation, or to go homeless and starving on city streets. The flesh of that child appears bruised and conquered on piles of trash in a fashion magazine.

T. S. Eliot once wrote that "the hint half guessed, the gift half understood, is Incarnation."[1] The hint, only just intuited by ancient Persian astrologers, that gift, only barely grasped by gospel writers, the epiphany still so desperately needed today appears as this: with us and among us and in our very flesh, God takes great delight. Not abstractly or generally or vaguely but in all the material details of human life, the magnificent and tender ones as well as the heartbreaking and tragic.

This half-understood gift resides at the queer heart of Christianity's peculiar faith, for the queerest thing about Jesus emerges not so much in what he said or did, though gospel accounts of his teaching can certainly scramble most contemporary religious assumptions and expectations. Queerer still than what Jesus said is the peculiar way others tried to speak about him as they struggled to render their experience into speech and stumbled over their own religious metaphors and literary tropes. In meeting this otherwise ordinary human being, they encountered God—no, something or someone like God, perhaps a vision of God-like life, or . . . well, what exactly?

Each of the gospel writers spins that question a bit differently, and biblical scholars propose a number of ways to describe those unique rhetorical

---

1. T. S. Eliot, "Four Quartets," in *The Complete Poems and Plays: 1909–1950* (New York: Harcourt, Brace World, 1971), 136.

rotations. We could find the new Moses in Matthew, for example, or a sage healer in Luke, and a didactic miracle worker in Mark. The community that produced John's gospel ventured rather boldly into metaphysical, some would say mystical terrain: In Jesus the Word of God became human flesh (John 1:14). If that sounds perfectly sensible, then the subsequent centuries of fierce divisions and contestations among Christians will seem quite peculiar indeed. How strange and startling if not terribly queer to suppose that humanity and divinity can reside together in a single person—if that even suffices to describe what John or Paul or Augustine or Athanasius or Tertullian, or many others meant to convey. Can we ever know precisely what those ancient writers intended? Would it make any difference?

Jesus more often provoked questions than provided answers, and still does two millennia later. Among the questions Jesus continues to pose, one in particular has grown in both severity and consequence over the last 150 years: How do we speak or even think "God" in a market-shaped world of disposable bodies? Tracing the arc of the modern West from Darwinian evolution through the industrial, technological, and now digital, cyber-space revolutions, voices tuned to the significance of Jesus fade to background noise in the cacophonous commodification of humanity itself. Apart from its profit value in vast systems of economic exchange—or more likely, *for* such profit—the human body carries not the imprint of divinity but the tread of a sneakered foot.

Trying to speak humanity and divinity together confounds linguistic convention. A bit more clarity from those first-century gospel writers might have spared us the confusions of theological speech, perhaps with a claim a bit easier to classify in today's marketplace of ideas. By portraying Jesus as Zeus, for example, or some other recognizably god-like figure, we might know better what kind of worship he deserves and in which kind of temple to ensconce him. Or by situating Jesus more firmly on the trajectory of human history's insightful prophets and spiritual teachers we would know where to find him on bookstore shelves, probably in the self-help section or among the "how-to" guides promising financial prosperity. Yet neither of those rhetorical strategies seems to have occurred to any of the four canonical gospelers. They insisted instead on some peculiar mix of both the resolutely human and uncannily divine, which carves out a rather queer, in-between space.

The gospel space of confounded categories energizes many of those engaged in "postcolonial" theorizing, an academic cousin to queer theory, and especially those who adopt notions of "hybridity" to describe the fluid flux of ethnic and cultural identities that resist Western colonial-era classification schemes.[2] Could this notion of the "hybrid" translate the gospel texts better, that space where human being mysteriously discloses divine life? Kwok Pui-Lan finds insightful theological possibilities in that kind of questioning, an exploration of what she describes as the space between Jesus and Christ:

> The most hybridized concept in the Christian tradition is that of Jesus/ Christ. The space between Jesus and Christ is unsettling and fluid, resisting easy categorization and closure. It is the "contact zone" or "borderland" between the human and the divine, the one and the many, the historical and the cosmological, the Jewish and the Hellenistic, the prophetic and the sacramental, the God of the conquerors and the God of the meek and the lowly. Jesus' question "Who do you say that I am?" [Matthew 16:15] is an invitation for every Christian . . . to infuse that contact zone with new meanings, insights, and possibilities.[3]

Kwok would have us consider here the multiple layers of identification that eventually coalesce around and attach to the first-century figure of Jesus, all those philosophical, metaphysical, and theological constructions signified by "Christ." Marcella Althaus-Reid proposed a similar approach to what she called the "systematically deviant Jesus." The fluidity and ambiguity of his identity, even within the gospel texts, constantly elude the orderly doctrinal categorizations of orthodox Christology. Citing the work of Robert Goss,[4] Althaus-Reid invites us to see in Jesus a divine moment of "coming out," a moment of God coming out as the "Bi/Christ." She does not mean to suggest anything about sexual performances of intimacy with this image; she wants to evoke instead the destabilizing character of bisexuality in a system constructed on binary terms. In ways similar to the notion of hybridity, the Bi/Christ unravels the tightly woven classifications of the "Systematic Messiah" to reveal "the Christ who is neither this nor that, a Christ who embraces and shows life

---

2. See Catherine Keller, Michael Nausner, and Mayra Rivera, eds., *Postcolonial Theologies: Divinity and Empire* (St. Louis: Chalice Press, 2004), and especially Mayra Rivera's contribution to this collection, "God at the Crossroads: A Postcolonial Reading of Sophia," 186–203.

3. Kwok Pui-Lan, *Postcolonial Imagination and Feminist Theology* (Louisville, KY: Westminster John Knox Press, 2005), 171.

4. Robert E. Goss, *Jesus Acted Up: A Gay and Lesbian Manifesto* (New York: Harper and Collins, 1993).

as fluid, changing, outside the reductionist patterns which confront people with irrelevant options."[5] In these musings, neither Kwok nor Althaus-Reid wish to reject the historical constructions of Christological doctrine out of hand but rather to appreciate the untidy edges that any hybridized identity necessarily creates, perhaps especially when the assumed purity of a timeless divinity mixes with the undeniably messy patterns, rhythms, and relationships of finite humanity. In that very mix, many stumble.

Humanity hardly seems a suitable vehicle for divinity. No one needs a crude fashion photograph to recognize the fragility of human flesh. Each of us sees its precarious character in the mirror, with each new wrinkle or gray hair, or feels it with each added ache or creak in aging muscles, or upon hearing a sudden and terrifying medical diagnosis. Human vulnerability appears at nearly every turn, whether in random violence on city streets or domestic violence in one's own home. Still more, the willingly vulnerable if not also silly bodily postures human beings adopt in acts of sexual intimacy surely settles the matter: human flesh belongs among the least likely places we should look to find "God." Queerly enough, precisely there Jesus continues to pose questions.

If "divinity" sounds antiquated in contemporary speech about Jesus, sexuality sounds fresh and compelling, or at least intriguing. Few churchgoers ask out loud a question that now occupies the attention of best-selling authors: Was Jesus ever sexually intimate with someone, anyone? Dan Brown's *The Da Vinci Code* persuaded more than a few people to believe that Jesus sired a child with Mary Magdalene.[6] Beyond the realm of historical novels and Hollywood films, some biblical scholars have persuaded a few others (but significantly, not quite as many) to believe that Jesus was sexually intimate with "the beloved disciple" (presumably John) or the intriguingly anonymous neophyte featured in the so-called "secret Gospel of Mark."[7]

How people respond to the question of Jesus's sexuality matters less than why so many care to ask. Until recently that question has been, quite

---

5. Althaus-Reid, *Indecent Theology*, 114.

6. Dan Brown, *The Da Vinci Code* (New York: Doubleday, 2003). Brown's book is of course a work of fiction, yet it draws from a long line of historical speculation and legends about Jesus, including that his heirs eventually sired the crowned heads of Europe.

7. See Theodore Jennings, *The Man Jesus Loved: Homoerotic Narratives from the New Testament* (Cleveland, OH: Pilgrim Press, 2003). Recent scholarship has mostly discredited the *Secret Gospel of Mark* as a hoax; see Stephen C. Carlson, *The Gospel Hoax: Morton Smith's Invention of Secret Mark* (Waco, TX: Baylor University Press, 2005).

literally, unspeakable (if not actually unthinkable). The presumption of an unmarried Jesus rendered any speculation about sexual intimacy moot, and for many, thankfully so. The legacy of Puritan hesitations over bodily life and Victorian-era propriety instilled a deep reticence in the modern West to speak about sexuality more generally. Christian piety preserved a mostly "sex-free zone" well into the twentieth century as the wider society gradually stripped away the scandalous character of public sex-talk.

Little seems surprising much less scandalous in today's world of social media discourses and the confessions of reality television shows. Yet Christian faith bears witness to a perduring peculiarity: the Word of God residing in human flesh. Repeating this claim for centuries has perhaps blunted its startling if not scandalous character. Discovering God in Jesus might still startle us into hopefulness by finding a fully sexual human being in God. Can I find myself at home in my fully sexual body, and thus blissfully at home with other fully sexual bodies, and still be at home with God? For the earliest centuries of Christian faith, the flip side of that question proved just as vexing: Can God really find a home with and among us? Questions like these lift the veil of silent propriety that Western Christianity cast over sexuality and disclose an ancient quandary made new: What does the particularity of Jesus have to do with the specific particularly of our own bodies, of your body and mine?

Human bodies resist abstraction, whether as philosophical data, legal subjects, literary figures, racial types, gender categories, or theological doctrines. Yet everyone, without exception, perceives human bodies through all of those philosophical, legal, literary, racial, gendered, and theological lenses. These many lenses, often layered, one on top of the next, nearly and sometimes entirely obscure the concrete, irreducible particularly of any given body in question. Whenever I think or speak about my body, I think and speak about a white and male body, the two defining characteristics of human flesh on which the modern West bestows most of its privileges. How easily I forget this: bodies always appear gendered and racialized. Laurel Schneider frames that ease by noting how difficult it is "to think around the corners of the world one inhabits, or to glimpse the limits and gaps in one's own inherited view." That difficulty becomes particularly apparent when trying to imagine modern Western categories of race, sex, and gender as anything other than biologically "natural" differences between human beings. To imply that those categories could be otherwise would mean "unmooring them from nature and thereby disrupting just about everything taken for granted in modernity."[8] And that "everything" would certainly include Christian faith.

The ease with which white men, like me, can forget the always-racially-gendered character of human interactions in turn tends to obscure something terribly odd about Christianity: white masculinity sits at the apex of Western society but *not* at the center of Christian faith. Surely here the peculiar queerness of Christian faith surfaces in vibrant, textured color. The Semitic brownness of the historical Jesus exhibits a maleness that rarely fits the standard expectations of masculinity, whether in his own society or in the twenty-first-century North Atlantic. This peculiar Jesus nonetheless—or perhaps ironically and implausibly—enjoys the status of "founder" in a religious tradition still in the thrall of Western patriarchal whiteness.[9]

Queer home economists scarcely know where to begin sifting through these complexities and contradictions in a household of faith where so many take so much for granted about Jesus and about bodies. They do know this much: speaking and hearing "incarnation" as genuinely good news will mean addressing simultaneously the unrelenting denigration of human bodies and the splendors of incarnate life as matters of profound spiritual *and* sociopolitical investment. Patrick Cheng describes that investment as "boundary crossing," whether those boundaries are marked socially, sexually, or with gender. He means especially the boundary-crossing God of the Incarnation:

> The story of Jesus Christ fundamentally changes the relationship between God and humanity. That is why, for Christians, Jesus Christ is considered to be the axis around which all of salvation history turns. No longer are "God" and "humanity" mutually exclusive categories, but they come together in the person of Jesus Christ, the God-human, who is fully divine and fully human.[10]

---

8. Schneider, "What Race Is Your Sex?" 142–43.

9. See Kelly Brown Douglas, "Black Body/White Soul: The Unsettling Intersection of Race, Sexuality, and Christianity," in *Body and Soul: Rethinking Sexuality as Justice-Love*, ed. Marvin M. Ellison and Silvia Thorson-Smith (Cleveland, OH: Pilgrim Press, 2003), 99–113.

10. Patrick S. Cheng, *Radical Love: An Introduction to Queer Theology* (New York: Seabury Books, 2011), 79.

Marcella Althaus-Reid and Lisa Isherwood describe the same thing but more succinctly: "That God is in flesh changes everything."[11] Perhaps so, but not without turning frequently to an ancient question with profound contemporary implications: As human beings hope to find a home with God, can God find a home with us, in our own frequently messy bodily lives? Richard Rohr poses that very question by noting how infrequently (if ever) we look to our own embodied selves to find God. This spiritual resistance to bodies, punctuated by institutional Christianity's rigidities and repressions, is in Rohr's view "evil's greatest triumph over Gospel freedom."[12] What might it mean for how Christians live if we returned to our bodies to find the God we seek? We could begin with a tantalizing if not queer possibility: bodily joy might actually constitute a Christian spiritual practice. This may seem queer for some, certainly, but not without an equally tantalizing historical precedent for that insight tucked away in the history of ecclesial councils and their creedal declarations. Some observations about both can help shape Christian witness in and from households of embodied desire.

RELISHING BODIES

In an episode of the television series, *Star Trek: The Next Generation*, a Vulcan admiral says something rather remarkable to Captain Jean-Luc Picard. "Relish in your body," he says.[13] Remarkable for several reasons, not least what this admiral's deceptively simple exhortation reveals about American popular culture and its posture toward bodies. In this episode, Captain Picard and his crew of the starship Enterprise have stumbled upon a conspiracy that threatens the future of the Federation. Small scorpion-like aliens have invaded the bodies of those highest in command. When Picard returns to earth to investigate, he shares a meal at Star Fleet headquarters with officers who have already been compromised. Uncompromised humans, like Picard, find the food at this meal thoroughly unappetizing if not revolting. The small aliens

---

11. Marcella Althaus-Reid and Lisa Ishwerood, eds., *The Sexual Theologian: Essays on Sex, God, and Politics,* Queering Theology Series (New York: T&T Clark, 2004), 7.

12. Richard Rohr, *Radical Grace*, ed. John Feister (Cincinnati, OH: St. Anthony Messenger Press, 1995), 230.

13. "Conspiracy," *Star Trek: The Next Generation*, DVD, directed by Cliff Bole, 1988; Los Angeles: Paramount Pictures, 2002.

now inhabiting the bodies of those present at the table chose this particular menu to enjoy the new range of sensory delights their captured bodies afford them. As a Vulcan admiral lifts a handful of slimy, worm-like food to his mouth, the alien inhabiting his body speaks through him and issues an invitation to Picard: "Relish in your body."

Few would mistake this moment for a friendly invitation, especially since the alien who extends it threatens what it means to be human. The invitation, after all, comes from an *alien*. This encounter with an alien life-form at least implies that relishing in one's body constitutes an inhuman act. For sexually queer people, the religious analogy readily appears. To relish in our sexual bodies of desire outside of religion's regulatory grasp can certainly feel alien, out of place, even dangerously exotic if not considerably "queer." To engage in such relishing openly (which might mean simply holding hands with someone in public) can and often does elicit a response of revulsion. Such an act might even qualify as a threat to the cohesion of Christian thought and ordered ministry.

The television writers added yet a further layer of exoticism to this scene as the invitation to "relish in your body" comes not just from an alien enemy but an alien who inhabits the body of a different "race," a Vulcan. Does this suggest perhaps that the humans of the Federation made a mistake in forging an alliance with Vulcans? Vulcans look mostly like human beings except for the pointy ears made famous by Leonard Nimoy's portrayal of Mr. Spock. That "nearly-but-not-quite" human familiarity poses a troubling question: Do Vulcans constitute a different *species* or a different *race*? What difference would it make? What difference has it made in Western culture? Less abstractly, what kind of "alien" bears the burden of dangerous embodiment in contemporary North Atlantic societies?

For decades that burden has fallen on the hypersexualized portrayals of the African-American male body while the failure of the modern welfare state sits at the tired feet of poor bodies, usually unmarried African-American mothers. The burden of a culture deeply ambivalent about embodied sexuality continues to weigh heavily on HIV-positive gay men (whose bodies, many believe, simply reap what they deserve from their alien practices) but even more so by hundreds of thousands of AIDS-inflicted bodies on the continent of Africa, whose black, impoverished bodies matter even less than the black bodies of the North Atlantic. Meanwhile, all the alien brown bodies south of the U.S. border and all the ones living "illegally" on the northern side shoulder the latest irruptions of immigration anxiety, rooted mostly in economic panic.

A single scene in just one episode of a science-fiction television series prompts queer people of faith to recognize a long-standing vexation in Western society. Bodies constitute highly charged sites for culturally constructed social hierarchies and institutional religious manipulation. Christians can turn to our own traditions for that reminder, which have playfully, creatively, and provocatively placed the human body at the center of theological reflection and spiritual practice. *Why* the body resides there, though, remains difficult to decipher as the body itself might appear explicitly, ambiguously, positively, and negatively, and sometimes all of these at the same time.

Turn to nearly any page in the gospel texts or any chapter in Christian history; bodily exultations and perplexities abound. Gospel readers meet the body of Jesus in the womb of his *virgin* mother, in a feeding trough for animals on the night of his birth, on a cross as an executed criminal, and a corpse tenderly wrapped in the arms of Joseph of Arimathea. Those same texts present the absent body in the image of an empty tomb or the unstable body of the risen Jesus who forbids Mary Magdalene to touch him. Dipping even briefly into church history exposes disciplined bodies in the ascetic practices of desert monasticism; the body unveiled in renaissance paintings of Madonna and child as Mary points to the naked infant's penis; in culturally marginalized but religiously valorized bodies of women mystics, who insisted on speaking of union with the divine with erotic speech; in terrified bodies of those classified as heretics and witches, whose ideas Spanish inquisitors not only banned but burned with the bodies that voiced them.

Bodies clearly matter, but why so terribly much? I mean, why so terribly and why so much? Human bodies matter, Christians might want to say, because our faith resides in the divine humanity of Jesus.[14] But what can this really mean in a Christian history littered with bodies treated so terribly? In the nearly seamless blend of Christianity and culture in Western society bodies punctuate some of the most distressing historical moments, from

---

14. Daniel Boyarin would qualify that claim significantly, arguing that for some early Christian communities "incarnation" functioned not so much as an affirmation of bodily life but instead perpetuated the dichotomy between "human" and "divine" as a way to refute the fleshiness of Jews (see *Carnal Israel: Reading Sex in Talmudic Culture* [Berkeley: University of California Press, 1993], 5–7).

the denigration of female bodies to the mass enslavement of African bodies, the colonization and extermination of Native American bodies, and the gassing of Jewish bodies in concentration camps. From these ruins wrought by misogynistic, racist, and anti-Semitic appropriations of Christian traditions, woven throughout the evolving cultural and political patterns of the West, the queer body now seeks to rise, phoenix-like, from all those ashes. It longs to rise but without at once being seized as a commodity to buy, sell, or trade in a vast marketplace of international sex trafficking, or as a field from which to harvest organs from the poor for transplanting into the rich, or as sweatshop labor making shoes to plant on the back of a woman's bruised body reclining on piles of trash in a fashion magazine.

Queer people of faith understand how terribly much bodies matter for nearly all the wrong reasons. We interrupt that socioreligious legacy whenever we seek to relish bodily life, not for profit or advantage or self-gratification, but because there, in the flesh, we meet God. Mostly uncanny, frequently veiled, tantalizingly aloof, God meets us there nonetheless in the exasperating vulnerability and erotically radiant flesh of human beings.[15] Bodily life queerly matters in Christian faith quite particularly there, in its allusively divine arousals. "Queerly" especially in a consumer-oriented society of instant gratification where bodies matter in their consumption, the consummation they provide for any given moment's desire. The queer body, by contrast, rises not as an object of satisfaction but as the occasion to awaken divine desire, the very *Eros* of God.

Queer people of faith, no less than anyone else, rarely think this way about bodies, the ones they meet in grocery stores, or barely notice in commuter traffic jams, or neatly lined up in church pews. Standing in the Household of God, surrounded by bodies of every imaginable type, queer home economists can barely fathom what in the world all these bodies have to do with the ecstatic hope of the Gospel. Yet they remain convinced that bodies do matter, and with profound implications for Christian witness. Convinced of this and often just as perplexed by it as any other household member, queer home economists will turn again to the familiar biblical texts in the opening chapters of Genesis. Making scripture from those texts quite properly defamiliarizes their meaning, and properly so for these iconic passages in particular, whose carnal qualities too often and ironically dissipate

---

15. See Mark D. Jordan, "God's Body," in Loughlin, *Queer Theology*, 281–92.

in Christian readings. Fresh readings can breathe new life into those ancient stories, just as God breathed life into the creature made from mud with something like a kiss (Genesis 2:7).

The divine kiss of life? Even this modestly fresh reading rather quickly sounds peculiar if not dangerously queer, especially in a society that reduces all things erotic to a shadowy world of the pornographic. If, however, divine creativity springs not from necessity or even design but from the depths of desire, Christians might find new reasons to animate their witness with Genesis. I mean a countercultural witness as God's own desire attaches to bodies. Bodies of all kinds, not just human bodies, emerge from divine *Eros*, whether the body of the earth itself, the bodies of sun, moon, and stars, or of plants and animals. In contrast to modern market mechanisms, the divine desire percolating in these stories of creation turns not to consumption but, as *Eros* instinctively does, to communion.[16] The biblical writer invites that insight with the very first question God poses to God's own creation: "Where are you?" (Genesis 3:9). Perhaps not only the first but also the perpetual question that rises up continually and in countless ways from each new chapter of God's erotic quest for intimacy and relationship, the divine desire for communion.

"In the beginning"—the biblical writer launches Genesis with those words, which John repeats to launch his account of the Gospel. Still more echoes from Eden as the questing God, John declares, appears among us at last, flesh of our flesh and bone of our bone. John answers the primal question in the Garden by awakening a seductive hope: God may actually want to make a home in, with, and among our bodies. This proves seductive in more than just one way. Queer home economists will take that Johannine hope with a dose of caution, reading it in the light of modernity's tendency to relish bodies by fetishizing flesh or adoring its commodification. The caution emerges from the gospel texts themselves: to relish bodily life makes us vulnerable to a desire that continually recedes from our grasp, from the urge to own and control. Embracing rather than resisting that vulnerability orients the Household of God toward the trail blazed by Jesus, who refused both fetishization and adoration and chose instead to follow the road leading to crucifixion.

---

16. See Daniel T. Spencer's account of an "erotic ecology" that extends well beyond humanity's relations with other humans (*Gay and Gaia: Ethics, Ecology, and the Erotic* [Cleveland, OH: Pilgrim Press, 1996], 322–24).

In all three synoptic gospels, the disciples catch a glimpse of God in the flesh, in flesh brilliantly and alluringly transfigured (Matthew 17:1–8; Mark 9:2–8; Luke 9:28–36). Momentarily unveiled, the glory of God radiating from this human Jesus inspires Peter to make a "booth," to capture, enthrone, and freeze-frame what will surely, at long last, satisfy his desire. But Jesus refuses. Jesus insists instead that he must suffer and die. How tempting to read Peter with condescension in that moment, the one disciple whose brashness continually runs past the insights Jesus offers. Queer home economists might find a fruitful and less condescending rereading of Peter with some help from the Rolling Stones and the lyrics made famous by Mick Jagger: "I can't get no satisfaction." Peter on the mount of transfiguration as Mick on our religious concert stage: he invites sympathy. Who could resist wanting to seize the satisfying object of desire as it appears in such tantalizing splendor?

The theological posture of my youth resisted finding Peter in any way sympathetic. That theological tradition mostly eschewed bodily glorification (with its attendant desire) and demanded instead the divine necessity of the cross (the punishment thrust on Jesus that I no longer had to bear). The polarity of glory and pain remained both stark and necessary in my spiritual imagination for years; either relish in the body's glory *or* offer it up as a sacrifice; only one of those choices leads to heaven. The dichotomy of that choice vexes many, not least those who intuit the spiritual significance of relishing bodily life on our journey homeward. A long history trails behind these vexations, a history stretching back to the earliest doctrinal controversies over bodily life itself and its contested relationship with divine life. That history, no less than Genesis and John, deserves a fresh reading.

FROM CRADLE TO CREED

At the center of my childhood faith stood the substitutionary sacrifice of Jesus on the cross for humanity's sin. The forgiveness wrought by this divine act—for those who believe—grants access to an unearthly place called "heaven," where the faults and foibles of a thoroughly flawed human life would be left behind, for good. This made perfect sense to me as I grew up, as it still does to many Christians today. It occurred to me only much later to wonder why Paul considered the cross a foolish stumbling block (1 Corinthians 1:23) or how Jesus managed to forgive sins before he died (Matthew 9:6 and Mark 2:5) or to question the disembodied character of this salvation if God intended to save God's own wonderfully physical, bodily creation that had been declared unreservedly "good" in the first chapter of the Bible. More simply, I grew up reading Genesis as "Plan A" and the Gospels as "Plan B" without ever considering that both might belong to the very same divine plan.

Joining the Episcopal Church, with its stress on incarnation repeated in mantra-like fashion, blurred the tidy outlines of my earlier theological world. I began to see the deep fault lines that world had drawn between the "spiritual" and the "physical," between "body" and "soul," between nearly everything "earthly" and all things "heavenly." The chant-like repetitions of incarnation rising up from Anglican texts and proffered from Episcopal pulpits slowly chipped away at my assumptions until it finally dawned on me that bodies matter. They matter not to the extent that we manage to distance ourselves from them. Bodies matter to the extent that we can embrace them, find a home in them and among them, precisely where, according to the Johannine writer, the Word of God chose to dwell. Or as the original Greek suggests, where God pitched God's own tent with us (John 1:14).

I gained something else by joining the Episcopal Church as well: a new appreciation for historic creeds and their bold declarations about incarnation. A bit uncomfortably bold, actually, given their accompanying denunciations of those who disagreed with their claims. Tucked away in the back of the 1979 Book of Common Prayer, for example, the section called "Historical Documents of the Church" includes the Creed of Saint Athanasius. This ancient statement of Christian belief begins with a dire warning: "Whosoever will be saved, before all things it is necessary that he hold the Catholic Faith. Which Faith except everyone do keep whole and undefiled, without doubt he shall perish everlastingly."[17] Still more uncomfortable, the didactic character of these conciliar statements tends to evacuate nearly all the fleshliness they ostensibly extoll. Running throughout these discomforts, the presumption of containing divine mystery in a doctrinal box seems quite at odds indeed with the fluidity of bodily life itself. How exactly did the story of a humble birth in Bethlehem take center stage in ecclesial councils, some of which the Roman emperor convened? How did we travel from that manger-as-cradle to these historic creeds?

---

17. The Book of Common Prayer (New York: Seabury Press, 1979), 864.

One possible answer to these questions lies in yet another question: How would the particular Palestinian Jesus become culturally portable? For some, not only institutional declarations but also Eucharistic worship provided the means. Rather than relegated to the first-century borders of Palestine, the risen Christ can cross both national and cultural boundaries by appearing in Christian table fellowship *and* residing in commonly shared assertions about his identity, assertions expressed in conciliar texts. More than a few theologians embraced this approach to universalizing the particular Jesus while others harbored rather severe reservations, especially those most often referred to as "apophatic" or negative theologians. Negative not in the sense of being disagreeable (though some undoubtedly were) but for their conviction that the categorical affirmations of human speech can never crystallize the mystery of divine life with any final conceptual clarity. Indeed, such positive affirmations actually risk distorting that mystery into which the creeds themselves otherwise invite us ever more deeply.

Queer theorists share a similar concern with respect to modernity's categorical classifications of both human sexuality and gender. Human identity and relationships will always resist the systems designed to contain their definitions. Gerard Loughlin would note, however, that Christian theology itself displayed this cautionary insight long before theorists adopted a queer posture. This applies particularly well, in his view, to the centuries of intense philosophical wrestling over Christology:

> Even when theology was culturally dominant it was strange, for it sought the strange; it sought to know the unknowable in Christ, the mystery it was called to seek through following Jesus. And of course it has always been in danger of losing this strangeness by pretending that it has comprehended the mystery, that it can name that which is beyond all names.[18]

Trying to name the unnamable sounds more like an ancient riddle than a foundation for theological belief. If life itself, whether human or divine, resists codification, must a queer theology for Christian witness abandon Christianity's historic creeds? More than a few find that a compelling solution, but to do so invites the further risk of missing the life-changing insight that enlivened those ancient debates in the first place: the possibility

---

18. Gerard Loughlin, "What Is Queer? Theology after Identity," *Theology and Sexuality* 14, no. 2 (2008): 144.

of encountering the infinite mystery of God in the fragility of finite flesh. The peculiarity of Christian faith and its transforming energy reside in that very possibility. In that light, queer home economists will ask not whether to retain ancient creedal statements but rather how to read and reread them. At least three ways for reading those creeds might queerly strengthen Christian witness: as a dance floor, as open-source software, and as my grandmother's recipe cards.

Consider first that human bodies appear to move rather naturally to the rhythms of music. Some bodies clearly do this a bit more fluidly than others and nearly everyone can benefit from lessons if they want to dance better. Learning various styles of choreography can seem quite complicated and some styles of dancing do require a great deal of work to learn. Dancers come to appreciate these often tedious, sweat-producing lessons not only when they move gracefully on the dance floor but also and perhaps especially when they feel free enough to improvise dance steps and confident enough to lead a partner in those moments of creativity. Improvisational theater companies know this as well; they work hard to build a sense of rapport with each other before ever trying to improvise on a stage. Even scripted plays are rarely performed exactly the same way twice as much depends on the energy of the audience and the connections among the actors. These performance artists might invite us to read Christianity's historic creeds as a dance floor for communal improvisation. The creedal "choreography" matters but only for the sake of the dance and even more for those moments when the Spirit might take what we have learned and inspire novel steps.

The technologically inclined might find a different image more useful. Baby-boomers will remember the days when "software" meant ordering a product from a company that arrived by U.S. mail on a disc. After loading that software on one's computer hard drive, it will do what the software engineers designed it to do, *and nothing more.* Today, "open-source" software provides something quite different: downloading basic coding from the Internet for doing something that remains malleable in the hand of the end user, who can change the code and adapt it for particular needs. Open-source software still comes with limits but not nearly as many as accompanied the older discs. Tech geeks and hackers might invite us to consider historic creeds as theological programming directions and functions, but with the pathways and outcomes in the hands of end users, in the hands, that is, of queer home economists and indeed the whole Household of God.

I appreciate both of those ways of reading but perhaps my favorite comes from my maternal grandmother. In her own handwriting, she made recipe cards with notes like these: "use some butter around the size of an egg or so"; and "stir until it looks like the color of our wheat field in September"; and "toss in some salt, stir, taste, add some more if you like." Those notes stand in stark contrast to the narrative instructions one finds in *Cook's Illustrated*, which leave precious little room for idiosyncratic innovation. If my grandmother ever cared to write creedal statements, I imagine her doing so the way she cooked, with broad and rather general directions, a few observations about what has worked well for her in the past, and plenty of room to toss in one's own flavorful ingredients along the way.

I am grateful for grandma's recipe cards, which I still have and still use, just as I am grateful for the historic creeds of Christianity's peculiar faith. Grateful most of all for the struggle those ecclesial councils embodied to address embodiment itself and its entanglements with the mystery of God. I see little evidence that the creeds produced by those councils resolved that struggle in any definitive way, either historically or today; we can be grateful for that as well. Prepackaged resolutions to the complexities of human life—not to mention divine life—risk doing violence to the unfolding epiphanies of being human with each other and with God. Irenaeus tried to make this point in the second century. "The glory of God," he wrote, "is the human being fully alive."[19]

What then does it mean to live fully alive? This question animates much more of Christian history than the Church captured in its creedal statements and, indeed, the creeds themselves would seem to urge us away from only textual responses to that profoundly fleshy question. As John might remind us, whatever God's Word means for us, we cannot simply hear it spoken or read it off a printed page. Whatever that Word "means" will only appear in how we live and bear peculiar witness to it. The Word can only be incarnated, and in that sense, God's Word remains "unspeakable." Reading and rereading, preaching, and teaching all orbit around texts, and all these texts and speeches play important roles in Christian witness as they move God's household further along the path toward transformation. Sooner rather than later, however, the unspeakably divine Word calls us beyond still more words, creedal or otherwise.

---

19. See Mayra Rivera's treatment of this concept from Irenaeus, and its complexities, in *The Touch of Transcendence: A Postcolonial Theology of God* (Louisville, KY: Westminster John Knox Press, 2007), ch. 7, "The Glory of God."

HOUSEHOLDS OF EMBODIED DESIRE

Cable television companies offer hundreds of channels. Grocery stores devote an entire aisle to breakfast cereals. By the time you unpack and set up a new smart phone or laptop computer, technology companies have already designed its next iteration, making your new device old before you even use it. A consumerist society runs on consumption, and runs best by multiplying choices. The next, the newer, the better thing keeps advertisers employed and corporate profits high. Christianity likewise sits on a shelf among other religious commodities from which today's spirituality shoppers may choose or perhaps mix and match to suit their particular inclinations. In this dizzying array of consumer choices populating a fast-paced, crowded world of options, why would anyone find Christian faith attractive? Does it respond to deep and perennial human needs? Can it fulfill the longings of the human heart? Do any of us know what we really want?

Since at least the sixteenth century these questions have generated not just one but many different Christian products, each with its own marketing slogan and sales pitch. Calvinists peddled divine providence while Lutherans purveyed justification by faith and Anglicans crafted a "via media," a middle way between Catholics and Protestants (in large measure to stave off an English civil war). In 2002 some Episcopalians changed the familiar slogan "The Episcopal Church Welcomes You" to "We're Here for You," prompting some to wonder whether any actual product came with that free-floating "we."[20] Today, corporate profits translate religiously into congregational membership rolls, measured mostly with the number of "pledging units." Clerical CEOs retain their positions only at the pleasure of share-holders, otherwise known as pew sitters.

This rather crude reduction of Christianity to market mechanisms rightly belongs in any catalogue of the symptoms defining modernity's dis-ease. Marcella Althaus-Reid identified that distress both cogently and provocatively:

> Economic desires walk hand in hand with erotic desires and theological needs. An economic model is a relationship model . . . based on the patterns of accepted and unaccepted needs in the market. . . . The theological

20. For more on religion as consumer product, see James B. Twitchell, *Shopping for God: How Christianity Went from in Your Heart to in Your Face* (New York: Simon and Schuster, 2007); see also his treatment of the slogan for the Episcopal Church, 87.

models are, in this sense, not far from the economic ones. Traditionally, we may consider that theology deals with a market of souls and the definition of their needs . . . in order to effectively distribute the spiritual goods of redemption or forgiveness or even eternal life amongst them, the spiritual clientele.[21]

Economic exchanges fail to address, much less satisfy human yearning, a failure typified by houses filled with countless products and occupied by "homeless hearts." Building houses in homeless spaces rarely soothes those questing hearts any better than building another house of worship in the vast marketplace of religious commodities. Both secular and religious commodification alike leave untouched the deep anxiety bred from this widely shared though mostly unspoken homelessness. Unspoken, perhaps, but nonetheless distressingly visible in the sharp stratifications of neighborhoods, towns, and cities delineated by bodily difference, whether in terms of race, sex, or gender or the inevitable overlaps and intersections of all three.

LGBT sensibilities infuse this analysis with bodily desire itself as a source of insight. The many failures to live at home among others cascade from the challenge of finding ourselves at home in our own bodies. Queer home economists render that insight as theological questions: Can the peculiar faith of Christians bear witness to the God who makes a home with and in our bodily life? How can we reshape our churches into households of embodied desire? Would this make any difference in a world of homeless spaces?

The modern edifice of institutional Christianity resists asking much less answering these questions that spring from bodies and their unruly desires. Both historical and contemporary anxieties fuel that reticence. The biblical writer may have insisted, for example, that in Christ "all the fullness of God was pleased to dwell" (Colossians 1:19) but apparently *only* there; evacuated to heaven, the body of Jesus leaves scant doctrinal traces in its wake. These traces do matter, or rather they can when queer home economists deploy them to break what Althaus-Reid called institutional Christianity's "monopoly" on Jesus and its strict control of the means of "spiritual production."[22] She has more in mind here than evoking a Marxist analysis of capitalism to critique the commodification of doctrine as an institutional product. The critique exposes the source of bodily desire and its anxieties

---

21. Althaus-Reid, *Indecent Theology*, 166.

22. Ibid., 95.

within institutional Christianity's own history. In her words: "Theology has its own deconstructive forces, its own instabilities and imprecisions which always create tensions and open new ways of understanding. This has made of theology something still worth the effort, a path of permanent revelation and rediscovery of the engagement between the sensual and the divine in our lives."[23]

Modernity's ambivalent if not troubled posture toward bodies and their untamable desires derives from a complex matrix of sources, not least Christian theological traditions and their entanglements with Western culture. Althaus-Reid would caution us, however, to distinguish between the institutional packaging of these traditions and the theological insights they might still prompt. Two theologians in particular and their multivalent legacies have stamped nearly every strand of contemporary Christianity with a recognizable brand, even when their names frequently go unmentioned: Augustine of Hippo in the fourth and fifth centuries and Thomas Aquinas in the thirteenth. How these theologians have been read and appropriated matters as much as what they actually wrote.

Since at least the sixteenth-century Protestant Reformation, Augustine has most often been read as the Christian champion of fastidious sexuality. Augustine's own checkered sexual history certainly contributed to his apparent disdain of nearly all things erotic. Carter Heyward frames this more pointedly, describing Augustine as "the first theologian to systematize erotophobia—fear of sex—as a staple (arguably *the* staple) of Christian orthodoxy." A brilliant and passionate man, as Heyward notes, he nonetheless lived with two competing passions: "his spirituality as a source of love and creativity; his sexuality as a source of shame and guilt."[24] More than a few readers, as Heyward would argue, extrapolate from Augustine's sexual anxieties and view human life more broadly as a set of fundamental, virtually insurmountable problems. Augustine did not seem to live very comfortably, either in his body or in this world. Instead, he wrestled with both, longing for release to the spiritual realm of the world to come. The human heart is restless, he would write in his *Confessions*, until it rests in God.[25] Humanity's fundamental restlessness expresses itself in countless ways, but quintessentially (as

---

23. Ibid., 148–49.

24. Carter Heyward, *Touching Our Strength: The Erotic as Power and the Love of God* (San Francisco: HarperSanFrancisco, 1989), 89.

25. Saint Augustine, *Confessions*, trans. Henry Chadwick (Oxford: Oxford University Press, 1998), 3.

Augustine would have it) in our continual acquiescence to lust. This unfettered pursuit after the objects of desire corrupts our ability to choose freely until at last, he supposes, we lose our ability to pursue the Good at all. At that point, only divine, gracious intervention can save us. Rather than mysterious and inexorable forces external to human volition, Augustine understood sexual desire as the result of humanity's fall from innocence in Eden. Sexuality itself marks humanity's ever-present estrangement from God. This Augustinian imprint on modern Christianity, in other words, places sex and sexuality between us and our true, eternal home.[26]

Thomas Aquinas presents similar vexations but for different reasons. Since the nineteenth-century revival of Thomistic studies in Roman Catholicism, Aquinas has most often been read as the champion of "natural law." Unlike Augustine, however, Aquinas did not view human life as fundamentally and essentially problematic, though certainly fraught with danger on every side. Aquinas understood humanity as naturally oriented toward the good, hard-wired by God's grace, as it were, to be at home with God. Rather than evidence of a corrupt will, Aquinas understood sin as a deviation from that natural trajectory. We can correct and even avoid such deviations through a committed, habitual participation in the sacramental community of faith, which provides the added or "special" grace we need to stay on course.

The Thomistic flavor of Christianity orbits perpetually around that deceptively simple word "nature," or more specifically *natural law*. Knowing right from wrong and good from bad depends on knowing the God-given purpose of things, the natural law operating in the universe directing things, and us, to specific ends. This qualifies as a *deceptively* simple reading of Aquinas given the vexations and ambiguities in discerning exactly what counts as "natural," not least with respect to sex and gender, to sexual intimacy and its peculiar bodily positions and conflicted intentions. LGBT people, for example, frequently hear Thomistic language about ourselves in institutional church descriptions of "objectively disordered" lives.[27]

Remarkably, if not surprisingly, these readings of historical traditions blended extraordinarily well with other developments in the modern West, including scientific studies of sexuality. Thomas Laqueur analyzes that potent

---

26. See Peter Brown, *The Body and Society: Men, Women, and Sexual Renunciation in Early Christianity* (New York: Columbia University Press, 1988), 416–19.

27. For more on the complexities and ample confusions in reading Thomas Aquinas, see Rogers Jr., "Bodies Demand Language," 176–87.

mix by noting how the "scientific revolution" stripped away much of the metaphysical veneer from our sexual desire, and he cites a particularly apt example. Elizabeth Blackwell, a nineteenth-century physician, understood those in her profession to contribute "very important aid" in the growth of "higher" forms of society. Nonhuman animals, she argued, possess no "mental component" in their sexual relations. "Primitive people" and the working classes have only a bit more, which makes them mostly unchaste. Chastity ranks the highest among civilized people, for whom the mental component predominates. For Blackwell (and a good many others) human progress relies on subordinating the "brutishly physical" in sexual relations so that chastity, what she understood as a "cultural triumph for the race," becomes "inseparably interwoven with the essential [biological] structure of our physical organization."[28]

The cultured high society of Blackwell's day was, of course, decidedly Christian, exhibiting a nearly homogenous blend of Christian faith and Western cultural values. Concerning sexuality, the Augustinian and Thomistic strands of institutional Christianity provided subtle but resilient threads to weave Christian practice and social mores together into a single fabric. Unfettered pursuit of sexual desire indicated, as Augustine had argued, a failure of will, which the lower classes of modern Europe so clearly embodied. Strictly defined, reified gender roles found theological support in a Thomistic-like appeal to the "natural order of things."

Few Christians could name these historical sources yet most readily recognize the brand of Christianity they generated, like the Nike "swoosh" logo or the partially eaten apple logo on computers and smart phones. Many have never known any other kind of Christian faith and more than a few have experienced how this Christian brand and its troubled posture toward bodies too often issues in violence. Demonizing bodily desire lies at the root of sexually gendered harassment and even more frequently fuels the mechanisms of white supremacy. Kelly Brown Douglas sifts through these many socioreligious contestations over race to uncover their source in what she calls "platonized Christianity." She means the philosophical equivalent of replacing the actual *body* of Jesus—in which the fullness of God was pleased to dwell—with a suitably sanitized *idea* of Jesus. An idea sufficiently suitable, that is, for denigrating black bodies as "bestial" in

---

28. Laqueur, *Making Sex*, 205.

their brutish sexual practices, nothing more than "mandingo bucks" and oversexed "Jezebels."[29]

In rereading these sources of modernity's distress, bodily desire clearly matters, but in ways that institutional Christianity has mostly failed to grasp. Queer home economists appreciate those sources for their cautions and even more for their invitations to listen carefully to the voice of divine desire in bodily life. Rereading Augustine's "restless heart," for example, surfaces a trenchant critique of today's consumerist society in the thrall of unabated desire. As human beings gobble up natural resources like a hoard of locusts descending on a grassy field, the Augustine who worries over unrestrained consumption sounds a surprisingly contemporary alarm. So does Aquinas, not for selectively describing just some members of the human race as "objectively disordered," but the whole human family as suffering from such wildly unfocused yearnings that very few of us can name what we really want or even need. Modernity's imprint on Christianity has rendered it virtually impotent to address these energies of human desire except to declare them dangerous or to restrict them with static laws supposedly drawn directly from "nature." With nowhere else to go, these energies erupt in the orgies of Western consumerism and globalized capitalism or languish as forbidden fruit in adult movie houses or the glossy pages of pornographic magazines.[30] Equally troubling, desire's bodily frustrations can quickly turn outward into blame and seek relief from designating and targeting particular scapegoats, especially the bodies most closely associated with dangerous desire, whether black, lesbian, gay, or "unnaturally" transgendered.

These cautionary tales invite not the wholesale rejection of desire itself (modern Christianity's profound mistake) but rather desire's recalibration, a theological rehabilitation of bodily eroticism. Putting this more simply but no less profoundly, the peculiar faith of Christians bears witness to love. Perhaps deceptively simple as well in the midst of love's reduction to greeting card sentimentality or its naïve exaltation in Hollywood romances. Ancient sources prove helpful here too. Werner Jeanrond invites us to recall ancient Greek approaches to *Eros*, the god of love, who seeks to unite what had been separated, to restore

---

29. Kelly Brown Douglas, *What's Faith Got to Do With It? Black Bodies/Christian Souls* (Maryknoll, NY: Orbis Books, 2005), 114.

30. Whether or not "pornography" with all its evasions of definitional precision deserves a sustained critique, a 2001 study should give everyone pause, a study that found pornography constituting a bigger business in the United States than basketball, baseball, and football combined (see Carr, *Erotic Word*, 47).

a long-forgotten wholeness.[31] To restore, perhaps, even the memory of desiring such wholeness in the first place, which animated Augustine's wrestling match with desire and, even more, the exultations of *Eros* among mystics. Writing in the seventh century, Maximus the Confessor imagined that the "eros or love that unifies all things is God." By "all" he meant to leave nothing behind, not angels, or birds, or sea creatures, or even inanimate, insensate things, all of which in their own way desire the desiring of God.[32]

Rather than consumption, in other words, erotic desire yearns above all for *communion*, a yearning that percolates in biblical texts, creedal traditions, and the long peculiar history of mystical musings. This history surely counts as peculiar if not queer in the modern West where *Eros* no longer percolates but languishes in mostly forgotten texts or lies hidden in familiar ones, veiled by institutional pieties. Meanwhile, the body of Jesus still speaks with the voice of divine desire, a voice echoed, if only faintly at times, in every moment of our own bodily yearning for intimacy and wholeness, for reconciliation and communion. This divine voice continues to speak with the first question humanity ever heard from the Creator: *Where are you?* The voice still speaks, as Althaus-Reid again reminds us, because when God chooses to speak, God does so with bodies.[33] And today's bodies speak with an unmistakable clarity for an end to violence; for an end to color-line stratifications; for an end to photographs of women tossed on piles of trash and calling it "fashion."

Queer home economists will hear in all these bodily voices not merely a complaint but a primal yearning for communion, and with it, an epiphany: in human flesh God takes great delight. This is the body's grace, as Rowan Williams so eloquently describes it, the grace to encounter in our bodily lives the God who does not merely tolerate us but who finds us desirable.[34] No less than the body of Jesus, in which the fullness of God was pleased to dwell, in and with *our* bodies God longs to make a home.

Queer home economists relish this epiphany, but cautions still persist here in the risk of idealizing bodily life or of denying the painful work of

---

31. Werner G. Jeanrond, *A Theology of Love* (London: Continuum, 2010), 14–15.

32. See Christos Yannaras, *Person and Eros*, trans. Norman Russell (Brookline, MA: Holy Cross Orthodox Press, 2007), 120–22.

33. Marcella Althaus-Reid, *The Queer God* (New York: Routledge, 2003), 34.

34. Rowan Williams, "The Body's Grace," in *Our Selves, Our Souls and Bodies: Sexuality and the Household of God* (Cambridge: Cowley Publications, 1996), 59.

reconciliation that wounded bodies demand in their quest for communion. The magi in Matthew's gospel remind us of this as they present their extravagant gifts to a Jesus already scarred by circumcision. Traditional Christian calendars marked that scarring with a feast day five days before Epiphany, called appropriately enough, the "Feast of the Circumcision," on January 1. Most liturgical calendars today obscure that genital wounding by renaming it the "Feast of the Holy Name." Does this liturgical shift reflect an ongoing discomfort with Jesus's genitals or a subtle denial of wounded bodies? Probably a bit of both, which carries implications for all the sexually and racially scarred bodies sitting in the pews of our churches.

Graham Ward agrees and locates his bodily reflections in both the scarring and the naming. Circumcision, as early Christian apologists argued, confirmed the genuine humanity of Jesus, but it did more than this; it marked a boundary of identity, specifically a Jewish male identity. At the very least, as Ward urges us to notice, theology always entails a "cultural politics."[35] We might take this still further and notice that God appears within this gendered and ethnic classification scheme through the act of *wounding*.

This bears repeating: to live in modern Western society is to be identified, and based on that identity to occupy one's proper place. It bears repeating with an addition: the process comes with wounds. Laurel Schneider's analysis of how race, sex, and gender mutually inform each other includes the bodily pain that accompanies those social constructions:

> The well-documented public sexual brutalization of black women in slavery, and particularly the legal prohibitions against slave marriage, further distanced slaves from dominant, colonial practices of sexualized gender (not to mention their own inherited gender practices). The result was to racialize gender all the more, in this case through prohibitions on gender practices for certain races. Such prohibitions served further to "feminize" slave men except where they could dominate slave women, and to "masculinize" slave women, except where they could submit to slave or free men.[36]

Even with all the pain associated with categorical identity placement, I cannot imagine many would choose to abandon their identities—whether racial,

---

35. Graham Ward, "On the Politics of Embodiment and the Mystery of All Flesh," in Althaus-Reid and Isherwood, *Sexual Theologian*, 77.

36. Schneider, "What Race Is Your Sex?" 157.

ethnic, sexual, or gendered—based solely on the many scars that inevitably accompany those social identifications. Not least, of course, God, who chose a path for identification that began with blood. The blood of childbirth, yes, and yet more blood in the wounded genitals, and still more as a criminal executed by imperial power.

Pursuing the bodily desire for communion always comes with a cost. That cost comes higher for some than for others, to be sure, but the pursuit itself will never unfold without expense. Queer home economists know this and relish even more the epiphany lodged in the liturgical feast of that very name: God deems bodily communion worth the fleshly price. They know and relish this bodily insight and, because of it, stand dismayed in Christian worship services where so few Christians actually touch each other.

In 1968, not long before his assassination, Martin Luther King Jr. preached at the National Cathedral in Washington, D.C. There he famously described 11:00 a.m. on Sunday mornings as the most segregated hour in America.[37] Ironically and also tragically for most white communities, that hour qualifies as the most severely disembodied one as well. A society that divvies itself up by color, and then even further sequesters human flesh itself behind touch-free pieties surely stands in desperate need of a peculiar, incarnational faith. All these bodies still speak yet in muted tones as the unspeakably divine Word that seeks incarnation resides mostly in words on a printed page of worship directions. If we heard them, all these scarred bodies would speak a deep longing for reconciliation, for intimacy, wholeness, and communion. Could the peculiar faith of Christians bear renewed witness in that racially segregated, touchless hour, a witness to the hope for communion? As ministers lift a loaf of bread, they repeat the words attributed to Jesus: "take, eat; this is my body." Would it matter if people touched each other at that moment? What might happen? Scandal might happen, or the thought of scandal, or perhaps an epiphany.

Perhaps the ancient scandal of finding God in human flesh—a scandal sufficient to inspire extravagant gift-giving from pagan astrologers—perhaps that scandal could suffice today, not only to transform Christian worship but because of this, to inspire Christians to transform society with a peculiar faith. Bearing witness to that faith will seem quite peculiar indeed, if not

---

37. See Tony Bartlett's reflections on that sermon and some of its theological implications in "Our Most Segregated Hour: Church, Black Theology, and Rene Girard," *God's Politics: A Blog by Jim Wallis and Friends* (*www.sojo.net/blogs*, April 24, 2013).

terribly queer, when Christians reject color-blind justice and relish skin color differences; when we relish diverse engagements with sexual intimacy among differently gendered bodies; and when we see the bodies of all the other-than-human ones as equally the cause of God's ceaseless delight.

Embodying this peculiar faith will certainly prompt further questions and quandaries, not least the ones orbiting around Christian proclamations of salvation. Just like incarnation, the notion of salvation itself carries a host of contemporary assumptions and modern distortions. "All flesh is grass," the biblical writer reminds us (Isaiah 40:6–8, KJV), and no matter how incarnate our faith, flesh will eventually decay and perish. In the midst of inevitable mortality, can salvation sound as peculiar as incarnation for Christian witness? Will flesh stand the test of eternity? Do we even want it to? If not, what happens to all that unspent and unrequited energy for communion? More than a few Christian communities today would find a felicitous entry point into these quandaries by pondering anew what in the world (quite literally) anyone means by the "Holy Spirit." Felicitous and also peculiar as God's household reflects on the perversely Pentecostal disruptions of ordinary life that compelled the earliest Christians to consider that Spirit "holy" at all.

Perversely Pentecostal

Sacrifice, Salvation, and the Body of Christ

*S*tables provide shelter for horses, sometimes cattle and sheep. They sit rather modestly on farmlands, sometimes in towns and villages, usually garnering little if any attention. Oddly enough, stables also punctuate some key moments in Christian history, beginning of course with the birthplace of Jesus. Twenty centuries after shepherds found their way to Bethlehem at the urging of angels, an odd mix of Angelenos found their way to an abandoned stable in an urban "black ghetto" of Los Angeles. William J. Seymour, an African-American preacher, drew them to that rickety, two-story building on Azusa Street. They came by the hundreds, not only for the preaching but for the ecstatic trances, speaking in tongues, and miraculous healings.

The Azusa Street revival began in 1906 and lasted, quite remarkably, until roughly 1915. This inspirited revival in turn launched a world-wide Pentecostal movement, today's fastest growing brand of Christianity. Fastest and perhaps also the queerest, at least in its humble and peculiar origins. Erupting in the midst of Jim Crow segregation, this revival attracted white, black, Latino, and Asian converts, all "intermingling," as one commentator derided at the time about their worship. Moreover, and fourteen years before suffragettes secured the right to vote in the United States, the Apostolic Faith Mission on Azusa Street encouraged women to take positions of leadership. This sufficed for some to dismiss the movement as "outrageous" and even "blasphemous." One minister at the time described the revival as "a freak imitation of Pentecost," and then added, "horrible, awful shame."[1]

---

1. See Jack Hayford and David Moore, *The Charismatic Century: The Enduring Impact of the Azusa Street Revival* (New York: Hatchett Book Group, 2006), ch. 4, "William J. Seymour and the Azusa Street Revival."

More than theology, this blurring if not erasing the color lines of racial distinction and rejecting the "naturally" gendered order of male privilege seized the attention of Azusa's detractors. Azusa's participants, by contrast, embraced those social disruptions as nothing less than a vision of heaven, a taste of salvation. Theologians have always struggled with such disorderly moments, especially those of us trained in *systematic* theology. The modern academic approach to systematics appeals to my own affinity for orderliness, the parsing of each doctrinal locus into interlocking modes of analysis and arranging them in a neatly organized religious filing cabinet. Etienne Gilson penned a less pedestrian version by describing medieval scholastic theology as a "cathedral of the mind," evoking the tight architectural reliance of each chiseled stone on all the others, and the whole structure supported by flying buttresses reaching toward the heavens.[2]

Queer theorists may appreciate the aesthetics of stone masonry yet insist on chipping away at mortared social systems and eroding the foundations of categorical classification schemes. Long before anyone thought to queer theological systems, however, the Holy Spirit had already provided good reasons to do it. "Holy," yes, but something like a prankster, a divine scamp in biblical accounts who fouls up tidy narratives, unsettles communities, and muddles common sense. Those departures from what otherwise seems reasonable and expected originally defined the word "perverse."

Perversity and sanctity rarely occupy the same sentence, yet this odd and challenging mix of the orderly and the queer animated the biblical writer known as Luke. The author of one of the four canonical gospel accounts as well as the Acts of the Apostles, Luke is sometimes referred to as the "historian." He lures my systematic sensibilities with his very first sentence: I decided "to write an orderly account" (Luke 1:3). In both style and structure, Luke manages to do precisely that. The content of his account, however, simmers with queer energy.

Luke begins his gospel, not with Jesus, as one might expect, but with the Holy Spirit. This Spirit empowers the son of an old and previously child-less couple (Zechariah and Elizabeth), visits a virgin with a divine pregnancy (Mary), and inspires that same young girl to declare that God has brought down the powerful and lifted up the lowly. In this, the very first chapter of his "orderly account" Luke confounds basic biology and overturns

---

2. Quoted in Alister E. McGrath, *Christian Theology: An Introduction*, rev. ed. (London: Blackwell Publishing, 2006), 29.

entrenched social hierarchies. Luke would have us see these disruptions as
the work of the Holy Spirit, who three chapters later animates the ministry
of Jesus to bring good news to the poor, release to the captives, sight to the
blind, and freedom to the oppressed (Luke 4:14–19); or more simply, social
chaos. This same Spirit plays a starring role in the opening chapters of Luke's
second volume, the Acts of the Apostles. There, this lover of orderly accounts
choreographs a tidy, albeit dramatic exit for the risen Jesus from center stage
only to depict a cacophonous scene of Spirit-filled disciples speaking multiple languages all at the same time. Witnesses to that scene dismissed the
disciples as drunk (Acts 2:13).

What Luke attempts in his two books foreshadows the patterns and
inclinations of institutional Christianity, and perhaps to Luke's chagrin.
I mean all the otherwise well-meaning attempts to order the disorderly, to
manage the unruly, to systematize the chaotic, to capture and harness that
divine breath called the Holy Spirit only to find again and again that it resolutely blows where it wills, as John's Jesus cautioned (John 3:8). Formal
liturgical commemorations of Pentecost repeat these inclinations with rituals
conducted "decently and in order" (as Paul advised in 1 Corinthians 14:40).
I certainly appreciate neatly arranged pews and reciting well-crafted prayers,
and yet I pause. When, I wonder, might the Spirit's soft breeze strengthen to
a gale of excited speech, or ignite prophetic visions, or erupt into dances of
ecstatic hope? The peculiar mix of Angelenos on Azusa Street knew to expect
such things at any moment, perhaps just as Luke had. Luke expected something else as well. The disruptive, untamable character of the Spirit serves
more than merely disruption itself but a divine purpose, nothing less than
salvation. "To you is born this day," Luke has an angel declare to startled
shepherds, "a Savior" (Luke 2:11).

LGBT people quickly recognize this Lucan posture in their own lives
of managed chaos. Those who spend years and enormous amounts of
energy trying to fit into social systems of sexual and gender conformity
know well what happens when they disrupt those systems: cherished expectations crumble; familial assumptions shatter; tidy narratives fall apart in
plot twists no one anticipated (or at least voiced). Some try to manage the
ensuing chaos by reassuring friends and family of their virtual normalcy
("it will still be a traditional wedding, but with two grooms") or with vocational overcompensation ("I'll be an even better minister now that I identify as a woman"). Others wonder whether restoring a sense of cultural and

religious order actually stifles the Spirit's work. Luke seemed to share a similar concern.

In the first chapter of Acts, the disciples ask the risen Jesus whether he will, at long last, restore the kingdom of Israel (1:6). Their question misses the point. Whatever else Luke understood the resurrection of Jesus to mean, it did not restore an orderly past. Indeed, the risen Jesus still bears the scars of his suffering at the hands of imperial power (Luke 24:39–40). Rather than erasing a painful history, much less inviting nostalgic dreams of a golden age, the resurrection opened a brand new horizon opening out from that traumatic history itself, a horizon marked by the unpredictability of the Spirit. Luke set the stage for this throughout his gospel account, the final chapter of which underscores the point rather dramatically. When startled disciples recognize the risen Jesus among them while breaking bread during a meal, in that very moment Jesus vanishes (24:31).[3] Few of us, I imagine, find in that story the "closure" so many of us seek for unspeakable grief, not least those disciples for whom any wistfulness over the "good old days" slips through their fingers with nothing to grasp or seize.

These reasons among others seal the bond between Luke's gospel account and his Acts of the Apostles. The former launches the particular body of Jesus into a ministry of social transformation; the latter chronicles the stitching together of Christ's body when Jesus disappears. One without the other leaves either unimaginable grief or naïve utopianism. In short, ignore your bound Bible that inserts John's gospel account in between "Luke" and "Acts." Unite those Lucan texts (as Luke himself intended) and notice what Luke's vanishing Jesus leaves in his wake: the very same Spirit who animated his own ministry among the poor, the captives, the blind, and the oppressed. As the rest of Luke's Acts of the Apostles amply demonstrates, taking up that ministry overturns economic systems that keep the poor in poverty (Acts 4:34–35); resists institutional authorities jealous of their own power (5:17–26); violates social and class boundaries (8:25–40); and rejects cultural and religious standards of propriety (10:9–30).

The inspired—literally "in-spirited"—Jesus of Luke's account of the Gospel shapes the peculiar faith and social practices of the similarly in-spirited community in Acts. The result, as Luke described it, is a world turned

---

3. See the commentary Robert E. Goss offered on this passage ("Luke," in Guest, Goss, West, and Bohache, *Queer Bible Commentary*, 545–47).

upside down (17:6), perhaps the most succinct biblical description of Christianity's peculiar faith and its queerly animating Spirit.

Institutional Christianity (to which the "orderly" Luke would surely not object) has always harbored a bit of reticence about Pentecost and the unruliness of the Spirit featured in that story, even though the Church canonized that very story. Or perhaps that reticence actually explains the canonization, the vain hope of containing the Spirit in a text, and even better, a doctrine. Imperial regimes, for example, generally look askance at sources of disruption. A truism, certainly, and a modest one at that, but a theologically vexing one in the wake of the Emperor Constantine's fourth-century edict of tolerance for Christianity in the Roman Empire. Constantine's socioreligious sea change rather abruptly posed a question that the gospel writers never would have imagined asking: Can Christian faith find a home in the courts of imperial power? The affirmative answer to that question should probably shock more than it does. The incongruity of a suffering Jesus appearing in the robes of an emperor abated with surprising alacrity, especially in the promulgation of the Nicene Creed. That statement of baseline Christian doctrine was produced by a council called by the emperor Constantine himself.

The development of Latin American liberation theology in the mid-twentieth century highlights particularly well the wide-ranging effects of imperial favor on Christian faith, both historically and today. Jon Sobrino, for example, rather pointedly notes that "forgetting the poor has gone hand in hand with forgetting the Kingdom of God." The galvanizing announcement of the Kingdom, which features prominently in Matthew, Mark, and Luke, gradually gives way to speculation on the relationship between Jesus and God and thus on his identity at the expense of what he announced. As Sobrino rather pointedly observes, by the time of the fourth-century conciliar debates the Kingdom of God plays no role whatsoever in Christology. The consequence of this, he writes, is that the title "Christ . . . ceased to express the fact that 'Messiah' was the referent of the hope and the salvation of the poor—that which points toward the Kingdom of God."[4]

Did Christians worry that the Gospel might destabilize the empire? Did the Council of Nicaea deliberately omit politically disruptive images from a statement being drafted at an emperor's request? Did Constantine urge them

---

4. Quoted in Jeff Astley, David Brown, and Ann Loades, eds., *Christology: Key Readings in Christian Thought* (Louisville, KY: Westminster John Knox, 2009), 85–86.

to set aside theological provocations that might lead to social unrest? We know nothing of Constantine's inner motivations and spiritual convictions, but we can surmise this: like every other astute leader, both historically and today, Constantine knew that political order depends on religious order, if not conformity. Notably, the creed produced by that fourth-century council linked belief in the Spirit to the Church where, presumably, the Spirit would rest comfortably and not cause too much trouble, religious or civic. Luke would likely fret over such attempts to institutionalize that untamable Spirit, the Spirit who can just as easily upend institutions as turn worlds upside down.

Does this sound troubling, even harsh? It does to me, a trained systematic theologian and a priest in the Episcopal Church. At the same time, those very theological systems infusing the liturgical rhythms that continue to nourish my vocation compel me to notice this: Luke's faith communities rarely appear orderly but instead compellingly perverse: unexpected, unreasonable, and disruptive. I notice this, and along with other queer home economists, I ponder what it might mean to nurture perversely Pentecostal communities as base camps for Christian witness. Whatever else this kind of work might entail, it will keep Luke's own caveat fully in view: God's unruly Spirit seeks to inspire and indeed to accomplish *salvation*.

That too sounds troubling and even harsh for many LGBT people who have too often fallen under the weight of doctrinal systems that demand our exclusion. Luke would interject here again. Neatly dividing the world between the saved and the damned, or the orthodox and the heretical, certainly protects institutional boundaries, but it does this only by ignoring some of Luke's most familiar and time-honored stories: Peter's encounter with Cornelius (Acts 10); Philip's encounter with an Ethiopian eunuch (8:26–39); and Peter and Paul's impassioned plea to include Gentiles (15:1–21). These stories, not to mention the Spirit who inspired them, rarely stay put on a printed page. The rainbow coalition on Azusa Street realized this quite acutely more than a century ago.

Like all good home economists, those called to queerly Christian housework appreciate the benefits of an organized household. As Luke would likely remind us, however, the Spirit will always disrupt any attempt to take institutional order as synonymous with salvation, or more severely, the impulse to sacrifice the disorderly few to save the well-behaved many. The deep divisions over slavery in nineteenth-century America turned as often on preserving church unity as on the morality of slave-holding itself, just as women's vocations to ordained ministry withered at the altar of institutional order in the mid-twentieth century, along with the lives of many LGBT people to this day. In the wake of Gene Robinson's election as bishop of New Hampshire, for example, some in the worldwide Anglican Communion called for a "moratorium" on any future such elections of gay or lesbian people until a wider consensus can be reached on questions of sexuality. The moratorium would, of course, serve the singular purpose of holding the institution together. By some accounts, however, few of us will live to see what critics of Bishop Robinson's election would take as sufficient agreement for affirming the vocations of LGBT-identified people.[5] In the wake of this modern history littered with racial, gendered, and sexual sacrifices, queer home economists may need to sacrifice standard notions of "order" for a lively witness to salvation. In relation to the wider society, in other words, the Spirit calls God's people to be "differently organized."

Here some additional pieces for the queer theology puzzle come more clearly into view, including the troubling notion of sacrifice and what it has to do with salvation. Paul linked these with his familiar image of the body of Christ and its many diverse members, which proves to be no less disruptive than Luke's perversely Pentecostal communities. In a first-century society just as rigidly stratified as the twenty-first-century North Atlantic, Paul insisted on the indispensable value of each member of the Body. Even more, he declared that the weaker among us are actually the most indispensable, clothed with the greatest honor (1 Corinthians 12: 22–26). Paul urged the Christians in Corinth to bear witness to this bodily life with faith and hope and most especially with love (13:13). These three ancient hallmarks of Christian witness still set a lively agenda for today's "differently organized" households, especially if we map those hallmarks to sacrifice and salvation, and even more to an embodied love.

SACRIFICE FOR LIFE

Mychal F. Judge, a Roman Catholic priest and chaplain to the New York City fire department, sacrificed his life on September 11, 2001, while ministering

---

5. See Oliver O'Donovan, *Church in Crisis: The Gay Controversy and the Anglican Communion* (Eugene, OR: Cascade Books, 2008), especially ch. 2, "The Care of Churches," 18–34, and ch. 3, "Ethics and Agreement," 35–53.

among fire fighters at the World Trade Center; Fr. Judge also identified as a gay man. On that same day, Mark Bingham sacrificed his life on United Airlines flight 93 to prevent even further loss of life; he too identified as gay. As most accounts of heroism do, these stories feature moments of profound sacrifice, and perhaps of more than one kind. Did Fr. Judge believe he had sacrificed his sexuality for the sake of his priestly vocation? Did mainstream media reports sacrifice any mention of Bingham's sexuality for the sake of telling a heroic story? Can American heroes live queerly sexual lives and still qualify as heroic? These questions pose still more, especially about the meaning of sacrifice itself.

Good home economists, queer or not, realize that thriving households rely on regular moments of sacrifice, both small and large. My parents sacrificed a portion of their retirement account to pay for my graduate school education. Children will sometimes sacrifice careers to care for aging parents. We sacrifice time for the sake of friendship, money for the sake of charity, and household space for companion animals. The theological question here turns not on sacrifice per se, but on its conditions and purposes. Does God, the divine home economist, make sacrifices? A standard Christian answer surfaces rather quickly. God the "Father" sacrificed his "Son" to atone for the sins of the world. Queer home economists, among others, find that answer deeply troubling.

Discerning how sacrifice relates to salvation presents significant challenges, not least is trying to avoid dealing with it at all. Some of the most familiar biblical texts, liturgical practices, and religious icons drip with sacrificial blood: Cain's murder of Abel; the (barely) averted sacrifice of Isaac by Abraham, his own father; the intricate temple rituals of ancient Israel; early Christian references to Jesus as the "Lamb of God who was slain"; Eucharistic prayers extolling the saving blood of Christ; and the ubiquity of graphic crucifixes in households of worship. Even that short list evokes varying types of sacrificial mechanisms with a range of diverse consequences. The Evangelical faith of my youth, however, reduced all these to just one, a direct link between the animal sacrifices of ancient Israel and the sacrifice of Jesus on the cross.

Decades ago feminist scholars rejected theories of sacrificial atonement in light of their disturbing social effects. Assigning spiritual, even ultimate significance to sacrifice can convince victims of domestic abuse, for example, to remain with a violent partner, to "sacrifice" for the sake of a marriage, or for children.[6] Liberal Protestants more generally have expressed similar concerns since at least the mid-nineteenth century. Many abandoned sacrificial language and imagery entirely, choosing instead to focus on the ethical teachings of Jesus as a guide for social justice ministries. Today, some LGBT-inclusive faith communities offer liturgical celebrations of Holy Communion that make no mention of the cross or the death of Jesus at all. Their history with institutional religion makes some pastoral sense from that otherwise odd omission as far too many have been told to sacrifice their sexually gendered lives and relationships for the sake of their faith.

Queer home economists sympathize deeply with these vexations even as they worry over wholesale dismissals of potentially insightful theologies. The multivalent character of salvation invites more than just one interpretive approach, even on questions of atonement and sacrifice. Most Christians either miss or overlook theological diversity in Christian history, due in part to the nearly irresistible temptation to think and speak correctly. In theological matters, especially in the modern West, correct speech means choosing only one among the possible ways to speak. Gustaf Aulen, for example, mapped a variety of historical approaches to the doctrine of the atonement in his oft-cited book *Christus Victor*, yet he left little doubt over which of those views he preferred as the best (the one enshrined in the book's title).[7] H. Richard Niebuhr replicated the same pattern with his even more frequently cited *Christ and Culture* in which the various models for Christ's relationship to the wider society all pale by comparison to just one of those options.[8] Following Robert Neville's lead proves far queerer and more fruitful. Neville proposes multiple entry points into the mystery of salvation through the variety of symbols for Jesus evoked by the Christian Testament (such as Friend, Lamb of God, and Cosmic Christ, among others). One of those symbols may work well for some but not for others or might operate differently over time. Neville does not mean to suggest that good theology is just whatever one happens to like. He does argue, however, that symbols in theology should not be mistaken for the reality to which they are meant to point. Under certain

---

6. See Rebecca Ann Parker and Rita Nakashima Brock, *Proverbs of Ashes: Violence, Redemptive Suffering, and the Search for What Saves Us* (Boston: Beacon Press, 2002).

7. Gustaf Aulen, *Christus Victor: An Historical Study of the Three Major Types of the Idea of the Atonement* (New York: Macmillan, 1968).

8. H. Richard Niebuhr, *Christ and Culture* (New York: Harper and Row, 1951).

conditions, some of those symbols point well, and under other conditions, not so well.[9] C. S. Lewis seemed to believe this too. For Lewis, the "how" of salvation poses in inexhaustible question, impossible to answer with any one model or mechanism.[10]

Queer home economists appreciate this rich historical diversity for many reasons, especially for the opportunity to speak more meaningfully and less harmfully about sacrifice. Given the ubiquity of the cross among Christian symbols and the modern reduction of its meaning to just one view of atonement, queer home economists will attend carefully to the complexities in relating Christ to ancient Israelite rituals of animal sacrifice. This will sound less arcane and more intriguing by saying it differently: how we approach the death of Jesus makes a difference in how we approach sex; sexual intimacy likewise sheds light on crucifixion. While a bit odd at first glance, lesbian and gay people need little prompting to make those otherwise curious connections. After all, the rituals of animal sacrifice appear in the very same biblical book that contains one of the most frequently cited verses to condemn "homosexuality" (Leviticus 18:22).

Ancient texts like Leviticus seem rather far removed from the cultural sensibilities of the modern West. The differences appear on multiple fronts, yet some of them can sound strangely familiar. The sensibilities of a tribal, warrior culture, for example, shaped those ancient texts. In that society, survival depended on what we might call an "economics of masculinity," or how the household called Israel would arrange its social patterns of relation.[11] Freed from slavery in Egypt, the command to conquer on the way to the Promised Land provided the "script" for the men of Israel, a way to perform their covenantal relationship with God. While this script eventually evolved into the textual elaborations of religious and cultural purity, those texts remain steeped in the rhythms of a warrior culture that made very little distinction between dominating an enemy and subduing a sex partner. Stephen D. Moore, quoting the work of Harold Washington and Harry

---

9. Robert Neville, *Symbols of Jesus: A Christology of Symbolic Engagement* (Cambridge: Cambridge University Press, 2001), 1–6.

10. See Michael Ward, *Planet Narnia: The Seven Heavens in the Imagination of C. S. Lewis* (Oxford: Oxford University Press, 2008), 70

11. Ronald E. Long has offered an intriguing analysis of religious masculinity in a variety of religious traditions, which can help to frame ancient Israel's sensibilities around the expectations of male/masculine warriors (*Men, Homosexuality, and the Gods: An Exploration into the Religious Significance of Male Homosexuality in World Perspective* [New York: Harrington Park Press, 2004], see especially 49–58).

Hoffner, makes the same point, not only concerning ancient Israel but the whole ancient Mediterranean world:

> The language of war in the Hebrew Bible and other ancient Near Eastern literatures is acutely masculinist. Warfare is emblematically male and the discourse of violence is closely imbricated with that of masculine sexuality. . . . The masculinity of the ancient was measured by two criteria: (1) his prowess in battle, and (2) his ability to sire children. . . . These two aspects of masculinity were frequently associated with each other. . . . Those symbols which primarily referred to his military exploits often served to remind him of his sexual ability as well.[12]

Linking sex and war sounds off key in contemporary contexts but only at first. Raping a conquered army belongs not only to an ancient past but quite uncomfortably in current events; witness the sexually scandalous behavior that came to light in 2004 at the Abu Ghraib prison in Iraq, operated at that time by the U.S. military.[13]

The particularly strange yet oddly familiar threat of enemy intrusion lurks behind a great deal of the proscriptions and ritual regulations in Leviticus. More than a few lesbian and gay apologists have highlighted that threat to help explain why the prospect of male same-sex behavior might trigger alarm and even disgust in those ancient communities with reference to wartime rape as well as peacetime slavery. In short, one does not do to one's own people what one does to one's enemies and slaves. Or more precisely, the *men* of Israel should avoid such behavior for fear of religiously disenfranchising their male partners, of excluding them from the covenant with their warrior god.[14] Performing that covenant necessarily means dominating the other, just as "Yahweh" himself eventually emerges not as just one god among many but the one god who tops any and all other divinities.

Constructing purity as a dynamic of domination sheds considerable light on the horror of the Babylonian exile in Israel's history, but it also appears at the heart of the Gentile controversy in the early Christian era. Paul appears

---

12. Moore, *God's Beauty Parlor*, 181–82.

13. For more on the subtle but pervasive links among gender, war, humiliation, and empire, see Zillah Eisenstein, *Against Empire: Feminisms, Racism, and the West* (London: Zed Books, 2004).

14. For a similar reading that takes these texts in a slightly different direction, see Daniel Boyarin, "Against Rabbinic Sexuality: Textual Reasoning and the Jewish Theology of Sex," in Loughlin, *Queer Theology*, 135–36.

early on as the champion of overturning the restrictions of the Levitical code that he once embraced. The evolutionary development on display in the Hebrew Bible itself, however, provides further texture to this queer turn in both Judaism and Christianity. Consider Isaiah, in many ways a stunning transformation of Levitical sensibilities no less radical than the one Paul attempts. For Isaiah, the character of covenantal performance shifts rather dramatically from the sensibilities of a tribal warrior, replete with a sacrificial system to ensure tribal purity, to the sensibilities of a universal, suffering servant. In this shift, Israel functions not as the means for Yahweh's domination of the nations but as the means to invite all the nations to the holy mountain where the people will learn war no more as they beat their swords into ploughshares (Is. 2:2–4, 25:6–10, and 65:17–25).[15]

Here the queer home economist returns to Luke, the queerly ordered evangelist, and underscores this: Luke inaugurates the ministry of Jesus by quoting Isaiah, not Leviticus. "The Spirit of Lord is upon me," Luke's Jesus says (4:18) as he reads from the scroll of Isaiah (Isaiah 61:1). This is the Spirit not of a domineering warrior but a humble servant, which sounds particularly queer in first-century Palestine. There, in that world described by the gospel texts, Palestine has been violently subdued by Rome, no less than a victim of rape. Given Levitical sensibilities, some of Jesus's own followers eagerly anticipated that Jesus would reverse this humiliation by leading an armed uprising against Rome. Jesus chose crucifixion instead, the path not only of a humble but also a suffering servant.

But wait—did he *choose* that path or was it thrust upon him? The difference matters, not only then but also today in societies that too often blame the victims of violence rather than the perpetrators (especially if the victims are women). The difference matters theologically, too. Did God demand this sacrifice? Much depends on the answer to that question.

Paul readily presents the cross as a scandal, a "stumbling block" (1 Corinthians 1:23), yet for reasons too often left unaddressed in the halls of institutional church power. Jesus did face a critical choice as Rome sought to kill him: Would he meet that imperial force with still more force of his own? He refused to do that, or rather he chose to exercise an entirely different kind of

---

15. Donn Morgan makes a similar argument by noting the differences within the Hebrew Bible concerning Israel's own self-perception of its mission before and after the exilic period. Will they be a people "set apart" (as in Leviticus and Ezekiel) or a "light to the nations" (as in Isaiah and Jonah)? See *Fighting with the Bible: Why Scripture Divides Us and How It Can Bring Us Together* (New York: Seabury Books, 2007), 36.

power, the power to sacrifice male privilege in an economics of masculinity. He chose the path pioneered by Isaiah centuries earlier rather than the path of a Levitical warrior. To miss the deeply gendered contours of that choice is to miss why the cross presents a multivalent scandal. Stephen D. Moore again reminds us of the gendered character of ancient social dynamics: "to be a man is to fight."[16] In today's parlance, the cross represents Jesus's refusal to be a "real man."

But the question persists: Did God demand this of him? I think not, no more than I demand sacrifices from my parents or they from me or any of us from our friends. The more vital theological question turns on how we respond to sacrifices born from love, whether we can make from them a sacrifice for life, for the sake of life itself.[17] Luke apparently agreed and wastes no time in presenting a queerly ordered economic system as one of the first things the disciples of this queerly gendered Jesus create. Rather than the tribal household of economic topmanship, Luke describes postresurrection, Spirit-filled communities sharing "all things in common" (Acts 4:32). Even more, they apparently understood this economic transformation as a matter of life and death, a matter central to salvation itself. Witness the truly queer story of Ananias and Sapphira, both of whom lied to their community about their "personal" finances and, then and there, dropped dead (Acts 5:1–11).

Most Christians would likely acknowledge the importance of economics for ethics but likely blanch at the peculiar mix of money, gender, and households that biblical writers seem to place at the heart of Christian theology itself. More recent American history might make that mix seem a bit more timely but not less peculiar. Consider the gendered transformation of "homosexuality" that transpired in the post–World War II era. Prior to that time only the receptive or "passive" partner in male same-sex activity was considered "homosexual," the one acting "more like a woman." In the 1950s, however, both partners suddenly lived with that sexual label.[18] Not merely coincidentally, this same era witnessed a flurry of cultural efforts to underscore the supposedly natural and self-evident gender roles of the American household,

---

16. Moore, *God's Beauty Parlor*, 179.

17. Another approach to atonement in Christian theology, one that resonates with this notion of locating atoning work in how we respond to tragedy, emerged from the work of American philosopher of religion Josiah Royce. See his *The Problem of Christianity*, 2 vols. (New York: Macmillan, 1913; reprint, one volume edition, with an introduction by John E. Smith (Chicago: University of Chicago Press, 1968), 143–63.

18. Chauncey, *Sexual Brotherhood or Sexual Perversion?* 315–16.

portrayed in such iconic television shows as *Leave It to Beaver* and in the figures of Ozzie and Harriet.[19] What began to emerge more distinctly in the
nineteenth century and in the wake of the industrial revolution becomes, less
than a century later, the very foundation of American society: the contained
nuclear family as the basic economic unit of a free-market, capitalist system.
Without these individuated economic units the system would collapse.[20]

Gendered economics shape both ancient texts and contemporary societies with equal force, albeit in different ways. The emergence of the so-called
"religious right" in the United States, for example, illustrates particularly
well the intertwining of money, gender, sex, and faith. At the heart of this
movement sits the "traditional" view of marriage, which relies especially on
the headship of the husband over the wife, or the economics of masculinity.
The otherwise excessive vitriol leveled toward gay male relationships in this
worldview has little to do with love and much more with the threat posed
by same-sex marriage to the gendered economics of the American family.
Perhaps even more than this, the risk of exposing the revolutionary gendered
practice of Jesus that Luke seemed so clearly to relish.

Ronald Long echoes these complexities in his interreligious study of the
gendered constructions of "homosexuality." For Long, the issue at stake in
these religious contestations depends entirely on the kind of masculinity male
same-sex relations perform. More pointedly, he argues that most religious institutions share a common concern to shore up the masculinity of socially superior males.[21] This alone ought to keep queer home economists anxious about
their own household economics but perhaps also oddly hopeful. Consider that
the undeniably patriarchal imprint of institutional Christianity includes the
oft-repeated image of the Church as the "Bride of Christ." Clare of Assisi
rendered that biblical image rather strikingly in the thirteenth century:

> Queen and bride of Jesus Christ, look into [a] mirror daily and study well
> your reflection, that you may adorn yourself, mind and body, with an
> enveloping garment of every virtue, and thus find yourself attired in flowers

---

19. For more on the idealization of the family unit configuration that appeared in the 1950s in the
United States, as well as how terribly strange this configuration is compared to most other times and
places in human history, see Stephanie Coontz, *The Way We Never Were: American Families and the Nostal-
gia Trap* (New York: Basic Books, 1992).

20. Marvin M. Ellison weaves these economic concerns throughout his careful assessment of marriage as
a civic institution in *Same-Sex Marriage?: A Christian Ethical Analysis* (Cleveland, OH: Pilgrim Press, 2004).

21. Long, *Men, Homosexuality, and the Gods*, 13.

and gowns befitting the daughter and most chaste bride of the king on high. . . . Consider also his indescribable delights, his unending riches and honors, and sigh for what is beyond your love and heart's content.[22]

Clare could well have been referring to herself, quite likely to the human soul, and probably had every Christian in mind. Could this traditional image of Christ as the heavenly bridegroom surface far more gender trouble in Christianity's own symbol set than most have perhaps realized? Do clergy-*men* really see themselves bejeweled and decked in the garlands of a bride? Surely many men, even gay ones, would squirm a bit at the prospect of male brides. Less severe but no less troubling (for some), the long history of ardent devotion to Christ in traditional spiritual practice would suggest something more than just "male bonding." How do otherwise "heterosexual" men understand the history of Christian spiritual practice that renders another man (Christ) the object of desire, affection, and even passionate love?[23] Read the rhetoric of traditional family values through the lens of that question; it helps to explain a good deal of the panic that often accompanies the denunciations of gay male sexual intimacy.[24]

Socioeconomic relations have always exhibited a deeply gendered character. This means more for theological notions of salvation than modern Christianity has been willing to admit. I sympathize with the kind of male anxiety that can attend this theological trajectory, yet countless women have paid an unspeakable price to keep that anxiety unspoken. Their sacrifice deserves one of my own: relinquishing the privileges I enjoy in today's economics of masculinity. More than this, and to follow Laurel Schneider's lead, the *racialized* gender privilege from which I benefit as a *white* male needs to end. Schneider puts this challenge bluntly: "Can we unman ourselves enough to begin to take the supremacy out of whiteness?"[25]

This theological commitment to sacrifice of course comes with risks, not least playing a zero-sum game with privilege. That game only perpetuates the

---

22. Clare of Assisi, "Fourth Letter to Blessed Agnes of Prague," in *Francis and Clare: The Complete Works*, The Classics of Western Spirituality, trans. Regis J. Armstrong and Ignatius Brady (Mahwah, NJ: Paulist Press, 1982), 204–5

23. See Stephen D. Moore's account of these peculiarities, including the more recent return to a Victorian ideal of "muscular Christianity" with images of Jesus as a "man's man" to assuage some of this ambient gender discomfort (*God's Beauty Parlor,* 105–8).

24. See Gerard Loughlin's similar musings in "Omphalos," in *Queer Theology*, 123–27.

25. Schneider, "What Race Is Your Sex?" 160.

mistaken portrait of life's blessings as scarce commodities. Augustine proposed a different way to conceive of sacrifice by reflecting on its Latin root, from which we get the word "sacred." He does this by recalling Paul's exhortation to present our bodies as a "living sacrifice, holy [sacred] and acceptable to God" (Romans 12:1). Paul then went on to explain what such holiness entails by encouraging the Romans to adopt a posture of humility toward each other, to avoid thinking of themselves more highly than they ought, and always to bear in mind that *each* of them belongs as members to a *single* body. "This is the sacrifice of Christians," Augustine writes, "'the many who are one body in Christ.'"[26]

Augustine invites a subtle but profound reorientation of sacrificial love, a recognition that the benefits of isolated privilege actually curtail the flourishing of the beneficiary. In short, Christians sacrifice whatever thwarts the thriving of the whole body, from which all the members draw life. Diarmuid O'Murchu lends additional and important nuance to that insight with his approach to the revolutionary character of both Jesus and the early Jesus movement. The complex entanglements of gender with empire demand more than redistributing power and privilege. The "more" begins by empowering invisible women with visibility and likewise recognizing the disempowerment of economically weak or socially inferior men. Systems of domination, in other words, always exhibit multiple layers of power exchange, to which Jesus responds with a radical envisioning of human identity, what O'Murchu calls the "companionship of empowerment" that extends to *all*.[27]

Luke would likely concur with that assessment. Today he might call it something like "sacrificial disruption." Whenever we disrupt categorical systems of exclusionary privilege, everyone gains, even those who previously benefited from those systems. Queerly enough, that kind of sacrifice can lead to life, not just for some but for all. Luke would and did call that kind of life "salvation."

A DIVINE SAVINGS ACCOUNT

Some years ago I stumbled on a theologically rich greeting card in San Francisco's Castro district. The card featured a cartoon depicting a vaguely Jesus-like figure in a tunic standing in front of a bank teller's window. A sack of

26. Augustine, *City of God*, Series 1, Vol. 2, 430

27. Diarmuid O'Murchu, *Christianity's Dangerous Memory: A Rediscovery of the Revolutionary Jesus* (New York: Crossroad, 2011); see ch. 7, "Decoding Gender Marginalization," 111–32.

money sat on the counter, which had just been presented to the teller. The caption read simply enough, "Jesus saves." That delicious pun speaks theological volumes, beginning with where I found that card, in the heart of the historically gay district of San Francisco. More than a few who have fled Christianity because of their sexuality populate that urban haven, where Christianity can still appear as a wolf in sheep's clothing. Poking fun at Christianity there makes sense, but not just any kind of Christian faith. "Jesus saves" bumper stickers appear on quite a few cars belonging to Evangelical and fundamentalist Christians, the ones most likely to condemn "homosexuality." That greeting card evoked all of this and a host of questions besides. From what does Jesus save and how does he do this and for whom?

A Jesus-like figure in front of a bank window offers more than a pun in response to those questions. Luke's two-volume account of Christianity's queerness ties salvation inextricably to economics, to the complex systems of exchange upon which so much of human flourishing depends. Luke certainly imagined salvation meaning more than economic justice, but never less. Saving "souls" while letting bodies starve, for example, would make Luke cringe, to say the least. In addition to crafting their own microeconomic system, the earliest Christian communities in Luke's Acts of the Apostles designated some among them as "deacons," those particularly charged with service among those who are hungry, homeless, widowed, or orphaned (6:1–6).

Christian communities have historically and today offered "works of charity" of precisely the kind Luke's "deacons" embodied. Luke likely imagined far more than this, however, just like Latin American liberation theologians of the mid-twentieth century did, theologians who took charitable service to a new level. Any theological reflection on salvation, they insisted, must include an economic analysis of *why* people are hungry, homeless, widowed, and orphaned. Queer home economists go even further: Why have these analyses of economic systems so often omitted sexuality and gender? Marcella Althaus-Reid and Lisa Isherwood locate their queer theological work in that question, in the relationship between capitalism and sexuality, between economics and "heterosexual" thinking. "To regulate sexuality in the name of divinities," they write, "means to regulate the order of affectionate exchanges but also other human exchanges [in] political and economic systems."[28] That sentence ought to deliver the theological equivalent of a wallop in the North Atlantic.

---

28. Althaus-Reid and Isherwood, *Sexual Theologian*, 3.

Most Christians in the modern West, especially those accustomed to relegating economics to banks or the financial markets on Wall Street, find it at least odd to weave economics into the theological fabric of salvation, not to mention sexually gendered economics. Althaus-Reid and Isherwood remind us, however, that economic systems not only draw theology into their operational effects, such as responding compassionately to poverty and hunger; theology also actively contributes to the economic conditions from which those effects spring. That reminder falls flat in a society accustomed to separating public rather neatly from private, in a society where most people link "the family" to "the economy" only by means of a paycheck. The modern invention of single-family residences only entrenched that link still deeper into Western markets. There, as Mary Hobgood argues, the binary division of gender lives rather comfortably in nuclear families. This arrangement seems not only natural, but it also naturally generates a gendered division of labor for the monetary benefit of a global market. This system, she writes,

> hierarchalizes the value of human labor and justifies the super-exploitation of female workers and racially subordinated men who are "feminized" insofar as their market work becomes associated with women's free (slave) household labor. Twenty-first century structures of class and race are overlaid with the gender system to create a super-exploited global working class comprised primarily of poor women of color.[29]

Queer home economists worry about many things here, not least about using the image of a "household" to describe Christian community and "housework" to describe theological reflection. These images could easily translate into further divisions of gendered labor. Moreover, while Christians historically built on the already culturally established multigenerational household to imagine "church" as an even wider household of faith, today's privatization of household life in Western society makes such imagination more challenging. Nineteenth-century liberal Protestants worried about similar things and responded with the galvanizing proposals of the Social Gospel movement. Those pioneers at the intersection of religion and society called into question the otherworldly focus in Christian accounts of salvation as well as the privatization of families. Their work set in motion a trajectory traceable through women's suffrage, labor reform, and the civil rights

---

29. Mary E. Hobgood, "Coming to Our Senses," in Ellison and Thorson-Smith, *Body and Soul,* 339.

movement. This historical precedent can animate today's queer theological critiques, but not without an important caveat: those formative decades of progressive Christianity failed to provide any substantive analysis (let alone critique) of the sexualized economics of marriage and family.[30]

Blurring the categorical distinctions between public and private causes consternation on multiple fronts, regardless of politics or ideology. The swiftness of securing a foothold in marriage equality for lesbian and gay couples makes that vexation even more tangible. Arguing for equal access to the many civil benefits of a marriage contract exposes the illusion of family as a purely "private" arrangement. Dawne Moon adds a further layer of analysis with her study of two congregations in the United Methodist Church, one of which identified as generally progressive, the other more conservative. Both of these congregations expressed a profound discomfort with politics, which they believed the church should avoid.[31] "Church," in other words, belongs to the same illusory private realm as the nuclear family does, the same kind of safe haven, not coincidentally, carved out for women in the nineteenth century, a domestic sphere where religion helped to tame the unruly tendencies of men. Mary Ryan traces these modern developments to the consequences of the New England revivals issuing from the Second Great Awakening in the early 1800s. As she puts it, the revivals and their effects illustrate how "the history of class and religion was hopelessly entangled with questions of family and gender."[32]

The modern sequestering of private from public manifests a symptom of a much deeper theological dis-ease, the discomfort of "homeless hearts," the very root of modern distress. Carter Heyward finds the roots of this distress in traditional systematic theologies that distinguish too severely between the doctrines of creation and salvation. This dichotomy projects "home" far into the future toward a disembodied heaven, quite literally out of reach. The pernicious effects of this doctrinal dichotomy appear quite readily in the nearly self-evident polarities with which so many Christians live, the ones between body and soul, or earth and heaven, and human and divine. These polarities bespeak yet another as the hope for the "world to come" emerges at the

---

30. See Ellison's analysis and critique of marriage as "private" (*Same-Sex Marriage?* 150–51).

31. Dawne Moon, *God, Sex, and Politics: Homosexuality in Everyday Theologies* (Chicago: University of Chicago Press, 2004), 5.

32. Mary P. Ryan, *Cradle of the Middle Class: The Family in Oneida County, New York, 1790–1865* (Cambridge: Cambridge University Press, 1981), 12.

expense of the world we currently inhabit. Heyward urges us instead to view creation and salvation as belonging to the same "sacred process" to which all can contribute.[33] This will sound familiar to the many advocates for LGBT-affirming theologies, which often stress the goodness of embodied, sexual life in God's own creation. Yet queer home economists, keen to account for the fullness of salvation, would not imagine having lots of sex or even guaranteeing equal access to marriage as a panacea for the world's economic woes. On a planet slowly dying from Western consumerist impulses, spending more, buying more, and having more simply perpetuates the very conditions from which all of us need saving. Queerly enough, the same can be said about sex and even marriage, both of which implicate every sexually active or married couple in those consumer-oriented market mechanisms.

Could marriage be the problem from which everyone needs saving? Perhaps not, but queer people of faith do find themselves sorely confused by the religious rhetoric that extols matrimonial bliss. Many of us fail to understand how the unqualified goodness of marital sexuality resonates in any meaningful way with Jesus and Paul, arguably the primary figures in Christian traditions, both of whom were apparently unmarried and childless. Whatever else queer people of faith will want to make of that biblical oddity, they will at least resist any attempt to abstract sex and sexuality from the vast economic systems and social hierarchies in which sexual intimacy transpires. "Intimacy" can easily mask the troubling history of the public institution of marriage, which the state has frequently exploited to maintain racial segregation, gender conformity, and healthy profit margins. These are the very dynamics from which human beings do indeed need saving.[34]

Jesus apparently said nothing about any of this, or perhaps he did in the way he lived. While we know virtually nothing about the sexuality of Jesus, we do know quite a lot about Jesus and food. Many of the social dynamics involving food appeared in ancient Mediterranean views of sex, which today's fast-food culture easily obscures. Contemporary North Atlantic societies have nearly evacuated shared meals of all their symbolic weight; sex has suffered a similar fate. Sex in ancient Mediterranean cultures maintained social hierarchies of power and value in ways that most people today cannot imagine. For the world inhabited by both Jesus and Paul, the gender

---

33. Heyward, *Touching Our Strength*, 91.

34. See Ellison, *Same-Sex Marriage?* 102–6.

of one's sex partner mattered far less than the social rank that person occupied. Recalling Stephen Moore's description of biblical sexuality, both culturally appropriate sexual behavior and proper worship depended on the social
inequality of the partners.[35] We can readily imagine what Jesus might have
thought about these dynamics given his apparent disdain of hierarchical systems of value. He put that disdain on display every time he ate with tax collectors, women, and prostitutes. Each of those shared meals disrupted the
social order as much as having sex with the wrong type of person.

Did Jesus refuse to marry for the same reason that he shared a meal with
tax collectors? If marriage inevitably reproduced male privilege, abstaining from that social and religious institution could well mark yet another
moment of sacrifice for the sake of life, if not for salvation itself. Salvation, that is, manifested as the overturning of systemic inequalities toward
a vision of abundant human thriving. Dale Martin takes this a step further and argues that Jesus may well have placed restrictions on divorce and
remarriage not to strengthen the institution of marriage but to do away
with it.[36] Paul seemed inclined in the same direction when he encouraged
Christians to remain single, like him (1 Corinthians 7:8). We might explain
this kind of encouragement by supposing that Paul lived with a number
of sexual neuroses himself. Even more likely, Paul found the institution of
marriage theologically troubling. For Paul's world, marriage belonged to the
same system of social value he sought to disrupt. Jew or Greek, slave or
free, everything attached to the neat divisions between male and female all
disappear in Christ (Galatians 3:28). Paul insisted on this for a simple but
profoundly Eucharistic reason: if those social distinctions remained in force,
Christians could not share a meal together.

Lisa Isherwood reads these texts and histories through both feminist and
queer lenses as she ponders the vexations inherent to sexual economics. She
ponders especially the theological fecundity of an "erotic celibacy."[37] More
disruptive than "homosexuality" or even "gay marriage," the refusal to engage
at all in the cultural rites of courtship, sex, and marriage bears witness to the
peculiar faith of Christians, a faith rooted in a "single savior," as Dale Martin
urges us to remember. Here the notion of sacrificing for life, for the sake of

---

35. Moore, *God's Beauty Parlor,* 153.

36. Martin, *Sex and the Single Savior,* 146–47.

37. Lisa Isherwood, *The Power of Erotic Celibacy: Queering Heteropatriarchy* (London: T&T Clark, 2006).

abundant life, takes on both compelling and troubling textures. Compelling, as it suggests new ways to read the gospel exhortation that only in losing one's life does one thereby find it (Luke 9:24). Troubling, as it unfurls an unexplored horizon for faith communities today where economic consumerism and the primacy of marriage no longer constitute what it means to live a "good" life, let alone a happy one.

As Isherwood likewise insists, however, and which queer home economists will want to highlight, the Gospel does not invite glorifying sacrifice for its own sake. Luke would remind us that the Spirit disrupts for a purpose, nothing less than salvation. We might reconstruct the institution of marriage to that end, but queer home economists will turn elsewhere. They will turn, rather surprisingly, to love. Few Christians would deny the centrality of love in the Gospel, yet hardly anything else has attracted so many unexamined assumptions or suffered quite as many clichés. In perversely Pentecostal communities, the queerness of Christian love will feature prominently in the theological work of accounting for salvation, and thus also in shaping Christian witness to a very peculiar faith indeed.

PERVERTING LOVE

A Latin American liberation theologian recalls being asked at a conference why she spent so much time on sexuality rather than the economic crises created and perpetuated by global capitalism. Bringing to mind the lyrics from a Tina Turner song, this theologian responded by saying, "You're asking me what love has to do with this."[38] The question might sound odd, yet the difficulties in responding to it seem queerer still.

Love's many confusions and reductions appear readily enough in religious wedding ceremonies. Clergy quite regularly recommend the thirteenth chapter of Paul's first letter to the Corinthians for those occasions, a biblical text commonly referred to as the "love chapter." The sermon on that occasion (if there is one) might provide a religious gloss on contemporary strategies for building a healthy marriage drawn from Paul's tribute to love: it is patient, kind, not envious or boastful, is not irritable or resentful (13:4–5). The preacher might even conclude with Paul's own crescendo where he extols love as greater than either faith or hope (13:13). The wedding guests will likely *not* hear that Paul

---

38. Althaus-Reid and Isherwood, *Sexual Theologian*, 1. (The theologian in question is clearly Althaus-Reid herself.)

had something other than marriage in mind when he wrote that chapter. The diversity of the Corinthian community, which Paul describes in the twelfth chapter, threatens to divide them into competing factions. Rather than encouraging either competition or conformity, Paul wants to show the Corinthians a "still more excellent way" (12:31) for living in unity, namely love.

Given Paul's apparent purpose here, queer home economists might liberate this love chapter from its restriction to weddings and imagine a broader household context. The 1979 Book of Common Prayer, for example, suggests that Pauline text for the celebration of Holy Matrimony but not for baptism. The prayer book does include a series of vows for both liturgical occasions, including this one for the baptismal rite: to "respect the dignity of every human being."[39] Yet that rite leaves unspoken what everyone needs in order to live that life in common with others. We all need divine grace, to be sure, but we need most especially love. Not just any kind of love will do for this kind of life, and certainly not the greeting-card variety that "means never having to say you're sorry." The naturally odd life of baptized Christians, springing from the incarnate hope of finding a home in our bodies, rightly belongs to any account of salvation. So too does the hope of being at home with others, a hope that only the Spirit's "perverse love" can fully inspire.

No less than the word "queer," God's household will need to retrieve the word "perverse" with both care and caution but also with boldness, especially in a society where love reduces to sentiment or the friendliness of affinity groups. Luke's Jesus disrupts love's domestications by extending its reach to the ordinarily unlovable. "Love your enemies," Jesus says, "do good to those who hate you. . . . If you love those who love you, what credit is that to you? For even sinners love those who love them" (6:27, 32). Safely ensconced on the printed page and bound in a gilt-edged book, those revolutionary words from Jesus no longer sound quite so perverse as perhaps they should. Luke provides at least a hint of what those words might launch with his portrayal of Pentecost in Acts 2.

Recall the scene: fifty days after Jesus's resurrection, many foreigners had gathered in Jerusalem for a festival while the disciples barricaded themselves in a locked room. Just then the Holy Spirit, the Breath of God, blows through that room and inspires the once-fearful disciples to preach good news in ways that all those foreigners could understand. Here I confess tendencies a bit

---

39. Book of Common Prayer, 305.

more orderly than even Luke seemed to demonstrate. I would imagine all those travelers to Jerusalem suddenly able to understand Aramaic, the language likely spoken by the disciples. But Luke describes it more queerly: the disciples suddenly spoke in multiple languages they had never studied so that all those foreigners could hear the Gospel in their own native tongue, or what surely sounded like a cacophony. One might suppose that love had something to do with this miracle of translation and proclamation; the kind of love, though, deserves careful attention. It was, apparently, the kind of love that refuses to erase linguistic differences or to insist on a single syntax.

Christians quite clearly speak faith not in a single language but many. That observation resides safely enough in most standard interpretations of this story from Acts, which in part has energized the translation of the Bible into nearly every human language on earth. But reading Pentecost through a queer lens suggests something more. My own wistfulness over writing the story differently reveals more than a penchant for orderliness. Or rather, my love of order discloses the many cultural biases that inform my understanding of Christian faith. Everyone of course lives with and from particular cultural perspectives, many of which remain implicit most of the time. These cultural peculiarities pose no theological problem per se until—and Luke helped me to see this—I impose my language of faith on others. In that very moment the perversely Pentecostal approach to the Gospel urges sacrificial love, the willingness to set aside my comfortable grammar and to let the Spirit teach me a new language. Again, this apparently animated Augustine to declare what Christian sacrifice entails: the many are one body in Christ.

"Language" can mislead us here, however, if it means only words. Translators know this better than most as their work involves far more than replacing one word with another, like the Spanish "salvación" for the English "salvation." Do those words mean exactly the same thing when the former resounds in the barrios of San Salvador and the latter echoes from the vaulted ceiling of Canterbury Cathedral? The language each of us learns from our biological families carries with it all the many culturally inflected ways of seeing and perceiving the world around us; speech rises up from culture, which in turns shapes our speaking. The marriage equality struggle in the United States casts these linguistic dynamics in bold relief. White lesbian and gay activists have too often failed to recognize how marriage, family, and religion intertwine in most African-American communities as a form of resistance to white supremacy. White and black people in the United States can use the same English word—marriage—and evoke significantly different historical and cultural meanings.[40]

Taking the complexities of language to heart, Luke's perversely Pentecostal vision issues a clarion call not only to speak but especially to listen. Attending carefully and deliberately to the many languages of faith ensconced in God's household will mean, at the very least, that no single account of Christian hope will suffice to capture the richness of divine grace, much less the peculiar character of divine love. Peculiar indeed in the midst of Western categorical classification schemes that render love synonymous with agreement if not conformity. Could love actually trump divergent points of view? What kind of love would seek the gifts of diverse perspectives? Might love inspire more than "agreeing to disagree" with each other? What if love compelled us to sacrifice the prevailing modern assumption that being "correct" means everyone else must be "wrong"?

Putting that kind of love into practice will likely provoke incredulity if not outright disdain. The urge to conform tugs at nearly every turn in both civic and religious movements. How much diversity can a single community absorb? Who will adjudicate conflicts over mission and strategy? What kind of criteria will help us discern a healthy mix of differences in contrast to a divisive or destructive one? Queer home economists appreciate these questions and even readily agree that Christian witness does not render salvation synonymous with libertine individualism. At the same time, queer home economists will also urge a radical reframing of how God's household assesses the standards of belonging, of being at home with others.

These many questions lead rather pointedly to this one: Why has institutional Christianity made creedal conformity the benchmark for membership in God's household? That qualifies a particularly peculiar question. Few in the modern West can imagine how to organize and maintain a religious community apart from conformity and fewer still recognize how often that organizational impulse obscures the Gospel's own fundamental creed, namely love. Here queer home economists will need the Spirit's gift of courage to adopt a rather bold posture: assenting to particular doctrines as the precondition of belonging to a loving household drains Christian witness of the queerly good news that first animated it. A bolder posture still: commit to loving people into belief.

---

40. See Kelly Brown Douglas, *Sexuality and the Black Church: A Womanist Perspective* (Maryknoll, NY: Orbis Books, 1999), 64–67.

Christian history certainly presents examples of people finding Christian ideas compelling enough to become Christian themselves. I find that rare today as far more adopt Christian faith because a Christian community loved them into it. Stanley Hauerwas realized this in his own approach to developing Christian ethics:

> I understand my own story through seeing the different ways in which others are called to be [Jesus'] disciples. If we so help one another, perhaps, like the early Christians when challenged about the viability of their faith, we can say, "But see how we love one another."[41]

As Hauerwas seems to suggest, nothing about this primacy of love over belief is terribly new or innovative; indeed, Jesus adopted this approach in nearly every gospel encounter. Gregory the Great, writing in the seventh century, echoed this theme by recalling the Emmaus road story in Luke's account of the gospel (24:13–35). In that odd story the disciples fail to recognize the risen Jesus, their dear companion, until they invite him to lodge with them and share a meal. As Gregory puts it, by extending hospitality they "discover the God whom they had failed to come to know in the explanations of the Scriptures. . . . The Lord was not recognized while he was speaking; he was pleased to make himself known while he was offered something to eat. Let us then, beloved, love to practice charity."[42]

To be sure, this ecclesial posture rooted in love carries risk. Most sexually intimate couples know that love may delightfully attract at first but it rarely yields harmonious agreement all on its own. Christians who worry about this risk might insist on conformity to shared doctrine as a condition for the love to continue; this of course amounts to little more than a religious bait-and-switch. The perversely Pentecostal love of the Gospel sacrifices that urge to conform for something both more compelling and more strenuous: learning how to love by being in relationships with people who are different.

Queer people appreciate, and often quite bodily, this challenge of loving the diversity of a community and the insights it can generate. Queer people can detect rather astutely, for example, when the rush to conformity signals a fear of difference, the fear of those "others" whose language, culture,

---

41. Stanley Hauerwas, *A Community of Character: Toward a Constructive Christian Social Ethic* (Notre Dame: University of Notre Dame Press, 1981), 52.

42. Gregory the Great, "Homily 23," *PL* 76, 1182–83.

perspectives, and relationships seem to threaten cherished assumptions and worldviews. Queer people of *faith* intuit something else as well: the resilience of divine love. They find helpful confirmation of that intuition from the Johannine writer, who actually cautioned against relying on anything at all except the love of God. Doctrinal acuity, creedal conformity, and proper worship all serve a shared life of faith. At the same time, none of those will knit diverse people together in the face of diversity's challenges. Only love casts out fear (1 John 4:18).

Not just any kind of love does all this, but only "perfect" love, or what Luke would call that perverse love of the Spirit who makes friends from enemies and family from strangers.[43] If such love can inspire the hope of at long last being at home among others as much as being at home in our own bodies, it rightly belongs to any account of salvation among those who hope to find a home with God. Not just any "god," of course, but the God whose own erotically social character both invites and inspires that very hope.

---

43. See Dale Martin's analysis of the kind of love that "works" rather than reducing it to sentimentality (*Sex and the Single Savior*, 165–69).

5

Erotically Social

THE LOVER, THE BELOVED, AND TRANSFORMING LOVE

he peculiar faith of Christians appears quite vividly in the queer-ness of its arithmetic. The one God in three persons defies most attempts to speak coherently, and mostly for the trouble "thirdness" causes. Consider that trouble in the 1949 film *And Baby Makes Three*, a romantic comedy starring Barbara Hale and Robert Young. Hale plays Jackie Walsh, who divorced her husband Vernon, played by Young. Jackie realizes, however, that she is pregnant with Vernon's child when she faints while walking down a church aisle to marry her second husband, Her-bert. To help him win custody of his child, Vernon decides to marry his ex-girlfriend Wanda. Meanwhile, Jackie regrets her divorce and tries to discourage Wanda's marriage to Vernon by telling her that she, Jackie, will be having triplets.[1]

Thirdness runs throughout this film, at times as a disruptive element in a couple's relationship and at others as comic relief in a potentially scandal-ous situation. The complex relational entanglements in this story—Vernon, Jackie, Wanda, and Herbert, not to mention the baby—would have troubled the cultural sensibilities of a post-War American society eager to extol "tradi-tional" families. These complexities would seem far less troubling however in the ancient Mediterranean world. In Greco-Roman society, marriage had less to do with the modern notion of romantic love than creating a stable house-hold for raising children. Romantic liaisons were best reserved for someone

---

1. *And Baby Makes Three*, directed by Henry Levin, 1949; Los Angeles: Santana Pictures Corporation.

other than one's spouse, to avoid destabilizing the household system and the wider community.[2]

Those ancient familial patterns involved what most people today would consider "adultery," which can carry severe social and legal consequences. But where exactly does "fidelity" end and "adultery" begin? Do we draw that line with physical intimacy or emotional attachment or both? Contemporary approaches to marriage differ significantly from those in the world of biblical writers, but the troubling "third" still lingers, though in largely unspoken ways. Some couples enjoy a rich sexual intimacy with each other but find deeper emotional intimacy with other people. Some couples flip that dynamic by developing deep emotional bonds with each other while finding better sexual compatibility with someone else. These patterns operate mostly outside the public spotlight where descriptions of marriage idealize the perfect match between physical and affective intimacy. Most Christians today assume that ideal relationship as an obvious, nearly self-evident ethical norm even though Christian history exhibits considerably more diversity. Some early Christians, for example, advised chastity in marriage, not fidelity in the modern sense but abstaining from physical intimacy even with one's spouse.[3]

"Thirdness" can indeed prove troubling when it emerges from mostly private realms and disturbs the public ideal. Alfred Kinsey discovered this with his pioneering research into actual rather than only perceived sexual practices, which scandalized many when he published the results in the 1950s.[4] Noticing and giving voice to the "third" can prove just as troubling for Christian theology when it makes the queerness of Christian faith more visible. I mean especially the queer resistance to both monotheistic and polytheistic understandings of God. Christianity occupies instead a thoroughly Trinitarian space. Most Christians acknowledge that odd space but rarely appreciate its disruptive potential.

Divine "thirdness" could challenge and disrupt more than a few fragile assumptions at the root of modern Western culture, including individual

---

2. This generalization of course risks distorting a much more complex historical terrain. See Louis Compton, *Homosexuality and Civilization* (Cambridge, MA: Harvard Unversity Press, 2003), ch. 4, "Rome and Greece: 323 BCE–138 CE," and especially, for romantic love's destabilizations, 82–84.

3. For an overview of some of the earliest Christian reflections on sex and marriage, especially in contrast to the wider Roman society, see Geoffrey S. Nathan, *The Family in Late Antiquity: The Rise of Christianity and the Endurance of Tradition* (New York: Routledge, 2002), 37–48.

4. For more on Kinsey's research in the context of Kinsey's own, often troubled life and its wider social effects, see James H. Jones, *Alfred C. Kinsey: A Life* (New York: W. W. Norton, 2004).

autonomy and self-sufficiency, the facile division between public and private, and the vital role played by "nuclear families" in free-market economies. The infrequency with which Trinitarian doctrine appears in relation to any of these cultural sensibilities speaks not so much to its conceptual complexity as to the risk it poses to the familial and economic patterns taken for granted in the modern West. The queerness of Christianity percolates there, not in the cognitive difficulty of Trinitarian faith but in how such faith urges a reassessment of the dynamics and parameters of our intimate commitments with each other, our societal patterns of relation, and even economic policies and environmental postures. Needless to say, few if any critics of Western culture cite Trinitarian doctrine as a source of inspiration, but Rodney Clapp thinks they should. Whether the "God" in whom Americans declare our trust by printing it on paper money has anything to do with the Holy Trinity deserves renewed and sustained deliberation in Clapp's view, not for the sake of correct doctrine but for exposing the religious patina brushed over cultural and political assumptions.[5]

To suppose that either biblical writers or theologians in the earliest centuries of Christian traditions harbored visions of cultural subversion for the Holy Trinity stretches the imagination, but perhaps not as far as one might suppose at first. God-talk matters, personally of course, but also and therefore socially. More pointedly for Western culture, because God-talk matters socially it therefore also matters in our conceptions of the "individual." How we think and speak about Unfathomable Mystery can marshal armies, fuel self-sacrifice, inspire courageous generosity, and forge enduring alliances, for both good and for ill. Queer home economists know all this about theology and its sociopolitical implications; they also know that particularly Trinitarian God-talk presents unique challenges, not least, the fear of getting it "wrong." The Christological and Trinitarian controversies that punctuated the first five centuries of Christian history present a dizzying array of "heresies" to avoid and "orthodoxies" to adopt. Sorting through those complexities can feel like a distraction, even an irresponsible one when so many homeless hearts cry out for more than "mere" doctrine. Just as challenging, nearly everyone fears looking foolish or sounding irrational. Proclaiming a one-and-three divine reality quickly travels from the merely peculiar to just

---

5. Rodney Clapp, *A Peculiar People: The Church as Culture in a Post-Christian Society* (Downers Grove, IL: IVP Academic, 1996).

bad math. Traditional images of the Holy Trinity in religious iconography only deepen the challenge, images I once heard described as portraying "an old man, his dying son, and a flapping bird." All of this springs from fourth-century responses to fourth-century quandaries, which poses a pointed question today: Do we really share those same ancient quandaries anymore?

Poor arithmetic, confounding art, historical irrelevance—each of these objections leaves unspoken the root of the problem. The "third" will always trouble and disturb a closed, binary system. Ancient writers knew this, and their often circuitous if not perplexing explorations of troubling thirdness actually provide a soothing balm: no one can speak correctly about Divine Mystery. To insist that Christians must provide perfectly accurate accountings actually misses the point of theological speech itself. After all, only God knows (quite literally) whether our intricate stammering about Trinitarian life rings even remotely true. Rather than doctrinal correctness, the adequacy of Christian speech and practice will turn on whether it invites any of us deeper into the mystery in which we already "live and move and have our being" (Acts 17:28). More simply and pointedly, can the Trinitarian imprint of Christian theology change lives? Queer home economists trust it can by relying on a startling claim: the word "God" points to an eternally creative, relationally dynamic, and erotically social reality as the Source of All. I caught at least a glimpse of that claim in another though more recent film, *Big Eden*.[6]

The film portrays a fictional, small mountain town called Big Eden as the residents welcome back one of their own, a prodigal-like character. He had been sojourning in New York City as a successful artist but returns home to care for an aging relative. Quite improbably but also believably, these characters eventually nurture a budding romance between this prodigal and a local Native American storekeeper. The story unfolds with humorous plot twists, miscommunications, and poignant family moments among this town's residents, who engage their own faults and foibles gracefully and with an astonishing honesty about human vulnerability and the human capacity for tender compassion. The plot relies on recognizable tropes for a romantic comedy, though this one focuses on two men in the leading roles. The rather casual treatment of gay romance qualifies as startling for some viewers of this film. Something else, however, seized my attention.

---

6. *Big Eden*, DVD, written and directed by Thomas Bezucha, 2000; New Almaden, CA: Wolfe Video, 2002.

In some subtle but powerful ways, the story's arc slowly unraveled the typical restriction of *Eros* to dyadic coupling. In this case, the "third" in that unraveling appeared not as another person but a whole community as it inspired what we might call a *social* eroticism. I do not mean anything as crude as desiring physical sexual intimacy with every resident of that mountain town. I mean rather to describe a yearning to give myself over to them, to be caught up in the multiple and varied relations of that community. Presumably, the producers of that film brought no formal theological education to their work, yet I could not help but see Gospel energy vibrating throughout. *Big Eden* offered a glimpse, in other words, of not only the Trinitarian imprint on Christian theology but also and especially on human life, on the kind of life eager for communion, restless with desire, and moving in waves of boundless love and generosity. An imprint, yes, but one that rarely surfaces from the reclusive and at times shame-based isolation of a world riddled with so many homeless spaces.

Queer home economists might imagine God's household as Big Eden, an imagination and its implications shaped by the Trinitarian history of our own religious backyard. Excavating that space for buried treasure proves worthwhile if the treasure itself inspires visions of a worship-worthy God, the God dwelling in us as well as among us and for us, the God whose worship animates socially transformative witness to the mystery of Love itself.

BEWITCHED, BOTHERED, AND BEWILDERED

The energizing Feast of Pentecost appears on the Christian liturgical calendar fifty days after Easter. One week later the Church celebrates Trinity Sunday. An odd day, to say the least, if not anticlimactic on the heels of resurrection praises and Spirit-filled speech. The calendar devotes this day to God-talk in the light of Jesus and the experience of the Spirit, a day unlike other liturgical feasts, as this one marks not an event but apparently a doctrine. Preachers find this doctrinal focus challenging, yet perhaps invitingly so if we take "God" to mean an event, just as we might likewise understand human life as eventful.

Static things stay put long enough to study them and to offer generally intelligible observations about them, like rocks and minerals. Eventful realities unfold over both space and time, making any speech about them always provisional, always subject to revision as they continue to unfold. How

plants grow, where babies come from, why people suffer with diseases, even
the origins of ostensibly static things like rocks and minerals all belong to the
unfolding event of life itself. A human being also qualifies as an "event" with
countless moments of unfolding, relational complexity. Falling in love, for
example, can confound anyone's ability to bring that moment into adequate
speech. Or in the words of an old Rodgers and Hart song, human life can
frequently bewitch, bother, and bewilder us; so also divine life.

Human understanding and speech about God has evolved over many
centuries, and still refuses to sit still. Biblical stories mark a time when such
developments reached a particular stage, which differs from the time when
the events that inspired those stories took place, which differs still more from
the time when some of the later stories appeared in writing. What "God"
means will sound different, and sometimes dramatically so, depending on
the source we explore, whether from Abraham or Moses or Mary or the
Apostle Paul, not to mention Irenaeus in the second century or Augustine
in the fifth or Julian of Norwich in the fourteenth or our own experiences in
the twenty-first. This bewildering array of sources might prove bothersome at
times, but hopefully also bewitching in the most tantalizing sense, especially
when dealing with the peculiarities of a Trinitarian faith. "Dealing" seems a
bit optimistic, though, as this peculiar faith tends to stretch our imaginations
and suspend our more ordinary, linear ways of thinking. Today's cosmolo-
gists invite similar stretches when they insist that the universe has no center
and no edge, or that the vast bulk of what exists remains so inscrutable that
scientists just call it "dark matter."

The controversial Episcopal bishop John A. T. Robinson challenged our
theological complacency back in the 1960s. Traditional theological language,
he noted, has barely caught up with the sixteenth-century Copernican revolution that put the sun rather than the earth at the center of our solar system. When Christians continue to talk about God in spatial terms, residing
somewhere above our heads or beyond the sky, Robinson noted, we sound at
least scientifically naïve.[7] Or perhaps better, we sound *understandably* naïve
as so much historical theology evokes a map of reality that plots earth "down
here" and heaven "up there" where God sits enthroned in unapproachable
splendor. Trinitarian language adds further, some might say unnecessary

---

7. John A. T. Robinson, *Honest to God*, 40th anniv. ed. (Louisville, KY: Westminster John Knox Press,
1963, 2002), 11–15.

complexity to these theological maps. But queer home economists appreciate that complexity whenever it interrupts habitual conceptions of the three divine "persons" as constituting a heavenly committee. Caricatures quickly spring from that habit. In the United States, we might be tempted to overlay images of a president, a vice president, and a secretary of state on these three divine figures, mapping out particular governance roles for each. More likely, images of the chief executive officer, the chief financial officer, and the chief operations officer, each with particular responsibilities for the cosmic enterprise. Absurd, of course, as Robinson observed decades ago. If we can draw it, map it, or make an organizational chart from it, then we have left the realm of Trinitarian Christian faith. The language of "up there" or "out there" fails if we do not also speak of God as "in," "among," "around," and "between." Trinitarian theologians have indeed tried to speak that way over many centuries, sometimes well, at other times badly, and often a mix of both.

"Charming bewilderment" might suitably describe encounters with the history of doctrine but even more with the Divine Mystery toward which all that doctrinal work has endeavored to point. "Mystery" can frequently mislead us in these efforts if we approach it as Sherlock Holmes might do, as something to solve. Theologians hope instead to evoke that which no one would ever want to "solve" but rather to worship: the very life of God in which we find ourselves caught up, entangled, enfolded, and embraced. How to speak about all this proves just as vexing as asking whether one should try to speak at all. The cautions that punctate nearly every text from apophatic theologians apply here quite urgently, the ones who insist that saying what God is *not* speaks more truthfully than saying what God is. Others would add cautions on the other side of that equation and insist that properly categorical speech guards against unethical and not merely heretical living, especially as these inextricably intertwine. As Gavin D'Costa notes, most Christian churches maintain a vigorous doctrinal vigilance for the sake of worshipping the living God rather than an idol. "Since all practice depends on the shape of God," D'Costa observes, "the life of the church would be severely dysfunctional if its God were not the true God."[8] Both apophatic and cataphatic theologians make persuasive arguments, but I mean to ask more pointedly here why we try to say anything at all, whether positively or

---

8. Gavin D'Costa, "Queer Trinity," in Loughlin, *Queer Theology*, 269.

negatively, about the Divine Mystery. That question haunted those labeled as "orthodox" in Christian history as much as it does many of us today, especially in the ancient refusal to define precisely the Trinitarian mystery of God.

The history of this doctrinal development presents not just one but many ways of speaking about the Trinity. "Father, Son, and Holy Spirit" rings in our ears and memories as the most familiar, and it appeared early enough in Christian traditions to sneak its way into the conclusion of Matthew's account of the Gospel (28:19). That formulation may sound familiar, but it by no means exhausts the possibilities for faithfully tuned speech. No less a classic figure than Augustine experimented with a range of ways of thinking and talking about the Trinity yet resisted choosing just one of them as the best. Indeed, Augustine insisted that whatever we grasp in our conceptualizations cannot be God since God cannot be grasped, or in his oft-quoted Latin dictum, *si comprehendis non est Deus* ("if you understand something, it's not God").[9] Nonetheless, Augustine kept experimenting with theological speech, with ways of thinking and believing that might lead one ever deeper into that ungraspable Mystery. One of his proposals for Trinitarian speech might sound surprising to modern ears and perhaps even inviting: the Lover, the Beloved, and the Love that binds them together.

A few centuries after Augustine, John of Damascus tried to inject a bit more dynamic motion into Augustine's Trinitarian speculation with the Greek concept of *perichoresis*.[10] That word admits no direct English equivalent, but some theologians have found in it a hint of the English word "choreography." Rather than monarchs seated on their thrones ruling a heavenly court, imagine instead the universe as a divine dance floor with creation itself as the perpetual music; the dancers blend seamlessly with the dance and the dance itself is endless, deathless love. These dynamic images highlight a consistent thread running throughout all this bewildering material in Christian history. Whatever Christians mean by the word "God" we do not mean a remote, isolated, self-contained individual. We need to find ways to speak of divine reality as essentially and erotically social, communal, open, dynamic, perpetually and forever welling up and spilling over with life itself. Cynthia

---

9. Augustine, "Sermon 52," in *The Works of St. Augustine: Sermons*, vol. 3, trans. Edmund Hill (New York: New City Press, 1991).

10. See Catherine Mowry Lacugna's treatment of this concept as it developed in historical theology, including the role played by John of Damascus, in *God for Us: The Trinity and Christian Life* (New York: HarperCollins Publishers, 1991), 270–78.

Bourgeault describes the urgent need for this kind of speech with her analogy drawn from the scientific challenge in trying to describe the character of light. The problem with categorical models for God, she writes, is that these become "a freeze-frame, one phase in a moving sequence. . . . [M]ost of the paradigm distress besetting contemporary Trinitarian theology has arisen out of trying to bottle into particle format what is intrinsically a wave."[11]

Given this unfathomable mystery, the question persists: Why try to speak of it? If we live and move and have our being in the mystery called God, then surely theologians are fish trying to describe water. What finally do we gain in the attempt? Perhaps the charming bewilderment of human life offers something like an answer to that question, especially the mystery of relating with friends, colleagues, lovers, spouses, and children. Can we ever speak adequately of these human mysteries? Pausing to say something *about* playing in a swimming pool with my eleven-year-old godson *while* playing seems quite beside the point of playing: splashing, diving, chasing, and laughing. Even so, here I am, writing about it. Why? We keep thinking and talking about human life as we try to work and play with each other, and eat meals together, and love and care for one another. We do this not for the sake of "correct" speech but perhaps "better" speech, a way to fine-tune our thinking and speaking as we seek to deepen our relationships with each other, so that we might continually learn new things about working and loving and playing and caring, so that we might enter more fully into the mysterious dance of being human with each other. The eventful character of human life invites no less; so also with divine life.

In Genesis we read that God made humanity in God's own image, the "*imago Dei*." Trusting that claim, we can make some good guesses about who God is by looking at ourselves and who we are. Just as much as Divine Mystery, the mystery of human life and relationships can bother, bewitch, and bewilder. In the remarkable energies of human creativity, in our capacity for love and forgiveness, in the deep human longing for communion and relationship—in all these mysterious features of human life we catch a glimpse of the mystery that Christians eventually called the Holy Trinity. These analogies eventually break down of course, and rightly so. Leaping from finite to infinite life presents a chasm even the most intrepid theologian

---

11. Cynthia Bourgeault, *The Holy Trinity and the Law of Three: Discovering the Radical Truth at the Heart of Christianity* (Boston: Shambhala, 2013), 200.

only dreams of bridging. But perhaps God dares to dream it. Perhaps the genesis of Trinitarian thinking, speaking, and praying lies not in *our* reach toward the unknown, but *God's* own dramatic reach toward us. The incarnation of the divine Word in human flesh bears witness to a God far more intrepid than any of us, a claim that fueled Trinitarian speculation in the first place. If encountering Jesus in some way signaled, evoked, or inspired something like encountering God, this would surely generate a bit of head-scratching if not the confounding of traditional theological speech. Sarah Coakley finds traces of this carnal insight in Paul's letter to the Romans. His description of the Spirit praying in us with "sighs too deep for words" (Romans 8:26) provokes an insight about God's desire much more than our own. Coakley quotes the fifth-century mystic pseudo-Dionysius to make her point:

> This divine yearning brings ecstasy so that the lover belongs not to self but to the beloved. . . . This is why the great Paul, swept along by his yearning for God and seized of its ecstatic power, has these inspired words to say: "It is no longer I who live but Christ who lives in me." Paul was clearly a lover, and, as he says, he was beside himself for God.[12]

"Ecstatic with love" might actually preach on Trinity Sunday and surprise both preacher and pew-sitter. Paul seemed to think so too when he reminded those Roman Christians that the word is very near to us, on our lips and in our hearts (10:8). He could well have added, in our bodily desires.

Do we really need to say anything more about this mystery that perpetually eludes our conceptual grasp? Yes, because God-talk inevitably shapes how we live. Theology sometimes informs our living in subtle ways, like barely audible background noise in our conversations, and sometimes quite explicitly, whether as justification for violence or inspiration for generous hospitality. Both are true for Western society, which evolved in tandem with the institutional Church, or more precisely, Christian theology wove Church and society together into a single fabric. Modernity never fully unraveled that socioreligious garment, which still retains considerable threads of theological influence. Queer home economists have no desire to repair that fabric but rather to unravel it even further, to tease out those theological threads

---

12. Sarah Coakley, "Living into the Mystery of the Holy Trinity: Trinity, Prayer, and Sexuality," *Anglican Theological Review* 80 (1998): 230.

and weave something new with them. Unraveling and reweaving the patterns of theological speaking and our theological living will always reflect the peculiarities of particular households. Even so, we might borrow from John of Damascus and suppose that all of our efforts will in some fashion resemble an invitation to dance.

TRINITARIAN TANGO

The ambient character of theology in Western society leaves much of it unspoken though easily tapped when needed, especially in the United States. A judicial ruling might cite "Judeo-Christian values" as part of its rationale and politicians will occasionally quote a biblical passage to support a social policy. These brief eruptions of religious rhetoric emerge from mostly unexamined theological assumptions that lie just beneath the veneer of an ostensibly secular country. We might visualize those assumptions circulating far below the cultural surface as water-table aquifers. Ensuring safe and clean drinking water requires regular testing, and the results might urge us to drill deeper or perhaps in another location entirely or to investigate whether potential contaminants have been running off from the surface above, polluting the aquifers below.

Queer home economists will test theological waters regularly for similar and often life-saving reasons, as Marcella Althaus-Reid argued in her queerly feminist approach to liberation theology. Her work skated close to what many would consider the obscene, and indeed she encouraged us to "talk obscenities to theology."[13] She did this not merely to provoke but to sound an alarm: our theological well has been contaminated with modern toxins and we must drill deeper. She urges us to consider carefully the collusion between institutional Christianity and Western sociopolitical institutions, what she calls "T-Theology" or the kind of theological system with a capital "T" that aligns itself with imperial power. This collusion, she argues, not only supports the oppressive structures of empire (regardless of the form such imperial forces take), it also represses the sources of liberation within theology itself. "What we need," she writes, "is to recover the memory of the scandal in theology, and with a vengeance. This is the scandal of what T-Theology has carefully avoided: God amongst the Queer, and the Queer

---

13. This is the title of her third chapter in *Indecent Theology*, 87–124.

God "present in Godself. . . . The theological scandal is that bodies speak, and God speaks through them."[14] God speaking through bodies hardly sounds scandalous, much less queer when spoken in the liturgical pieties of modern Western versions of institutional Christianity. That is precisely Althaus-Reid's point as she nudges us to drill deeper. Recovering a scandalous memory within familiar pieties would, for example, alert us to the God not only speaking *through* bodies but the God speaking *as* a body, as Jesus, which charted a theological path leading to the queerly Trinitarian God.

Doing Trinitarian housework can feel like any other kind of housework, a necessary but tedious chore. Also like housework, it comes with its own rewards. Encouraging Christian faith communities to delve into the complexities of theological history can unearth forgotten treasures, like finding an old trunk in the attic or a misplaced duffle bag at the back of a closet. These treasures appear not merely as keepsakes to trot out during family reunions or as memorabilia to perplex grandchildren about a bygone era. Bringing these treasures out from their dusty storage lockers can illumine the past with fresh insights for the present. These insights, queer home economists would quickly note, can both inspire *and* disturb. Kelly Brown Douglas, for example, adds a cautionary note to our treasure-hunting among relics. Returning to the aquifer metaphor, she worries about certain trace elements in the deeper wells of history that continue to infect us with a subtle poison. Those ancient elements of what she calls "platonized Christianity" implicitly sanction racial and sexual violence.[15]

Douglas complicates the Trinitarian imprint of Christian faith by insightfully locating a problematic turn in early Christian arguments for monotheism. She means especially to highlight a "closed monotheism," a rhetorical posture that emerged to refute Greco-Roman polytheism. The foreclosure of all other divine options, she argues, creates a binary theological system easily translatable to human systems of classification. Not even the Incarnation can break open this system, which theologians protected by treating Christ as a "paradox."[16] Althaus-Reid analyzes that same history of what she called the problem of "mono-loving."[17] An isolated God, safely sequestered from human interaction, provided a suitable icon for modernity's exaltation of the

14. Althaus-Reid, *Queer God*, 33–34.

15. Douglas, *What's Faith Got to Do with It?* 9.

16. Ibid., 10.

17. Althaus-Reid, *Queer God*, 55–58.

autonomous individual, a monad. But Althaus-Reid sees something else in this theological history as well. This history carries with it the potential for its own undoing, what she refers to as the "closeted Trinity" within theological traditions, something like a Trojan horse in institutional Christianity ready to undo the Church.[18] More than the incarnation, yet still because of it, Trinitarian speculation destabilizes the mono-loving practices associated with the self-sufficient autonomous God preferred by the forces of empire. The closed monotheism described by Douglas may have ensured the cultural hegemony of Christianity in the West but the Trinitarian foundation of that institutional power continually threatens to undo it from within. Thirdness, in other words, always causes trouble.

Much more, of course, than individual self-sufficiency lies at the root of modern distress. By the same token, much more than doctrinal orthodoxy hangs in the balance when sorting through Trinitarian peculiarities. To recall David Matzo McCarthy's felicitous phrase, the peculiar faith of Christians "disturbs the world with God." The queerness of theology disturbs the modern West by bearing witness to the God whose very essence is relation itself. Augustine struggled with this and worried most about preserving the unity of God in our theological speech. He proposed thinking of divine reality as a single substance—"God stuff," as it were—which three divine "persons" share equally among them, a proposal to ensure that the oneness of God remains securely ensconced in our theological systems.

Other ancient sources reflect a different kind of anxiety, the concern about reducing divine life to a static thing, a "substance." Three theologians known collectively as the Cappadocians (Basil the Great, Gregory of Nyssa, and Gregory of Nanzianzus) preferred to conceive of God's unity much more dynamically. Rather than supposing that divine oneness resides in a substance, they argued that such unity emerges only from *relation*. To speak of a person at all in that ancient worldview is to speak of relationships, or the relational dynamics that actually constitute who a person is. Apart from relations, persons cease to be persons at all, and this, the Cappadocians supposed, must apply equally to whatever Christians mean by "God."[19] More simply but no less profoundly, divine substance *is* relation.

---

18. Ibid., 58–59.

19. As just one treatment of the problematic aspects of "personhood," see David Cunningham's analysis of modern individuality vis-à-vis Trinitarian notions of communication and participation in *These Three Are One: The Practice of Trinitarian Theology* (Oxford: Blackwell Publishers, 1998), 165–95.

Significantly, and also rather queerly, the word "person" proves to be problematic in these ancient Greek views. These early Christian apologists worried about the word "person" nearly as much as today's postmodern critics of modern individualism, but for deeply theological reasons. Long before twentieth-century feminist theologians rightly critiqued the patriarchal imprint of Christian ideas, the Cappadocians found themselves vexed by the traditional theological language they had inherited. They certainly did not entertain explicitly the idea of abandoning the language of "Father, Son, and Holy Spirit" as appropriate for Trinitarian faith. Nevertheless they did worry that this traditional language implied if not demanded the power dynamics of subordination within Trinitarian relations, the dynamics with which they would have been quite familiar from actually living them in patriarchal households. A hierarchy of power relations in God's own life would subvert the commitment to unity that Augustine had so carefully tried to protect in Christian theological speculation.

Supposing that relationality itself describes the heart of reality inspired still further speculation. For some, like John of Damascus, this vision kindled images of reality in motion, a fluid dynamism that never sits still. To describe what he meant, John turned to the Greek concept of *perichoresis*. If "choreography" really does lurk around that ancient word, as Catherine Mowry Lacugna believed, then queer home economists will want to prepare for a theological dance party. Lacugna describes it like this:

> Choreography suggests the partnership of movement, symmetrical but not redundant, as each dancer expresses and at the same time fulfills him/herself towards the other. In interaction and intercourse, the dancers (and the observers) experience one fluid motion of encircling, encompassing, permeating, enveloping, outstretching. There are neither leaders nor followers in the divine dance, only an eternal movement of reciprocal giving and receiving, giving again and receiving again. . . . The divine dance is fully personal and interpersonal, expressing the essence and unity of God. . . . The idea of Trinitarian perichoresis provides a marvelous point of entry into contemplating what it means to say that God is alive from all eternity as love.[20]

To put this in another way, when speaking of divine reality we cannot distinguish the divine dancers from the divine dance; indeed the dancers *are* the

---

20. Lacugna, *God for Us*, 272.

dance and vice versa, and that dance is love. Or perhaps this: while it takes two to tango, it takes three to be God. And thirdness always causes at least a little bit of trouble.

It will take more than words like these on a printed page to disrupt modern Western individualism and even more to soothe its effects: homeless hearts. Queer home economists will need to draw on the talents of musicians, visual artists, and theater producers to disturb the world with God more fully. Theological theorizing nonetheless matters in all those efforts when ancient ideas inspire fresh ways to speak but also to paint, and sing, and especially to dance. Among the many possibilities, we might consider speaking of the ecological, the ecstatic, and the eschatological life of the Holy Trinity. Consider a few reasons why this might matter.

Consider first the God "up there" actually here, with us, for us, among us, and in us. Speaking of divine *ecology* might help us do that, and in the process help us break the modern habit of exiling earth from heaven. Help us, that is, to take seriously the prayer attributed to Jesus and repeated regularly by Christians to this day: "Your will be done on earth as it is in heaven" (Matthew 6:10). Ecologists might recognize in that prayer what they realize about their own scientific discipline: studying the vast web of organic relations necessarily entails studying ourselves. To speak of "divine ecology" can thus prompt deeper reflection on our own participation in God's Trinitarian relations as those relations both create and constitute the environment from which all life springs and in which all life flourishes. Divine ecology can likewise enrich our reflection on what we really mean when we speak about salvation and sanctification. Rather than describing moments of divine condescension to otherwise undeserving creatures (as they have too frequently been interpreted to mark), these doctrinal touchstones instead signal God's faithfulness to God's own expansive and expanding ecological life in Trinitarian relation. More simply: God the divine householder wants every creature to thrive and to feel perfectly at home.

Ecologists would also remind us about a key feature of this "home" as ecosystems exhibit constant motion. We might extrapolate from that deceptively simple observation and ponder divine life as *ecstatic*. This image proves a bit more challenging, perhaps, as we try to imagine God "standing outside" God's own self. The ancients nonetheless imagined precisely that and reflected on the whole creation as the ecstatic "overflow" of relational love.[21] Theologically speaking, all that is and all that will be is the result and manifestation of God's own ecstatic and creative energy, the inevitable yet also gratuitous superabundance of divine love within God's own self. Trinitarian theologians try in various ways to stimulate this profound insight: whatever "God" means that word points to the ecstatic outflowing of God's own self in relation. Or we might say the same thing like this: God just cannot contain herself.

Toward what end, then, does this ecological ecstasy reach? Undoubtedly only God knows, but the *eschatological* character of divine life suggests that even God might not yet fully know. "Eschatology" literally means "words about last things," but Christian theology employs that word to mean much more than chronologically final things. Think instead of goal and purpose rather than "last." Or think about dancing. We dance for many different reasons and God might well share at least one of those with us: God dances for a love not yet consummated. In the erotic rhythms of a tango still unfolding, the reach of God's own ecstasy has not yet achieved that for which it strives: the ecological fullness of communion in the deathless energies of love.

The fifth-century mystic pseudo-Dionysius reflects that eschatological reach but in far more startling terms. As one might expect from mystical inclinations, this Dionysian writer insists that we cannot fully know God. More surprising, this same writer suggests that God does not yet fully know us! As John Blevins describes it, "God cannot figure us out."[22] This, Blevins muses, could infuse Christian claims about incarnation with much more erotic and therefore queerer energy. God incarnate embarks on a quest marked by a passionate yearning, the longing to know us just as a lover seeks to know the beloved. Or to return to John of Damascus, God the Holy Trinity invites us to join the Divine Dance for the same reason we might invite a date to the prom, to get to know someone we find attractive, enticing, and enthralling. We invite someone to dance, in other words, not to categorize, classify, or conceptualize but to pursue where our desire leads. Doctrine can help us in our theological pursuit just as dance lessons can help us before we get to the prom. The point of both, however, is to dance.

Gregory of Nyssa, while no stranger to the conceptual intricacies of theological speculation, nonetheless cautioned his fourth-century readers about

---

21. See Lacugna, *God for Us*, 158–64.

22. John Blevins, "Uncovering the Eros of God," *Theology and Sexuality* 13, no. 3 (2007): 298.

theology's purpose. "Concepts create idols," he wrote, "only wonder under-stands anything." Jürgen Moltmann includes that quote in his reminder that reality will always prove more surprising than we are capable of imag-ining. By "reality" Moltmann means God, of course, but he also means us. Approaching one another with wonder rather than prejudice (literally "pre-judgment") preserves the possibility of relationship, the freedom to encoun-ter what lies beyond our conceptual grasp.[23] When even our closest friends and colleagues can still surprise us, can still appear to us as mysterious, we can begin to relax our grip on the host of preconceptions that divide our communities and breed only suspicion, hostility, and even violence. So also with God when divine encounter renders even our most familiar theologies as little more than idols.

The queerness percolating in all this Trinitarian speech leads to some-thing potentially queerer still. The image of the ecological, ecstatic, and eschatological God resides in us, God's creatures. Rather than referring only to the *imago Dei*, our lives bear the stamp of the *imago Trinitate*, a queerly divine life animating our own. But does this queerness matter? Can it make a difference in how we shape the relations in our households of faith? How might it energize a socially transformative witness in the world? Questions like these set an agenda for the preacher on Trinity Sunday far more daunting yet also more compelling than worrying about doctrinal acuity. We might prayerfully worry instead about whether our worship is sufficiently Trinitar-ian to threaten the forces of empire.

WORLD-CHANGING WORSHIP

When theology reaches its conceptual limits, what then do preachers say? When preachers stammer with wonder, what happens to Christian worship? Recall the cautions: seven centuries ago Thomas Aquinas insisted that *all* theology remains analogical. We cannot speak directly of the infinite mystery of God but only indirectly, through the analogies that populate metaphorical speech. More recently, Robert Neville has encouraged us to think of theol-ogy as "symbolic engagement." Rather than *describing* reality, symbols *evoke* reality for the sake of a deeper engagement with what Neville calls "ultimate

---

23. Jürgen Moltmann, *God for Secular Society: The Public Relevance of Theology*, trans. Margaret Kohl (Minneapolis: Fortress Press, 1999), 151–52.

matters."[24] Both Aquinas and Neville, among others, would thus counsel us to remember that when Christians speak of the Holy Trinity, we speak symbolically not descriptively. This cautionary note applies particularly well to Christian worship, one of the most symbol-heavy spaces Christians occupy while frequently mistaking that space for a *description* of reality.

Peter Rollins frames these theological and liturgical limits more succinctly if not provocatively: Christians need to disbelieve our own beliefs. That sets not merely a daunting agenda for a preacher but nearly an impossible one. Rollins sympathizes with that anxiety and rehearses the traditional dichotomy between apophatic and cataphatic theologies. He argues that these negative and positive modes of speaking about God actually intertwine with each other for a single purpose, to guard against idolatry.[25] Since we cannot speak directly of God but only of our understanding of God, Rollins would have us disbelieve our own beliefs, and he would have us do this for a single purpose: *encounter*. Rollins worries, in other words, that even belief itself can take the place of the God Christians worship and seek to proclaim. If so, then both conservatives (who seek to grasp God through conceptual knowledge) and liberals (who seek to grasp God through ethical practice) must recognize instead that all of us can only be *grasped by* God. Christian faith perpetually encourages that kind of assessment not only of our theological speech but also our practice of worship to ensure that nothing prevents God from grasping us with divinely transformative love and grace. All symbols need that kind of assessment, especially when they come freighted with tightly woven conceptual systems, like the Holy Trinity.

These theological and liturgical cautions inspire queer home economists to approach worship as primarily an occasion for life-changing encounter. This will mean preparing for the unexpected, for the real possibility of being grasped by what lies beyond the symbols that make our worship spaces recognizably worshipful. More queerly, all the symbols that populate our liturgical prayers and gestures aim for their own subversion, to dissolve in the light of that toward which they point. That kind of worship proves not only life-changing for worshippers but, and equally important, for world-changing witness. Biblical writers make that vital link at nearly every turn.

---

24. Robert Cummings Neville, *On the Scope and Truth of Theology: Theology as Symbolic Engagement* (London: T&T Clark, 2006), 1.

25. Peter Rollins, *How (Not) to Speak of God* (Brewster, MA: Paraclete Press, 2006), 11.

Isaiah begins his description of a remarkable, life-changing vision of God with these words: "In the year that King Uzziah died" (Isaiah 6:1). That detail matters, the death of a monarch. He may have been loved by some, hated by others, but in any case, a significant political figure in that community had died. Nearly every biblical writer provides that kind of potent reminder about the importance of context when trying to think and speak about God. For all of them, historical, geographical, political, and religious context matters. For Isaiah, his own context had devolved into quite a mess, just as Luke's had centuries later. Luke offers even more contextual details when situating the birth of Jesus: "In those days a decree went out from Emperor Augustus that all the world should be registered. This was the first registration and was taken while Quirinius was governor of Syria" (Luke 2:1–2). Luke's first-century readers would know exactly what that meant: the birth of Jesus occurred within the context of Roman imperial power and all the cultural and political effects it generated. It would be like saying today, "those years when Kennedy was president" or "that day MLK was shot" or "that night when Obama was elected."

Details like these connect our spiritual lives with God to the wider world, which nearly every religious tradition aims to do. "Connect" seems a bit too modest, however, given the queerly disruptive qualities of divine encounter. Notice how this unfolded for Isaiah, who was apparently attending to rather routine religious matters of worship in the Temple. In the year that King Uzziah died those familiar patterns of worship quite dramatically changed his life. The God who resided safely "up there" suddenly appeared "right here," and not just right here, but filling the whole temple (Isaiah 6:1–4). The distance between heaven and earth dissolved; the tidy boundary so frequently drawn between the "religious" and the "secular" faded away; what matters to God and what therefore ought to matter to religious people appears to Isaiah in that moment as absolutely *everything*.

Not coincidentally, the Revised Common Lectionary, shared by a number of Christian denominations, recommends that passage from Isaiah for Trinity Sunday. Queer home economists will certainly want to avoid reading later Christian doctrine into ancient Israelite texts, but they will also want to draw attention to the context of worship in that text. Queerly enough, worship might actually change the world if it can help us dissolve the contrived boundaries between "spiritual" things and merely "physical" ones, or more provocatively, between personal pieties and social policy. Here too the doctrine of the Trinity can infuse that posture with renewed vigor, as Catherine Mowry Lacugna tried to evoke with her book on the Trinity by calling it *God for Us*. As her careful analysis in that book over hundreds of pages makes clear, Christians insist on speaking of the God not just *for* us but also *in* us, *among* us, and *around* us. Like Isaiah's vision of God filling the whole Temple and extending to the heavens, speaking of God the Holy Trinity speaks the God who is everywhere active, everywhere calling for dance partners, everywhere calling us to join in the work of remaking a heartbroken world into a home.

Perhaps relatively few reflect on Trinitarian doctrine in that way, yet Lacugna evokes still more with the subtitle of her book: "The Trinity in Christian Life." Rather than an intellectual abstraction, she invites us to approach such doctrinal musing as a way to worship, a way to love, and a way to live. Queer home economists would add an important caveat to that insight: doctrine ought to provide a way to *disrupt* our usual ways of worshipping, loving, and living with a vision toward which our theological and liturgical symbols can only point. This recalls Marcella Althaus-Reid's provocations and her invitation to speak obscenities to theology, or less severely, Peter Rollins's exhortation to guard against idolatry. The religious challenge here intensifies when we consider the long history of interlacing institutional Christianity and Western sociopolitical structures. More precisely in the United States, the challenge emerges acutely whenever the cross sits in our churches draped in an American flag.

The risk of mistaking Gospel proclamation for patriotism has plagued Christian traditions since Constantine's fourth-century embrace of Christianity as the religion of the empire. Augustine fretted over that wedding of church and state, especially after the sack of Rome by the Visigoths in the year 410. That historical moment rattled both Christian and non-Christian alike, not unlike the shock and dismay that followed the terrorist attacks on New York City and Washington, D.C., on September 11, 2001. Some preachers blamed those attacks on American apostasy and immorality, calling for a renewal of the values that would once again make the United States a "Christian nation."[26] Augustine confronted similarly religious interpretations of Rome's calamity in his now classic *The City of God*. Whatever Jesus meant by the "Kingdom of God," Augustine argued, it will

---

26. See David John Marley, *Pat Robertson: An American Life* (New York: Rowman & Littlefield, 2007), 273.

not materialize among us as an earthly city, let alone a nation, much less an empire.

We know very little about the effects of Augustine's theological analysis among average fifth-century Christians as the Roman Empire continued to crumble. We do know that the decades and centuries that followed witnessed an ever tighter bond between European culture and Christian faith. Postcolonial theorists have been making that bond more visible in recent years, exposing the extent to which the North Atlantic can scarcely imagine Christianity apart from the social patterns, linguistic cadences, and political institutions of Euro-American history. Associating the powerful imperial inclinations of Western civilization with a religious tradition rooted in Semitic resistance to empire surely qualifies as ironic. That irony proves tragic when viewed through the dynamics of race and ethnicity. Richard Dyer explains, succinctly and uncomfortably:

> [N]ot only did Christianity become the religion, and religious export, of Europe, indelibly marking its culture and consciousness, it has also been thought and felt in distinctly white ways for most of its history, seen in relation to, for instance, the following: the Manichean dualism of black : white that could be mapped on to skin colour difference; the role of the Crusades in racialising the idea of Christendom (making national/ geographic others into enemies of Christ); the gentilising and whitening of the image of Christ and the Virgin in painting; the ready appeal of the God of Christianity in the prosecution of doctrines of racial superiority and imperialism.[27]

Queer home economists take this troubling legacy with them into worship, not with despair but rather with the queerly hopeful conviction that the Gospel can still inspire both constructive critique and a revolutionary imagination. Queerer still in some respects, liturgical patterns animated by a Trinitarian faith invite ways of thinking and of living that carry the potential to dismantle the seductive lure of Western imperialism and its corrosive partner, consumerist individualism. This approach to worship will necessarily entail fresh ways of framing social analysis with doctrinal insights, not for the sake of ensuring religious orthodoxy but for a compelling invitation to join the Divine Dance. Planning for that kind of worship will return frequently

---

27. Quoted in Moore, *God's Beauty Parlor*, 64–65.

to key questions, such as: Can a queerly Trinitarian theology contribute to Christian witness in a society where the commitment to the "common good" continues to erode? What could engagement with the Holy Trinity offer to the apparently intractable color lines that divide White from Black, or citizen from immigrant, or native from colonizer? How can the choreography of Trinitarian living inspire deeper commitments to ecological sustainability?

Modestly but still significantly, a Trinitarian witness might begin by recalling the ancient Mediterranean conception of personal identity, which relied first and foremost on relationality. Persons in that worldview did not actually exist apart from those relations; there is no "me" without an "us"; only a "we" can bring forth an "I." Augustine endeavored to take that insight into his musings on God as the Lover, the Beloved, and the Love that binds them. That kind of irreducibly relational language renders "person" as a thoroughly social reality; "Lover" makes no sense without either the "Beloved" to love or the "Love" itself.

Patrick Cheng finds in these ancient musings an image of "radical love." Radical, because this doctrinal hallmark presents communion as internal to God's own life, which in turn "collapses the usual difference between the self and the other (that is, otherness as being 'external' to one's self)."[28] This sounds less abstract in a society of gated communities where actual physical walls mark the difference between the self-at-home and all "others." Fences, enclosures, border checkpoints, guard towers, green cards, passports, and so much more populate the human propensity to stratify and divide ourselves into countless distillations of an "us" against all those who are "them." Less visible but no less divisive and destructive, a society of factory farming sequesters the animals it will torture for food, removing them far from the view of grocery shoppers on Main Street. Queer theorists most frequently turn their critical gaze there, on the distorting effects of polarized, binary constructions that frequently resort to violence to maintain them. Queer home economists find that critique firmly rooted in the "troubling third" of a Trinitarian faith.

This social view of reality matters in a world where bookstore shelves overflow with self-help books encouraging *self*-actualization yet no section at all devoted to books on *social* actualization. As social creatures of a social God, Christians have important *religious* reasons to object whenever

---

28. Cheng, *Radical Love*, 56.

political institutions permit every man, quite literally, to live for himself, or more precisely, that every rich, white man may live for himself without any concern for others. Still more: not even the rich-white-man can thrive and flourish as an island unto himself; in an age of global climate change and vanishing species, island-living of any kind proves unsustainable. Our lives are deeply intertwined with each other, friend and stranger, lover and enemy, human and other-than-human. We are bound together with those we like and love and those who perplex and irritate us; without all those others we would not be us. God knits us together in some truly uncanny and inscrutable ways precisely because of the Trinitarian image in which God keeps making and remaking us, and likely unraveling us first to reweave us together yet again into the divine dance of unimaginable and truly radical love.

A challenging view of reality, to be sure, but also compelling and inviting in a world littered with so many homeless spaces. Home-building will sound even more attractive if we engage in it together and still more intriguing to dance while we do. Lacugna believed John of Damascus sought to do precisely that with his image of the Trinitarian persons as a dance, as a fluid, energetic, perpetually dynamic motion of reciprocal giving and receiving. Imagine watching a ballroom dancing competition. Imagine, if just for a moment, losing yourself in the gorgeous lines of movement, or longing to join the dancers, or feeling the urge to gasp or shout at the end of a tango. Imagine this and you have touched on what the symbol of God as Trinity ought to inspire. On such doctrinal topics, Buddhists would remind us that the "finger is not the moon." Nonetheless, Trinitarian finger-pointing can inspire awe, praise, and worship, which just might change the world.

Queer home economists facilitate these sustained efforts of theological reflection, which leads rather queerly to praise. This will seem queer indeed to many self-styled "progressive" Christian communities who understand Christian life as more directly related to social activism and justice-making. Praise-filled worship, by contrast, seems too far removed from the "streets," where that spiritual activism ought to transpire. This binary distinction, along with so many others, deserves significant queering. Lacugna did not use that word, but she did devote the penultimate chapter of her book on the Trinity to praise, to doxology, as an indispensable ingredient in our theological housework. She notes how often biblical writers linked salvation and praise, not only in the sense that Christians give thanks for salvation but indeed that God saves us for the sake of giving God glory. She draws the same conclusion from later traditions as well:

> The language of praise is the primary language of Christian faith, and for that reason the liturgy is sometimes called "primary theology." . . . The language of praise and worship is a type of *theologia*, a way of speaking of God by speaking to God. In the early church, especially in the East, liturgy was understood as source and norm of doctrine. For Orthodox theologians even today, the idea of theological reflection disjoined from worship is unthinkable. . . . The worship and praise of God is the living context, the precondition even, for the theological enterprise as a whole. The theologian cannot stand "outside" the praise of God to speak about God.[29]

Lacugna's clarion endorsement of worship as the foundation for theology sounds compelling even as it raises more questions. As an Episcopalian, steeped in the formal rhythms of text-heavy liturgical rites, I often struggle with any direct link between worship and social transformation. At the same time, I have also experienced some remarkable moments in communities generally labeled "charismatic" in which those hesitancies dissolve. The praise life in some of these communities leads rather organically into ministries of service: ministries of caring for the least among us; ministries of extravagant welcome and hospitality; ministries that make visible the outrageous generosity of God's own self-giving dance of life, the very life in which the worshippers are caught up.[30] The life of praise offered to the Triune God can be only that, a life given over, ecstatically and generously, to ministry and service.

Worship matters when it draws us ever more into the very life of the Lover, the Beloved, and the Love overflowing, a life where hate becomes intolerable. We cannot easily give ourselves over to praising divine love and acquiesce to hateful speech or racist violence or genocidal madness. Worship matters when it catches us up into that divine dance where we cannot bear to leave anyone behind. Our praise will feel diminished if we see even just one who fell through the cracks, even just one left to die on a Wyoming fence post, even just one tortured by our own government, even just one literally

---

29. Lacugna, *God for Us*, 356–57.

30. One of several examples of this kind of community is City of Refuge United Church of Christ in Oakland, California (*http://www.sfrefuge.org*).

dying to cross a border, even just one who cannot afford life-saving medications. The God "for us" is the God for *all* of us, no exceptions.

Isaiah did not live with an explicitly Trinitarian faith, but he did discover why worship matters. His vision of God resplendent in divine glory enabled him to say *yes* to God. In the midst of his own society, a community falling apart and losing its way, the divine voice spoke: "Whom shall I send, and who will go for us?" Animated with praise and worship, overcome with the vision of God filling the Temple and divine glory reaching to the heavens, Isaiah responds without a moment's hesitation: "Here am I! Send me!" (Isaiah 6:8).

Among the many things worship can inspire, queer home economists will return repeatedly to Isaiah's reminder. Worship helps us to say yes to God. Each will say yes in different ways, each according to the gifts the Spirit gives to each person, and each gift blended with all the others in a single dance of life and love. The impetuous Isaiah does, however, give me pause. Given my proclivities for orderly systems, for making plans before leaping into action, I would prefer a bit more forethought prior to embarking on a divine adventure. What will be expected of me? How should I prepare? Where do I go next? Isaiah asked none of those questions before he said "Yes." Caught up in that moment of divine worship, he just blurted it out: *Send me!*

God provided exactly what Isaiah needed as God will for all others. God the Lover, who makes each of us the Beloved, will animate us with the Love we need to change the world. As we do this work of thinking and speaking and living, we eventually come back yet again to worship. When all of our words are spent, when we have nothing left to say because what matters most cannot be spoken, when the deepest pain and the richest joy alike pale in the light of God's own mysterious life of deathless love, then we shall know what praise really means. In the words of a hymn by Charles Wesley, then we shall know what it means to be "lost in wonder, love and praise."[31]

Queer home economists will shape their transformative work with such praise always in view. Praise to God, the Lover, the Beloved, and the Love Overflowing; praise to God, whose love makes each of us and dwells deep within all of us; praise to God, who makes each of us the Beloved to all others; praise to God, whose transforming love spills over every

---

31. The Hymnal 1982 (New York: Church Hymnal Corporation), 657.

boundary we construct or can even imagine into lives joyfully spent and lost in ministry and service.

Clearly, such a life of praise takes time to cultivate. Socially transformative worship takes sustained educational efforts and a renewed sense of communal spiritual discipline. And these are the very marks of the religious vocation to which queer home economists feel called. For them as well as for the whole household, that calling receives its shape from the intricate patterns of Trinitarian doctrine, the choreography of the Divine Dance that continually beckons and lures the whole creation deeper into the life of God. "Luring" of course implies all the erotic rhythms of seduction; this too shapes the historical pattern of Christianity's peculiar faith even as its modern expressions tend to mute it. Retrieving those rhythms may well mark the most effective means for revitalizing Christian witness today, a witness animated and sustained by a ritually aroused life of communion.

6

Ritually Aroused

PERFORMANCE ANXIETY, HUMAN RITES, AND BECOMING UNDONE

*I*f the socially erotic God yearns above all to dance with us, should we start with a bit of courtship? If that sounds too old-fashioned, we might try speed dating. Many in the North Atlantic already do this, testing a Methodist church one Sunday and a Buddhist sangha the following weekend, perhaps a yoga group in between and maybe a charismatic black Baptist congregation a few weeks later. The growing number of those who check "none" for their religious affiliation on national surveys nearly matches the equally growing number of spiritual "seekers" who yearn for, well, what exactly?[1]

More than a few theologians insist that God will surely find all those who long to join the Divine Dance no matter where they might look to find it. Christian traditions bear witness to that assurance, but it barely soothes the anxiety of queer home economists, the ones who worry about presenting a community attractive enough for the next blind date. Mapping the dynamics of a faith community to the rhythms of romantic desire may seem odd to some, yet the rituals inherent to both highlight the challenges in bearing witness to Christianity's peculiar faith—not only challenges but also opportunities to seduce the world with God.

I went on what might be called my first date during the summer after the sixth grade with a girl who lived only a few blocks from my house. Having saved some money from my allowance, I decided to take her to

---

1. See the 2012 results from a study by the Pew Research Center that shows one-fifth of Americans and one-third of adults under the age of thirty indicated no affiliation with any particular religious tradition: *http://www.pewforum.org/2012/10/09/nones-on-the-rise/* (accessed November 1, 2013).

lunch at the local diner downtown, also in walking distance. My mother made this the occasion for introducing me to proper courtship etiquette. "Be sure to compliment her outfit," my mother told me, "and when you're walking to the diner, stay on the street-side of the sidewalk" (this, I later learned, would ensure that a man shielded his date from any splashes of street water caused by a passing car—or a horse-drawn carriage). "Pull out the chair for her at the diner," my mother continued, "and let her order lunch first. If the conversation goes well and seems friendly," she concluded with a gleam in her eye, "you can hold her hand when you walk her home."

These instructions seemed rather complex to my twelve-year-old mind, but I dutifully remembered each one. Dutifully and also, it turns out, thankfully when I spied my parents about twenty-five yards behind Jane and me as we walked to the diner. They perched there in the family car to enjoy witnessing their son's first "date." To me, however, their hovering presence just felt like still more parental monitoring. That moment distills in microcosm what every community seeks to do with ritualized social customs—witness and monitor.

Well-ordered societies rely on countless social cues and gestures, instilled in most of us from an early age as ritualized patterns of behavior. Some of these customs help us feel at home among others by offering prearranged and time-tested methods for fitting in. Other cultural choreographies may strike us as odd or we chafe against their antiquated values, but most people accept them (if only grudgingly) as a way to preserve social harmony. Cultural habits achieve this harmonious effect in part by preserving the sense of an unnamed "they" who both witness and monitor our collective behaviors, like my parents in the family car down the street. To this day, even after many years of delving into a critical social analysis of gender roles, I still instinctively take up the street-side position whenever my mother and I walk down a sidewalk together. I do this even during times of California drought when few can remember rain let alone puddles.

Well-ordered churches leverage the same behavioral mechanism, especially for worship. Few occasions achieve that ambient sense of being "watched" more acutely as the divine "parent" hovers over and monitors the religious habits of the divine household. Worship styles can vary widely yet explicitly designated worship spaces nearly always prompt an altered bodily comportment. I remember pondering this as a child while watching my parents bow their heads rather oddly when we went to church. Uncannily, everyone else in that church did it in exactly the same way and at precisely the same time.

Mainline Protestantism in the United States owes its precipitous decline over the last thirty years to more than one thing. Among those factors, the blending of Western social customs with liturgical performance created an impression of Christian worship as merely the religious expression of North Atlantic cultural values. For the post-War generation of the 1950s, going to church on a Sunday morning belonged to the same cultural cloth as baseball and Fourth of July parades. The church-going subculture of my youth made no distinction worth mentioning between practicing good American citizenship and living as a disciple of Jesus. Pastors in that cultural milieu preached the Gospel and lived as paragons of social respectability; they did the former to support and express the latter. The emerging threat of Communism strengthened that bond even further as Christian clergy provided a religious embodiment of patriotic values and their twin expressions: free-market capitalism and participatory democracy.

Not all clergy baptized Americana in those years, to say the least. More than a few embraced the 1960s "counterculture" for Gospel witness, especially in the civil rights movement and among those opposing the Vietnam War. Many of these peculiar clergy, however, found themselves ostracized by the religious institutions they ostensibly represented, especially white clergy fighting against Jim Crow and men advocating for women's ordination. The progenitors of the "religious right" seized on that divide, securing an image of *institutional* Christianity belonging to the *establishment* of Western, and especially American culture.[2] That socioreligious bond seems weaker today as young Evangelicals tend to modify the social conservatism of their parents and mainline Protestant congregations serve mostly aging baby-boomers.[3]

---

2. For more on these mid-twentieth-century developments, their complexities and nuances, see Mark A. Noll, *The Old Religion in a New World: The History of North American Christianity* (Grand Rapids: William B. Eerdmans, 2002), esp. ch. 8, "The Recent Past: 1960–2000," 161–85.

3. Some research indicates that younger generations who continue to identify as "Evangelical Christians" still embrace broadly "conservative" theologies and social policies; see Buster J. Smith and Byron Johnson, "The Liberalization of Young Evangelicals: A Research Note," *Journal for the Scientific Study of Religion* 49, no. 2 (2010): 351–60. Evangelicals and mainline Christians who now associate with "emergent" forms of Christianity, however, tend to adopt more broadly "liberal" positions. For illustrations of the inadequacy of all these labels, see Bo Sanders' defense of "progressive" distinctiveness: *http://homebrewedchristianity.com/2013/02/11/there-is-a-difference-between-liberal-and-progressive/* (accessed November 1, 2013); and Matthew Schmitz's dismissal of "emergent Christianity" as liberalism in a new guise: *http://www.firstthings.com/blogs/firstthoughts/2012/09/25/brian-mclarens-liberal-christian-revival/* (accessed November 1, 2013).

Queer home economists wonder what all of this means for the Church, for the meaning of the word "church" itself. The wondering comes with some anxiety as well. The language of "households" in relation to church can easily evoke the modern conflation of Gospel and culture that so many have found problematic, and even more, the image of a congregation as a "family" of faith. Families of all kinds carry at least some troubling baggage, especially when freighted with "biblical family values." Prior to the Protestant Reformation those values coalesced around chastity and celibacy; today they serve as cultural shorthand for opposition to "homosexuality" and, more subtly though no less galvanizing, the submission of women to their fathers and husbands.[4] Binding the culturally familial to the congregational church convinces more than a few to abandon institutional Christianity entirely, to embrace the spiritual but not the religious.

All of these cultural complexities have been pulling on the loose threads in Christian ministry for decades, a religious fabric woven together with denominational structures, pension plans, and the professionalization of clergy as both organizational managers and theological therapists. That fabric now appears rather threadbare; for some it has unraveled entirely. What remains from that once seamless garment inspires spiritual seekers to seek community even if they cannot bear to call it "religion." What remains lingers in dwindling congregations that still draw people away from coffee shops to Sunday morning worship, even if they cannot name precisely why. What remains populates Facebook posts, tweets, and blog entries by disgruntled and disaffected Christians who at least intuit an untapped potential in the peculiarities of Christian faith.[5]

What remains from the crumbling edifice of modern institutional Christianity is the hope for home in a world of homeless spaces. This hope, as queer home economists realize, stubbornly resists settling for the artifice of homemaking proffered by Western consumerism. Hopeful resistance of that kind also appears among LGBT people who insist on creating "families of choice" in households that the U.S. Census Bureau scarcely knows how to categorize. What any of this portends for "church" few can say with any

---

4. Phyllis Schlafly and the Eagle Forum has promoted these traditional gender roles religiously and more broadly socially since 1972 (*www.eagleforum.org*). See also Focus on the Family (*www.focusonthe family.org*) and the Family Research Council (*www.frc.org*).

5. See for example Darkwood Brew (*www.darkwoodbrew.org*) and the Wild Goose Festival (*www. wildgoosefesitval.org*).

certainty, yet queer home economists know this much: the peculiar faith of Christians matters most visibly when it creates communities of hopeful resistance, or home-base communities for socially transformative witness to the Gospel. Elizabeth Stuart frames this witness a bit more pointedly by citing the theological projects of Richard Cleaver, who draws on methodologies that emerged among Latin American liberation theologians and especially their energetic critique of socioeconomic structures. Cleaver's chief theological point, Stuart notes, is that salvation is never an individual matter but rather emerges from political action, by acting in solidarity with others in ways that create new types of family. This reconfiguration of the ubiquitous image of family life extends well beyond whether lesbian and gay people can find a place at the table in Christian faith communities. Resisting the temptation to achieve cultural respectability animates what Stuart and Cleaver want to present as the Gospel call to subversion:

> One way of [responding to that call] is by building solidarity through liturgy and ritual, through a sense of embodiment and through a fearless formation of friendships. This is the completion of Christ's resurrection in community, the creation of a community of lovers out of a lover who gave his body to be touched and to touch, to eat and to be eaten, to die but to be never separated from his friends. Jesus is known through liturgy.[6]

Queer home economists can and will respond to that Gospel call and do their theological housework in recognizably Christian congregational spaces yet increasingly in many other locales as well, whether strip-mall storefronts, repurposed warehouses, public parks, or even bars and taverns.[7] Regardless of the venue, however, and as Stuart highlights, queerly Christian householding will rely on the rather traditional hallmarks of religious leadership: theological education and ritual formation. These twin hallmarks of institutional Christianity still matter, perhaps especially and more clearly in the light of Judith Butler's invitation to consider the performative character of gender.

The social cues and gestures instilled in our customary interactions with each other appear vividly and mostly unconsciously in their gendered

---

6. Stuart, *Gay and Lesbian Theologies*, 43–44.

7. Witness the circuitous evolution of "Revolution Church," founded by Jay Bakker, son of television evangelists Jim and Tammy Faye Bakker (*www.revolutionchurch.com*).

expressions. This, Butler proposes, exposes gender itself as the result of repeating a cultural script rather than denoting a biological "essence." Describing this proposal in another way, individual identities do not somehow float free from the cultural categories we use to articulate them, and each cultural system presents varying ways to express what only appear to be stable features of the human body. This approach matters to Butler, as William Turner notes, because it ensures possibilities for resistance to and subversion of oppressively limited forms of gendered expression. Rather than a static, bodily origin, in other words, "daily practices of socialization result in the body's signification of gender."[8]

Consider what it might mean to reread Butler's analysis of gender-as-socialization by replacing gender in that analysis with religion. Religious identifications operate in much the same way as Butler's depiction of gendered identifications, and religion does this most effectively through worship, or the repetitive communal performance of a religious script. Over time, and just like gender, religious identifications feel and seem "natural," which recalls the origins of the word "religion" itself. Combining the Latin *relegere*—to "reread" or pass on—and *religare*, or "to bind," as bones attached by ligaments, produces what so many spiritual seekers treat so warily: the scripted conformity of an institution.

Queer home economists share that wariness but temper it with a critical insight that nearly every household of nearly every kind appreciates: shared ritual strengthens communal bonds. That insight makes theology even more important for the patterns and rhythms of queerly Christian householding. As repeated ritual performance lodges texts, ideas, and behaviors in both cognitive and bodily memory banks, the content of those scripts demands careful scrutiny and deliberate reflection. What kind of religious identity does Christianity's peculiar faith invite and even coax and compel us to express? How would this make any difference in the socioeconomic systems of Western culture? To what exactly might "church" still bear witness in a world that has grown ever more suspicious of institutional authority?

Addressing those three questions sets a daunting agenda for the educational and formative character of queer home economics. Daunting for the potential it carries to crack the institutional amber in which modern Christianity has been caught for decades—to crack it open and release its

---

8. Turner, *Genealogy of Queer Theory*, 110.

transformative energy. Those queerly called to this work already know what that energy portends, not least in the transformation of their own vocations of theological and ritual leadership. It begins with an incredulous posture toward Church and what Christians believe about it—or rather, whether we believe *in* it. If so, then how we live will seem quite perverse indeed, to recall Luke's Pentecostal communities, and ritually shaped with peculiar patterns. Considering both of these in turn can recall David Matzko McCarthy's succinct description of Christianity's queerness and its purpose: "to disturb the world with God."[9] To that description I would add this: To disturb the world with the *seductive* God.

INSTITUTIONAL INCREDULITY

Christians and non-Christians alike harbor more than a few complaints about the institutional church. A short list would begin with the still-unfolding scandal of sexual abuse among clergy, most visibly in Roman Catholicism but certainly not in that denomination alone. The wealth of some churches likewise grates against the cries of those trapped in cycles of poverty while the perceived Victorian-style morality of ecclesial pronouncements exiles entire segments of the population. These contemporary reasons for incredulity likely pale by comparison to ancient sources, where Christian theology sounds queer mostly for its excessive claims. Two claims in particular about the Church raise modern hackles and, for some, outright disdain. The first comes from Cyprian, in the third century: "Outside the church there is no salvation."[10] The second appears in the fourth-century creedal statement of the Council of Nicaea: "We believe in one holy catholic and apostolic Church." The latter statement makes perfect sense if Cyprian's claim actually holds true—wherever our salvation resides deserves our belief.

Many Christians recite the Nicene Creed every Sunday in worship and likely do so without thinking about Cyprian, and even more without noticing the rhetorical excess of the creed itself. Notice the creedal progression: we believe in one God; we believe in one Lord, Jesus Christ; we believe in the Holy Spirit; *we believe in the Church*. Do Christians really believe *in* the Church the same way or to the same effect as we believe *in* God? Those who

9. McCarthy, "Desirous Saints," 307.

10. See the explanation of this claim from a Roman Catholic perspective in *The Catechism of the Catholic Church*, 2nd ed. (New York: Doubleday, 1995), 846.

try to live that pattern of belief may find their incredulity seasoned with profound disappointment.

Belief itself creates some of the trouble here, which many use as a synonym for knowledge. In contemporary English usage, "I believe the earth is round" conveys mostly the same conviction as saying that I *know* it is. Ancient Mediterranean societies lived with a bit more nuance. Recall biblical Hebrew, for example, in which the verb "to know" sometimes stood euphemistically for sexual intimacy. Knowing someone intimately may involve a collection of facts but usually extends beyond the cognitive and into the affective and the bodily. In that light, "knowledge" looks and feels more complicated, less tidy, and often more vulnerable to both ambiguity and ecstasy than *scientia*, the Latin root for the knowledge known as science. To know someone in ancient Hebrew more closely resembles the Germanic origins of the word "belief"—to hold dear and to love. To believe is to give one's heart, in other words. These distinctions may help but can still prove troubling. I might gladly give my heart to God but I would at least pause before giving it to an institution.

Robert Neville's approach to theology as a form of symbolic engagement might help even more. Christians readily recognize the cross as a symbol, perhaps also the bread and wine sitting on the Eucharistic table. But Neville wants to push us further to see so much else, indeed nearly *all* theological language as thoroughly symbolic, including "church." This can sound disconcerting in a society that so often appends the word "just" before the word "symbol," usually to dismiss a moment or object as irrelevant. "Oh, that's just symbolic," someone might say. A genuine symbol, however, creates the conditions for encounter and, if the symbol works appropriately, for actually engaging with and interpreting some aspect of reality truthfully or authentically. As Neville carefully points out, symbols do not merely stand in for something else, like money standing in for exchangeable value. Symbols instead *invite* in through direct encounter. In that sense, theological or religious symbols have less to do with "true description or explanation" than with bringing people, under certain conditions, into a truthful encounter with God. Symbols in that way connect people to the symbol's objects, or we might say they point effectively toward the reality they evoke.[11] Reading ancient theological claims as

---

11. Neville, *Symbols of Jesus*, 5. I do not mean to imply that my own approach to symbolic engagement replicates Neville's, only that it receives its inspiration from his work.

thoroughly rooted in symbolic speech may mitigate some of their excesses, and perhaps render the excess itself as a hope-filled encounter.

Disappointments, unsettling scandals, gut-wrenching betrayals—all these can and do attach to institutional Christianity. For many, these failures suffice to dismiss Church entirely; for queer home economists those same failures crack open the institution to reveal an invitation. Church-as-symbol invites us in and over a threshold littered with human faults and foibles, and there to catch a glimpse of the hope for home. Underscore "glimpse," for if theological speech turns always on the symbolic it turns especially on the eschatological. Theological symbols always point toward a horizon over which we cannot see, toward that hope which Paul insisted remains invisible (Romans 8:24–25). Standing, as it were, on this side of that horizon, the unseen excites our imaginations as we engage with the symbolic character of faith. Thomas Aquinas, for example, tried to imagine what church-as-symbol invites us to glimpse:

> [E]ternal life consists of the joyous community of all the blessed, a community of supreme delight, since everyone will share all that is good with all the blessed. Everyone will love everyone else as they love themselves, and therefore will rejoice in another's good as in their own. So it follows that the happiness and joy of each grows in proportion to the joy of all.

Significantly, John Laurance included that quote from Aquinas in his theological treatment of the Eucharist, a vision of the love of God being shared equally by all at the table of a shared meal.[12] Sharing meals with friends and family can certainly evoke those bonds of loving communion, yet the Eucharist invites us to stretch the vision further, to imagine both a broader and deeper level of shared love among a much wider communion. Wherever I can catch a glimpse of that kind of expansive harmony, or whatever inspires me to imagine it at all, to that I would gladly give my heart. Indeed, as Christians share that vision we might still believe *in* Church even as the depth of institutional incredulity today continues to mount a significant challenge to even the most willing believer.

As queer home economists attend carefully to an understandably incredulous posture toward Church, they take the symbolic richness of theological speech as necessary but not sufficient for bearing witness to Christian hope.

---

12. John D. Laurance, *The Sacrament of the Eucharist* (Collegeville, MN: Liturgical Press, 2012), 36.

More severely, the church-as-institution has shackled the church-as-symbol for too long, at times evacuating the symbol of its evocative power. Or in the language of digital media, Church today too often presents the WYSIWYG problem; what you see is what you get, and nothing more. Queerly enough, religion provides some assistance, or better yet, the queerness of the religious identity generated by Christianity's peculiar faith might help us sort through these complexities more effectively.

No less than spirituality, religion resists precise definition. Catherine Albanese embraced that resistance, abandoned definitions, and offered a description instead. For Albanese, religion distinguishes itself with *boundaries*. Physical and geographical boundaries have always been highly charged spaces for human beings, as Albanese notes, for reasons of safety but also of identity. We are here and not there; this space is safe, that one is dangerous. Crossing boundaries has been equally charged, whether in neighborhoods, or towns, or nations, or the boundary between my own skin and someone else's in sexual relations. "Ordinary religion," as Abanese calls it, provides assistance for living well within such particular boundaries of day-to-day life, which are often marked by the cultural customs of good manners. "Extraordinary religion" on the other hand offers guidance for navigating the boundary crossings outside the quotidian circles of ordinary life. In Western religions, this refers to how one encounters God, or how one successfully crosses the boundary between this world and the next, or how one respects sacred moments and locations as opposed to otherwise secular spaces. As Albanese quickly notes, ordinary and extraordinary religion rarely proves quite so easy to distinguish as they tend to blur in cultural institutions and practices.

How then do religious traditions monitor and navigate all these diverse and often overlapping boundaries? Albanese believes every religion does so with four component parts: creed, code, cultus, and community. The various beliefs about reality (creed) shape behavioral interactions (code) while ritual (cultus) reinforces that creed-code bond in the formation of community.[13] Notably, this descriptive analysis of religion applies just as well to civil society as it does to the institutional church. The monumental design of Washington, D.C., the speeches and gestures of political conventions, reciting the pledge of allegiance with hand placed over heart, watching a Fourth

---

13. Catherine L. Albanese, *America: Religions and Religion*, 2nd. ed. (Belmont, CA: Wadsworth, 1992), 9–10.

of July parade—all of these touch on the creed, code, and cultus that create an American community. Whether these component parts of a civil religion actually achieve communal cohesion matters less than their ubiquitous symbols, especially when they mark boundaries—border checkpoints, "green cards," and gated walls around embassies.

Albanese further notes that "ordinary religion is at home with the way things are . . . because it is about living well within boundaries, it values the social distinctions that define life in the community and respects the social roles that people play." Extraordinary religion, by contrast, exists and lives outside the ordinary circles of society. This kind of religion can take many different forms, yet Albanese argues that it always involves an encounter with a form of "otherness," whether natural or supernatural, and thus "encourages a special language that also distinguishes it from the rest of culture."[14]

Queer home economists will likely pause here and ponder some key questions that quickly surface from Albanese's analysis. Does Christianity express the *ordinary* religion of North Atlantic culture or does it still carry the transformative power to shape an *extraordinary* religious life? Can the Christian Church remain "at home with the way things are" and still proclaim the Gospel? Could the symbol of "Church" itself inspire countercultural witness? Christian worship offers a mostly untapped array of resources to address that range of vexations. Queerly enough, Christian worship can do this through rather traditional patterns and rhythms. Turning those resources into effective tools for transformation will mean attending carefully to the power of religious/social scripts to shape our identifications and relationships in the wider society. Albanese thus draws our attention to the religious significance of boundaries in much the same way Judith Butler invites us to see the scripted character of gender; both exhibit a performative quality subject to perpetual scrutiny. Whether anyone wants to be religious, in other words, poses the wrong question; each of us already is. Queer home economists will focus instead on the *kind* of religion Christianity's peculiar faith ought to produce, a seductively disruptive religion sufficient to inspire homeward belief. In that way, the traditional patterns of institutional Christianity disclose the potential not for a well-ordered institution but for the kind of hopefulness that rises up from and fuels a *disorderly* witness—the hope, in other words, of "extraordinary religion."

---

14. Ibid., 7.

DISORDERLY CONDUCT

Going to church on a Sunday morning rarely feels culturally subversive; should it? A charge of sedition has never resulted from making a tax-deductible donation to a congregation; why not? Christian clergy mostly enjoy widespread social respectability; does this seem odd? Christians outside the United States, whether in Somalia or North Korea, would pose decidedly different questions about their socioreligious contexts.

Extolling the freedom of religious expression in Western society tends to gloss over the privileges Christianity enjoys in the North Atlantic, especially in the United States. Mostly unspoken, that privilege nonetheless ripples through city councils deliberating over proposals to build a mosque and in questions raised about the patriotism of a politician who just happens to be a Muslim. That privilege comes with a cost to Christians too: mistaking the "American dream" for Gospel vision. Discerning where that vision departs from the dream depends on who benefits the most from conflating them. Yet even the dream's beneficiaries can pay the price of that mistaken confluence by missing the disruptive, disorienting, and therefore hopeful vision of home.

Queer theology inspires Christian witness by destabilizing what it means to be "at home" in our own naturally odd bodies and perhaps especially among all those other bodies drawn together in perversely Pentecostal communities by the erotic God. Drawn together, that is, by being "called out," to recall the root meaning of "ecclesial." LGBT people know something about destabilized lives. Few if any of us planned a life of living differently, yet our own bodies and desires as well as our relationships and households called many of us out of the expected and into the peculiar. Most of us live differently not for the sake of difference alone but for our thriving and the hope of flourishing. That hope has in turn inspired some activists to eschew cultural difference and pursue an "assimilation" agenda. The struggle for civil marriage equality illustrates that posture particularly well, a struggle not for "gay marriage" but simply for marriage for all couples.[15] Many religious activists aim for the same parity in their rejection of liturgical rites of blessing for lesbian and gay couples that fall short of "holy matrimony."[16] The question of

---

15. Michael Warner argues, for example, that the "rush" toward marriage equality too quickly cedes control over sexuality to the state (*Trouble with Normal*, 88–89).

16. In 2012 the Episcopal Church, for example, approved a liturgical rite for the blessing but not the marriage of same-sex couples; see The Standing Commission on Liturgy and Music, *I Will Bless You and You Will Be a Blessing* (New York: Church Publishing, 2013).

whether difference itself carries spiritual significance emerges here in a double sense. In the first, as to whether religious marriage differs in any way from the civil contract of marriage, and as to the second, whether the relationships of lesbian and gay couples are identical to those formed by "heterosexuals."

Queer home economists recognize in these vexations the hopeful energy that first animated their vocations, the energy of Christianity's peculiar faith, peculiar enough to call Christians out as Church. The interweaving of that faith and culture in the modern West thus poses an ongoing challenge for queer home economics: Can Christian witness disturb the world with God? Institutional Christianity actually carries within its traditional patterns at least one response to that challenge by issuing a regular invitation to "come out." I mean the way Christians worship together. This includes, certainly, the actual content of Christian preaching and the theological ideas expressed in liturgical texts. Even more, though, the rhythms of Christian worship itself invite us into a pattern of ritual formation set apart from the pattern of our daily routines. Catherine Albanese would describe this as crossing from the ordinary to the extraordinary in our religious practice. Worship, in other words, carries the potential to mark Christians as at least peculiar if not rather queer: to live like the peculiar Jesus did by eating with the wrong kind of people (Matthew 9:10–11) and perhaps by overturning the tables of profiteering that exploit the poor (Mark 11:15–17); to live queerly enough to make others wonder whether we might be drunk (Acts 2:13) or to stand accused of turning the world "upside down" (Acts 17:6).

Most Christians likely find worship an unlikely mode for queer living, especially in light of Paul's exhortation to do all things "decently and in order" (1 Corinthians 14:40). Much depends of course on the definition of decency and what qualifies as orderly. Paul himself apparently struggled with what this might mean as he urged the Galatians to overturn the cultural decency of gendered orderliness (Galatians 3:28) while instructing Corinthian women to stay silent (1 Corinthians 14:35). Queer home economists appreciate that struggle with order itself, especially as it illumines an otherwise unremarkable source for queer living in the Christian liturgical calendar.

The liturgical year plays a role in Christian life most often at Christmas and Easter, and perhaps during the seasons that precede them: Advent and Lent. Fewer Christians locate this temporal pattern in the complex intricacies of the Christian "Ordo." The Latin word *ordo* means "series" or "row" or "regular arrangement," which sits at the root of the Middle English word *ordren* from which today's word "order" comes. In the history of Christian worship, the Ordo most often refers to the invariable elements of the Eucharist, things like the Gloria, the Creed, the Lord's Prayer, and the Agnus Dei. The Ordo distinguishes these invariable elements from the variable ones, or the "Proper," the various readings and prayers properly attached to a particular season or day on the calendar. Ordo can also refer to a collection of ceremonial instructions and particular texts for both feast days and fast days, either for corporate worship or individual devotion, on virtually every single day of the year. The ebb and flow of all these texts and practices depends on the larger seasons of the liturgical year itself, which developed around two major cycles: Advent-Christmas-Epiphany to celebrate the Incarnation, and Lent-Easter-Pentecost to commemorate the death and resurrection of Christ and the gift of the Spirit. Some of the major feasts in these cycles fall on fixed dates based on the solar calendar, like Christmas. Others vary, based on the lunar calendar, like Easter.

In short, the complexities of the Christian liturgical year rival the labyrinthine instructions produced by the Internal Revenue Service. Unlike filling out tax return forms, however, the highly choreographed rhythms and patterns of the Ordo lend a sense of rootedness to the fluctuations and vagaries of a swiftly moving cultural climate. The Ordo does this by providing a rather queer structure for the patterns of daily life and inviting us to live a bit out of synch with the temporal rhythms of secular society. Sometimes these temporal modes overlap, as they do at Christmas, but they usually grate against each other with some dissonance. Rather than January 1, for example, the Ordo's new year begins on the first Sunday of Advent, four weeks before Christmas. Even more, New Year's Day on the Ordo features apocalyptic texts about the second coming of Christ rather than birth narratives about the first one.

Following the Ordo's peculiar patterns in the midst of wider society's scheduled rhythms can feel like dancing to music no one else can hear. Abstaining from meat on Fridays during Lent or decorating a Christmas tree on December 24 rather than the day after Thanksgiving or the traces of an ashy smudge on foreheads that one Wednesday every year—all these nearly clichéd markers of a slightly queer temporal rhythm appear in equally queer geographies. An Ordo-ordered life unfolds not in towns, cities, and counties, but in congregations, parishes, synods, deaneries, and dioceses. In this queerly ordered ecclesial world, some are called to "holy orders" in a ritual act called "ordination." In the development of the Latin tradition in Western Christianity, the bishop of a diocese became known as the "ordinary" by virtue of a bishop's holy orders to oversee these peculiar rhythms of Christian witness.

The wider world cares little about ecclesial geography and probably even less about calendrical mismatches. But queer home economists take even this modest queerness as an opportunity. Shaping God's household with asynchronous rhythms and peculiar spaces can start to disentangle church and culture. Slowly at first but over time the Ordo invites countercultural formation in the style pioneered by first-century evangelists. Their otherwise orderly portrayals of Jesus suggest at the very least a disorienting posture toward the ordinary structures of both society and religion. Luke extended his portrayal into post-Pentecost communities populated by trouble makers. More than a few times in his Acts of the Apostles Luke features yet another round of incarceration for those earliest followers of "the Way," a trail blazed by Jesus whose life led to charges of sedition against imperial power.

Karen Trimble Alliaume considered that biblical arc of what today's courts of law would classify as "disorderly conduct." She brought that with her into an analysis of the well-ordered ecclesial world of Roman Catholicism and its exclusively male priesthood. That world, as she describes it, illustrates the intractable vexations of categorical identities. More simply, only men can "stand in" for the male Jesus at the Eucharistic table, which is itself a "stand in" for the Last Supper over which Jesus presided. One could of course wonder why the maleness of Jesus matters more at that table than his Jewishness or his skin color or the language he spoke. Alliaume, however, wonders why all those things would matter more than his *conduct*. She wonders this by recalling Judith Butler's approach to identity as the repetition of a cultural script, or what she came to call "citational performances."[17] Just as books (like this one) provide bibliographic citations for quotes and ideas from other authors, usually in footnotes, so also live performances, or ways of living in the world can "cite" the lives of other people or communities. Moviegoers can appreciate Butler's point by watching Tom Hanks as Forrest Gump. "Stupid is as stupid does," Gump rather wisely observes.[18] For

---

17. Karen Trimble Alliaume, "Disturbingly Catholic: Thinking the Inordinate Body," in *Bodily Citations: Religion and Judith Butler*, ed. Ellen T. Armour and Susan M. St. Ville (New York: Columbia University Press, 2006). See especially Alliaume's helpful distinction between imitation and performance, 102.

18. *Forrest Gump*, directed by Robert Zemeckis; Los Angeles: Paramount Pictures, 1994.

Christians, both lay and ordained, the Gospel turns not on whether any of us can replicate the *identity* of Jesus but whether we can *perform* Jesus as the body of Christ; Jesus is as Jesus does, in other words.

As Alliaume's analysis implies, ritual formation in disorderly conduct implies much more than addressing institutional access to ordination; it invites renewed scrutiny of the table over which the ordained preside. Christian table fellowship traces its roots not only to the "last supper" but also to the many other meals Jesus shared freely if not rather promiscuously with others. Today's fast-food culture tends to miss the scandalous character of those ancient stories. For first-century Mediterranean societies, shared meals carried both social and religious significance and especially for the maintenance of social hierarchies of value. Jesus—and the stories told about him—disrupted that social significance with a profound realignment of what counts as decent let alone orderly. Luke's introduction to familiar parables about a lost sheep, a lost coin, and the prodigal son illustrates that disruption well: "Now all the tax collectors and sinners were coming near to listen to him. And the Pharisees and the scribes were grumbling and saying, 'This fellow welcomes sinners and eats with them'" (Luke 15:1–2).

Imagine someone completely unfamiliar with Christian history. Imagine this person reading for the first time these ancient stories of extravagantly if not wantonly hospitable meal sharing. Then imagine introducing that same person to the institution that preaches from those stories yet regulates and governs who may and may not participate in its shared meals. Would this not seem bewildering? Who could blame such a person for failing to see any connection between the ancient texts and the contemporary institution? How did those stories of gracious generosity give rise to meticulous institutional monitoring and sacred scrupulosity?

Queer home economists appreciate that experiment even as they worry about its implications. Precisely because Western society has drained much of the social significance of shared meals, the table of divine encounter struggles to find traction on a landscape littered with drive-through fast food. Practicing a generous Eucharistic hospitality on that landscape risks blending in with helpfully convenient but not terribly meaningful food options; a quick trip to Saint McDonald's will do in a pinch. Queer home economists thus navigate a challenging terrain marked by a twin impulse: to extend a generous hospitality without cheapening what they offer. Or more queerly perhaps, Christian table fellowship bears witness to a hunger not easily sated.

Following the queer Jesus into a ritually formed life of disorderly conduct charts a quest, one marked by hunger, yes, but a hunger never fully satisfied at the table. Whether formal and stately or relaxed and casual, the ostensible order of Eucharistic liturgy always carries at least a trace of disruptive desire; that desire springs first from God's own deep yearning for communion. Christians bear witness to that desire with oddly ordered lives tuned to the patterns of the Ordo. We do this to disturb the world of homeless hearts with God, with the God who seduces homeward.

EROTIC ENCOUNTER

Paul knocked off his feet and blinded by light; Mary Magdalene disoriented by a "gardener"; Thomas Aquinas unraveled by a Eucharistic vision; Teresa of Avila pierced by an angel's spear; John Wesley's heart strangely warmed at Aldersgate. These religious stories could easily pass for romantic ones. Or rather, what usually distinguishes religion from romance blurs in the haze of erotic madness. Relatively few of these iconic Christian characters would use the word "erotic" to describe their life-changing encounters yet most of them would certainly acknowledge the ecstatic character of those moments. Falling in love often involves both, the driving urge for union with another and its accompanying rupture of the status quo.

Some enchanted evening, wrote Oscar Hammerstein, you may see a stranger across a crowded room. Somehow you will know in that moment, even just then, that you will see that stranger again and again.[19] Or so it happens on the stage of a Broadway musical. On the Eucharistic stage Christians perform an encounter that may on occasion resemble those fabled moments of falling in love at first sight. More often the repetitive rhythms of Christian liturgy set that stage for a life-altering realization that dawns over time: through all the circuitous interactions of even the most quotidian moments in our lives, God has been pursuing us, God's own cherished beloveds. Realizing this can flood the theater of human life with uncanny light, illuminating not only the props and relationships we place on center stage but also everyone in the wings and all the leftovers in the shadowy spaces backstage.

---

19. Oscar Hammerstein II, Joshua Logan, and Richard Rodgers, "Some Enchanted Evening," in *South Pacific: The Complete Book and Lyrics of the Broadway Musical*, The Applause Libretto Library (Montlcair, NJ: Hal Leonard Books. 2014).

Like falling in love, divine revelation often feels sudden and unexpected, as if everything that came before contributed little or even nothing at all to that illuminating brightness of insight. But theater companies know better. They know the kind of painstaking preparation that fuels the most moving performances, even and perhaps especially when they generate unscripted illumination. Paul's rigorous devotion to his religious tradition; Mary Magdalene's discipleship; Thomas Aquinas's assiduous study; Teresa of Avila's contemplative practice; John Wesley's faithful exercise of priestly ministry—playwrights, directors, and actors would refer to all those religious rehearsals as "workshopping." That work matters for those unexpected and unplanned moments when scripted relationships fade into the background of encounter.

If theological education provides a script and ritual formation offers stage directions, queer home economists will engage both of those hallmarks of leadership to prepare for the unexpected. Or more queerly perhaps, the routinized rhythms of a liturgical production and all those stylized patterns of worship prepare us to leave them behind for good. Hymn writer Harry Turton gave voice to that moment like this:

> So, Lord, at length when sacraments shall cease,
> may we be one with all thy Church above,
> one with thy saints in one unbroken peace,
> one with thy saints in one unbounded love;
> more blessed still, in peace and love to be
> one with the Trinity in Unity.[20]

Turton clearly envisioned that day dawning on the other side of the grave and over the horizon where we cannot presently see. Yet Christian history, from Paul to the Wesley brothers and to this day, bears witness to heaven peeking through on this side. To put this in another way, queer home economists know that theological education and ritual formation turn often on texts *about* God, but they mean to create occasions for *encountering* God and, as John Blevins describes it, finding ourselves "undone."

Blevins cares about care itself, especially the kind practiced by pastors, and even more about the mostly unexamined assumptions that have seeped into pastoral care from modern Western cultural sensibilities. Blevins

---

20. Hymnal 1982, 315.

analyzed these dynamics by drawing on the critical theories of Michel Foucault, who investigated the social functions of modern sexual categorizations. Both medical and religious "experts" deploy these categorical classifications to tell us not only who we are but how we ought to behave. Foucault referred to this as "pastoral power," not just the kind exercised by clergy but the power running throughout most cultural institutions as they try to provide an answer to a fundamental question: What does it mean to be human?

Foucault believed that question resists definitive answers just as much as the question of God eludes systematic expression. If we cannot speak categorically about God, neither will all the many modes and roles Western society creates for speaking meaningfully about humanity suffice to capture what human life actually entails. Human beings, both individually and collectively, live in and through an ongoing process of being made, of becoming. To embrace that process more fully, as Blevins suggests, we must be willing first to become "undone." He means the willingness to set aside all the categorical identities that most of us have been trained to adopt for the social benefits those identities procure for us. Blevins explains by noting the weight of "truth" these social identities tend to carry: "the socially approved self—the upstanding citizen, the all-American hometown hero, the attentive wife, the successful business person, the beloved pastor—is the payoff for agreeing to abide by that so-called truth. If we refuse to follow the rules of this kind of power, we will pay a price."[21]

Couples in love have a sense of what Blevins means. The ecstasy of erotic encounter can make us vulnerable. Pursuing one's desire and being pursued as desirable creates a remarkable willingness to know and be known, even while the willingness itself carries considerable anxiety. How much of what lies beneath my categorically constructed identity am I willing to expose to another? Do I even know what resides underneath all those publically presented layers of the self? What will it take to bring more of "me" to the surface? What will my vulnerability cost and am I willing to pay the price? Questions like these circulate through every liturgical production of worship, though few of us pause to consider them.

I imagine relatively few Christians attend worship actively seeking to become undone. In similar fashion, few if any can predict when and with

---

21. John Blevins, "Becoming Undone and Becoming Human: Sexual and Religious Selves in the Thought of Michel Foucault and Judith Butler," in Boisvert and Johnson, *Queer Religion,* 13.

whom they will fall in love. The dividing line between worship and courtship queerly blurs in the light of the God who tirelessly seeks us, longing to
seduce us away from all that prevents our thriving and flourishing. To entice
us, as a lover would the beloved, and to bring us home, to our bodies, among
others, and with God's self.

Do Christians seek that kind of seduction in worship? Do we imagine
seduction as part of our spiritual practice? Why does anyone go to church
on a Sunday morning? Perhaps better, why does anyone *want* to? Nearly
as many answers can be heard to that question as there are people in the
pews to ponder it. Some may go to church from a sense of obligation or
religious duty. Others may attend sporadically, out of curiosity perhaps, or
on special occasions. In a society built on the centrality of nuclear families,
most of them located in "single family residences," quite a few probably go
to church for a sense of community, or more directly in response to an often
unspoken erotic desire for communion. I mean more specifically the longing for an end to isolation; the desire for a deeper engagement with social
realities than casual conversation at the workplace can provide; the yearning
(often unarticulated) to give one's self over to a world bigger than the self. A
consumer-driven culture, while temporarily satisfying the desire for things,
leaves untouched that vast, arid space of modern loneliness that advertisers
and merchants want us to believe they alone can touch and soothe if we buy
still more trinkets and gadgets. The decision to share a meal with others,
which already qualifies as an odd choice in a fast-food culture, rises up from
this deep, erotic longing for intimacy, communion, and union with another.

But communion with whom? Jesus, most certainly, but anyone else?
Paul reminded the Christians in Rome that they themselves are members
of the "body of Christ" (Romans 12:4–5). Perhaps the familiarity of that
image has sapped its startling character. Did Paul mean that the body we eat
at the Eucharistic table is somehow our own? Does this make the cultural
aphorism—"you are what you eat"—profoundly Christian? Or would Paul
suggest that we eat at that table what we hope more fully to become? Andrea
Bieler and Luise Schottroff would counsel us to remember the "real bodies"
at that shared meal; they mean the body of Christ as it is constituted by all
the other bodies just like our own at that table.[22] As a rite of "holy communion," we commune not with an idea or a concept but somehow and

22. Andrea Bieler and Luise Schottroff, *The Eucharist: Bodies, Bread, and Resurrection* (Minneapolis,
MN: Fortress Press, 2007), 127–34.

in some fashion with bodies, with Christ's body to be sure, but also the many other "real bodies" at the table, each of which contributes to the "remembering" of the Christic body. Even this kind of Eucharistic reflection only begins to tease out the queerness of that liturgical moment when the body we consume is not only our own but is also strangely gendered by its diverse members.[23]

Questions persist here. Skipping the coffee shop for worship on a Sunday morning may spring from a desire for companionship, but do Christians find that desire *erotic*? How often do Christians reflect on the Eucharistic table as their own performative participation in the *body* of Christ, a performance that relies on all the other bodies gathered with them? What are we eating there? Or rather, *whom*? For centuries, Christian ministers have lifted up bread and repeated the words attributed to Jesus in the Gospels: "Take, eat; this is my body given for you." If that invitation were spoken in any other public context, it would surely make most people blush. Perhaps the highly stylized gestures of that rite now obscure the erotic undercurrents in the rite's invitation. "Undercurrents" likely understates the case, as Marion Maddox tried to provoke rather explicitly concerning the intimacy of Eucharistic celebrations. "If you are male and heterosexual," she writes, "there is only one activity for which you kneel down in front of another man, his crotch close enough to touch, in an atmosphere of dim light and soft music, while something is placed in your mouth. If you are female and heterosexual, there are potentially two."[24]

Maddox's provocation signals more than a potentially tantalizing (and for some, scandalous) possibility for erotic encounter in worship. Prevailing statistics suggest the likelihood that some members of every Christian congregation have experienced a form of sexual trauma, domestic violence, or a type of hate crime. Consciously or not, those members of the body will bring their bodily experiences with them to worship where the queer home economist may well trigger traumatic memories or even retraumatize sexually wounded

23. See Gerard Loughlin, "Sex After Natural Law," in Althaus-Reid and Isherwood, *Sexual Theologian*, 88, 95–97. See also Mark D. Jordan, *Blessing Same-Sex Unions: The Perils of Queer Romance and the Confusions of Christian Marriage* (Chicago: University of Chicago Press, 2005), 166.

24. Marion Maddox, "'Nor Ever Chast, Except You Ravish Mee': Sexual Politics and Protestant Pieties," in *Claiming Our Rites: Studies in Religion by Australian Woman Scholars*, ed. Morny Joy and Penelope Magee (Wollstonecroft: Australian Association for the Study of Religions, 1994), 50. I am grateful to one of my students, Carolyn Lesmeister, for her observation that "Maddox still presumes that the person distributing communion is always male" ("Consuming Ritual: The Eucharist and Its Queer Implications," unpublished paper [Berkeley, CA: Pacific School of Religion, 2008], 2).

people with evocations of a divine erotic encounter.[25] The erotic character of Christian faith may read like good news on paper but feel like bad news to people whose sexual histories have unfolded with physical harm. Relishing bodies as an incarnational spiritual practice in shared ritual can liberate some while pushing others deeper into the pathological rhythms of today's cult of youth and beauty, replete with eating disorders and cosmetic surgeries.

What then do any of us want from worship? Or should we ask instead what *God* might want from our patterns of theological education and ritual formation? Some queer home economists would prefer that latter question to the former. The pressure to create and lead worship services compelling enough to attract people to church on a Sunday morning can easily trump the need to interrupt cultural noise for the sake of hearing the voice of divine desire. The vast American marketplace of "family-oriented activities," consumer goods, and entertainment venues presents a formidable alternative to what appears by comparison as "just" a religious obligation on Sundays. This cultural landscape presents a nearly irresistible temptation to compete for attention by replicating the very styles and sensibilities of a marketplace we might otherwise feel called to challenge.

William Cavanaugh intensifies that marketplace challenge by drawing our attention to the sociopolitical significance of Eucharistic liturgy in the church-state relationship. Cavanaugh reminds us that what we mean by a "nation-state" may seem elusive, yet it exerts considerable influence on how all of us see the world around us and our various roles in it. The state can inspire us to treat strangers with compassion and generosity as well as convince us to join the military and take up arms against a faraway enemy. The state can wield this influential power because of its ability to make us *believe in* it, just as the hopeful vision of communion can compel us to *believe in* the Church. The tightly woven bond between Western society and institutional Christianity, however, tends to blur the distinctions between the state's interests and Gospel values. Cavanaugh worries, for example, about a nation's power to define who counts as an enemy of the state and thus the power to justify oppression, torture, and violence. In contrast to that power, Cavanaugh urges Christians to retrieve the image of the Church as an "alternative social body," one that transgresses national borders and embraces both friend and stranger

---

25. See Dirk Lange, *Trauma Recalled: Liturgy, Disruption, and Theology* (Minneapolis: Fortress Press, 2009); and Serene Jones, *Trauma and Grace: Theology in a Ruptured World* (Knoxville: Westminster John Knox, 2009).

alike. The Eucharist, he argues, presents that theological and spiritual vision in particularly galvanizing ways, a liturgical act that can resist the power of the state to define reality for us.[26] Diarmuid O'Murchu agrees with that perspective, noting the ways in which the earliest traces of Eucharistic meal sharing exhibited politically and culturally subversive qualities, especially in relation to the oppressive power exerted by the Roman Empire.[27]

Embracing Eucharistic liturgy as countercultural practice will demand sustained attention on multiple fronts, whether economic, social, or political. Even the familiar patterns and rhythms of the liturgical act itself deserve renewed scrutiny, as Marcella Althaus-Reid observes:

> At its best, the sacramental ceremonies in the churches work as acts of exemplary colonial orderings, but not of solidarity. The body gestures of silence, of receiving the bread with cupped hands, and passing [it] to another person on your right or left, can become military operations of precision and discipline not too distant from poorhouse workers at the beginning of the [twentieth] century passing bowls of gruel under the vigilance of the bosses.[28]

The ritual gestures of Eucharistic sharing may well demand revision, but Althaus-Reid remains convinced that Eucharistic texts themselves carry a subversive energy, especially when we view the table where Christians share a meal through the lens of erotic encounter. People who have fallen in love know what this means. Pursuing the bodily desire for communion rarely conforms to the ordinary patterns of daily living. *Eros* always manifests a disruptive energy that first unravels our usual and expected relational engagements before weaving us into a new pattern of intimacy.

Translating erotic disruption into a shared meal sets a rather queer liturgical agenda. It invites at the very least a careful assessment of institutional Christian patterns of worship to discern where they might harbor the corrosive elements of Western culture. Diarmuid O'Murchu returns to the parables and miracle stories in the gospel accounts to make a similar point. Rather than texts that will confirm our preconceptions, the strangeness of these biblical texts, like the strangeness of the liturgy itself, compels

---

26. William T. Cavanaugh, "Torture and Eucharist: A Regretful Update," in *Torture Is a Moral Issue: Christians, Jews, Muslims, and People of Conscience Speak Out*, ed. George Hunsinger (Grand Rapids, MI: William B. Eerdmans, 2008), 110–11.

27. O'Murchu, *Christianity's Dangerous Memory*, ch. 6, "Companions Breaking Bread," 94–110.

28. Althaus-Reid, *Indecent Theology*, 92.

a dramatic reorientation of perspective. He describes these peculiar texts and their effects like this:

> They defy the criteria of normalcy and stretch the creative imagination toward subversive, revolutionary engagement. They threaten major disruption for a familiar, manageable world, and lure the hearer into a risky enterprise, but one that has promise and hope inscribed in every fiber of the dangerous endeavor.[29]

If worship ought also to inspire a risky enterprise and dangerous endeavor, then for the sake of truth in advertising queer home economists might include a warning label on worship bulletins: "Prepare to be undone." Annie Dillard issues the same advice more pointedly by imagining going to church in crash helmets where ushers distribute life preservers and signal flares. After all, she writes, "the sleeping god may wake someday and take offense, or the waking god may draw us to where we can never return."[30]

"Draw us to where we can never return"—this can happen when we fall in love. The mystics in Christian history agreed, and they frequently remind us that no one can predict how erotic encounters will change us. That reminder likewise includes an additional and perhaps even queerer caution: becoming "undone" will not leave us satisfied in the usual sense of that word. Encountering the erotic God will instead strip away the many desires that the wider culture trains us to harbor as well as their sources of fulfillment. What remains after that stripping away will seem profoundly dissatisfying and therefore potentially intriguing, compelling, and seductive in a society accustomed to near-instant gratification.

What remains once all the props and accoutrements on our life's stage fall apart—and indeed when the stage itself crumbles in a heap—what remains is a clearer view of the horizon. We cannot presently see over that horizon-line, yet God continually lures us toward it, the horizon that all of our theological ideas can only evoke and our lives of faithful worship can only stir with arousal. What awaits us beyond that eternally queer horizon, no one can say with any certainty. The peculiar faith of Christians, however, can bear witness to its hopefulness and, quite remarkably, bear that witness in the world with a posture of trust.

---

29. O'Murchu, *Christianity's Dangerous Memory*, 192.

30. Annie Dillard, *Teaching a Stone to Talk: Expeditions and Encounters* (New York: Harper & Row, 1982), 41.

7

Eternally Queer
LOVE, DEATH, AND DIVINE JUSTICE

*A*dolescents rarely feel at home, least of all in their own bodies. After roughly twelve years or so of figuring out how to navigate an incarnate life on this planet (and fortunate children in loving homes do so quite happily), something rather queer happens: one's own body no longer feels very homey. Rendered more like an alien landscape ravaged by an uninvited onslaught of hormones, a teenager's body no longer feels at home with other bodies, either. Acne-covered faces, awkward postures, peculiar urges, hair where no one imagined it really belonged—these feel less like the component parts of an intelligent design than a lab experiment of a mad scientist.

Few adults reminisce over puberty with much fondness. Those hormonal surges infuse most memories of adolescence with an unsettling if not an "apocalyptic" quality, to evoke the original sense of that Greek word: to uncover or reveal. Coping with the startling revelations of a maturing sexual body proves challenging enough for most. The Evangelical Christianity of my teenage years added yet another layer to that potent mix by filtering all of it through the fantastical lens of the Apocalypse in the more biblical and religious sense. Hal Lindsey's commentary on the Revelation to John sat on my bedside table throughout high school, which I consulted regularly during my daily Bible reading and study.[1] Neatly underlining key passages from Hebrew Bible prophecies and making occasional marginal notes about current events (with Lindsey's help), I worried that Christ would return before I

---

1. Hal Lindsey came to prominence with his bestselling *The Late, Great Planet Earth* (Grand Rapids, MI: Zondervan, 1970), which appeared shortly after the Arab-Israeli war of 1967 and helped to popularize a particular version of apocalyptic Christianity that interpreted events in the Middle East as particularly potent signs of the imminent return of Christ.

had the opportunity to have sex. That concern was muted, of course, by the deep suspicion of bodily pleasure in that apocalyptic worldview, not to mention the prerequisite of marriage. Only years later did I learn that the word "rapture" could describe sexual ecstasy and not just that moment of religious ecstasy when believers would be caught up at the end of time to "meet the Lord in the air" (1 Thessalonians 4:16–17).

I joined the Episcopal Church in college, believing that I had left such apocalyptic Christianity behind. Yet there too the Apocalypse waited to greet me at nearly every turn. Christian faith and theology generally present a worldview rooted in a peculiar construction of time. History has an end in this worldview, not merely or even mostly in the chronological sense of an ending, but in the sense of a purpose or goal. This claim of an "end" belongs to the branch of Christian theology known as eschatology, which derives from the Greek word *eschaton,* or "last thing." "Last" can mislead us just as much as "end." Rather than referring to something like a final chapter, "last" more queerly refers to a fresh beginning; the end of this world inaugurates new life in God. "World" deserves further scrutiny as well. That word in biblical texts rarely if ever refers to planet Earth. The Greek word usually translated as "world" in those texts is *kosmos,* at once more expansive than this planet (the whole of reality) and much smaller than Earth (one's own social location or neighborhood). In that sense, all sorts of "worlds" come and go with some regularity, whether the world of one's personal relationships, or of one's biological family or a professional career, or the world of commerce, of nation-states, and ecosystems. Many LGBT people know what it means and what it costs to bring a world of conformity to an end by "coming out," which can at times feel like an apocalyptic moment in its own right.

Christian congregations confront these peculiar temporal rhythms whenever they try to attend carefully to the Ordo calendar, especially toward the end of November. Recall when the Christian liturgical year begins, with the first Sunday of Advent, four weeks before Christmas and right on the heels of Thanksgiving Day in the United States, when the holiday shopping season lurches into high gear. The biblical texts in each lectionary cycle for that day invariably include selections from the apocalyptic literature in the Hebrew Bible as well as gospel passages describing various cosmic catastrophes as the prelude to the second coming of Christ. Rather than preparing to celebrate the birth of Jesus in Bethlehem, the lectionary urges readiness for the "end" of time. I imagine few Christians relish hearing about the end of the world on a Sunday morning while thinking about buying a Christmas tree that afternoon. Queer home economists, however, do relish this rather queer calendrical quirk as a disruptive opportunity. By putting eschatology up front, right at the beginning of the new year, the Ordo sets the stage for noticing all the apocalyptic sensibilities percolating throughout the entire liturgical cycle, from Christmas through Epiphany and on into Lent, Easter, and Pentecost. The Ordo invites us to do this, to put "last things first," not for the sake of making better sense of eschatology, nor merely to dismiss it as worn-out mythology from an ancient worldview we no longer share. Above all, Christian eschatology invites sustained reflection on hope itself and whether it makes any difference for Christian witness.

The first Sunday of Advent reminds us that a great deal of both the Hebrew Bible and the Christian Testament are riddled with eschatological claims and, one should note, confusions on nearly every page. The galvaniz-ing gospel announcement that the "Kingdom of God" is at hand oriented the lives and practices of the earliest Christian communities in some profound ways, not least in the expectation that Jesus would return at any moment to establish, once and for all, a new world order. Many centuries later, Alfred Loisy observed that "Jesus foretold the kingdom and it was the Church that came."[2] Protestant Christians likely read Loisy's observation wryly, and indeed, Loisy offered rather trenchant critiques of institutional Christianity throughout his career. But as a Roman Catholic modernist, Loisy also under-stood the Church as the very point of the Gospel's historical development. The anticipation of the Kingdom is lived socially and historically by those among whom the announcement is made. What then do we make of that anticipation's perpetual disappointment?

Most biblical scholars place Paul's letters to the Thessalonians among the earliest in the Christian canon, and there Paul addressed directly an eschatological disturbance. The community in Thessalonica appeared deeply troubled over the death of some of its members, which scrambled their bur-geoning apocalyptic hopes. What could this mean for our friends and loved ones? Will they miss the new world about to dawn? Not at all, Paul writes, because they have not really died. They are merely "asleep," and when Christ returns—at any moment, in the twinkling of an eye, with the sound of a

---

2. Alfred Loisy, *The Gospel and the Church*, trans. Christopher Home, 2nd English ed. (New York: Charles Scribner's Sons, 1908), 4.

trumpet—they will rise first and "meet the Lord in the air" (1 Thessalonians 4:16–17). Anticipation for this moment of spiritual rapture dwindled in the centuries that followed but occasionally resurfaced. Rather surprisingly to some, apocalyptic anticipation has regularly punctuated American history as well.

Eighteen centuries after Paul calmed Thessalonian anxiety, an itinerant evangelist by the name of William Miller began preaching in upstate New York about the imminent return of Christ. Revivalist preachers of the Second Great Awakening had made that time ripe for apocalyptic musings and Miller's interpretation of biblical prophecies attracted a loyal following of "Millerites." Miller's study of the Bible led him to suppose that the year 1843 might mark the advent of Christ's definitive reign on earth. The idea gained momentum and generated conferences, tracts, and newsletters in a broader movement of "Adventists." Some of the more enthusiastic members started pressing for specifics, as apocalyptic desire so often demands. Miller resisted that call at first, but eventually joined the rapidly expanding debates over temporal calculations based on the Jewish calendar and the rhythms of the vernal equinox. Revisions to Miller's original suppositions pushed the Advent moment into the spring of 1844. Finally, more calculations, many public disagreements, and still further biblical study yielded a definitive date for the Second Coming: October 22, 1844.[3]

The fateful autumnal day approached and many of the Millerites refused to harvest crops. They paid their debts, sold their property to help others pay their debts, and gathered to wait. The day arrived and, needless to say, transpired much like any other day, which they then referred to as the "Great Disappointment." While the Millerites quickly disbanded under the weight of public ridicule, their disappointment fueled further revisions. A remnant regrouped around the leadership of Ellen G. White, whose own visions gave birth to the Seventh-day Adventist Church. These Adventists were less inclined toward apocalyptic precision, but its attractive force proved irresistible. A smaller group splintered off in the 1930s to become the Branch Davidians, who later gathered around the charismatic leadership of David Koresh and moved to Waco, Texas. As their shared compound went up in flames in 1993 and reports surfaced of the peculiar sexual practices taking place among its members, the news media made no mention of

---

3. For more on the Millerites, see Stephen D. O'Leary, *Arguing the Apocalypse: A Theory of Millennial Rhetoric* (Oxford: Oxford University Press, 1994), 93–133.

nineteenth-century farms in upstate New York or the socially provocative revelations of William Miller. I saw no mention of "rapture" in those reports, at least not of the kind Paul wrote about to the Thessalonians.

Apocalyptic movements vary widely, both in theological ideas and social practices. Thankfully, few of them end as violently as the Branch Davidians did. Oddly enough, nearly all of these movements do share at least one thing in common: sex, whether in the form of severe ascetic renunciation or its exuberant embrace.[4] Odd perhaps, but also spiritually intriguing as both apocalyptic religious faith and sexual desire continually pose the same questions: Will we remain homeless forever? Can we anticipate a homeland of genuine belonging? Where will erotic desire finally lead? Why does the fullness of communion seem so fleeting and out of reach? I mean that tantalizing hope of being at home in our bodies, among others, and with God all at the same time. Is this just impossible?

Queer theorists might appreciate the poignancy of those questions even as they fret over the social and cultural effects of Christian eschatology, which seems by definition to rely on binary, dualistic thinking. Dividing reality between this world and the next, separating soul from body, and heaven from earth, and of course the saved from the damned, presents a rather obvious target for critiquing rigid dichotomies. This theological topic has further divided today's religious landscape between liberal Protestants, who typically eschew eschatological thinking as a mythological distraction, and Christian fundamentalists, for whom a thoroughly apocalyptic worldview belongs among the essentials of Christian faith. Like most binary systems, eschatological categories demand vexing choices. Do we sacrifice the body for the sake of the soul? Must we abandon earth to enjoy heaven? Does my salvation require the damnation of others? We might ponder what kind of theology might respond to those questions by refusing to make a choice, a refusal more consonant with the peculiar faith of Christians even as it sets a challenging agenda for Christian witness.

Christianity's own backyard sprouts a wild array of eschatological and apocalyptic speculation with roots that tap into a perennial human longing. Eschatology most often appears on the terrain of humanity's tenacious and

---

4. See, as just one example, Charles B. Strozier's study of Christian apocalypticism in which he includes a chapter on the Hopi tribe of Native Americans. Like some Christians, the Hopi exhibit, Strozier argues, an acocalyptic worldview yet with decidedly different approaches to sex and sexuality than most Christians (*Apocalypse: On the Psychology of Fundamentalism in America* [Boston: Beacon Press, 1994], 219–21).

insatiable yearning for justice, whether social, economic, or more personal. Queer home economists confront that craving at nearly every turn, whether in social service agencies, public advocacy organizations, or congregational ministry. Those moments constantly refresh in new guises an ancient quandary. In the midst of injustice and in a world of so much pain and suffering, can we really place our trust in God? Biblical texts, theological traditions, liturgies, and hymns all invite that posture of trust toward divine faithfulness. The credibility of that posture, however, can feel quite tenuous in the wake of tragedies both small and large. Sooner for some than for others but eventually for all the frustration of hope raises critical questions about the very notion of fidelity itself. To be clearer, I do not mean first of all *human* fidelity, but rather *God's* fidelity to God's own household of creation.[5]

Meaningful sermons on the first Sunday of Advent need not turn to elaborate charts mapping ancient prophecies to current events. Preachers can instead focus their attention much closer to home and draw on the eschatological perplexities they face quite regularly throughout the year. Quite apart from the peculiar biblical texts of the Advent lectionary, members of God's household already know what those quandaries entail, whether from a failed marriage, the death of a friend, or the intractable mechanisms of social injustice. The ending of even the smallest "world" can send vexations rippling throughout God's household, which biblical writers and later theologians tried to soothe. Those attempts turned often to fantastical apocalyptic scenarios that many queer people of faith today find at least embarrassing in a post-Enlightenment world of empirical science. Yet the vexations persist, not least why apocalyptic forms of Christianity have remained so resilient over the centuries. As Stephen D. O'Leary notes, "Apocalypse has been a dominant theme in Christian culture for over two thousand years." He cites New Testament scholar Ernst Käsemann's even more sweeping claim: "apocalyptic was the mother of all theology."[6]

Queer home economists may not find much solace in apocalyptic prophecies, but they do recognize the perduring questions from which those apocalyptic traditions so often spring and which likely fuel their longevity.

---

5. John Polkinghorne, a physicist and priest and in the Church of England, believes that both cosmic and human death pose this very question of God's intention for God's own creation, or the question of divine faithfulness (*The Faith of a Physicist: Reflections of a Bottom-Up Thinker* [Minneapolis: Fortress Press, 1996], 163).

6. O'Leary, *Arguing the Apocalypse*, 7.

Few escape those questions that bubble up inexorably from moments of crisis, and especially crises that unravel the standard modes of making meaning from and for our lives. Elizabeth Stuart noticed this in the wake of the HIV/AIDS crisis of the 1980s and 1990s. That crisis, she argues, exposed the weakness of lesbian and gay theologies in the face of death and, more broadly, the failure of modern Christianity to address genuine tragedy. Stuart cites the work of Michael Vasey to describe what gay responses to AIDS might actually remind the Church about its own theological traditions. In brief, Vasey contends that Western Christians have mostly absorbed modern approaches to death and sex that render both as simply "natural" parts of life; facing the former with meaning relies on the fulfillment provided by marriage and children. This "naturalization" process, Stuart believes, not only unraveled for gay men dying with AIDS but also for the wider society that witnessed it; even more, it exposed the inability of most Christian churches to speak in an eschatologically meaningful way in the midst of that crisis.[7]

Stuart does not mean to encourage a "happily ever after" version of Christian faith that merely glosses over Good Friday with the promise of Easter. She means instead to draw our theological attention to the widespread denial of death in the modern West and the implications of that denial for the meaning of sexual intimacy. She wants especially to highlight the role played by death's denial in the cultural elevation of marriage, even in locations where marriage had not previously featured very prominently at all, including among lesbian and gay people. Queer home economists notice this peculiar link between death and sex and realize where Stuart wishes to point: queering theory not only destabilizes sexual identities; it also queries unexamined assumptions about mortality.

Queer home economists notice something else as well: the eschatological and apocalyptic imprint of theological traditions has already and long ago clothed Christianity in stunningly queer garments without any help from queer theorists. The transformative potential in that queerness lies not in the answers it ostensibly provides to vexing questions. Painful perplexity rarely finds solace in explanations when tears of grief, inconsolable loss, or expressions of outrage in the face of oppression demand more than "answers." In that light, a queer theology for Christian witness invites an approach to eschatological quandaries that demands considerable courage. Rather than

---

7. Stuart, *Gay and Lesbian Theologies*, 65.

offering unbelievable answers to intractable questions, queer home econo-mists can instead create space in the Household of God for acknowledging the irresolvable. Opening up that space would invite household members to bear unbearable burdens by sharing their weight. Burdens do not disap-pear when shared, but the sharing itself deepens and enriches the pecu-liar character of Christian faith; it releases the compulsion for certainty to make room for the vulnerability of trust. The need for courage in that space appears quite readily, even frequently when we confront the insecuri-ties in life's deepest vexations, the ones that orbit most especially around love, death, and justice.

UNCANNY YEARNING

Love and death queerly intertwine. Ancient societies knew this in ways that modern Western culture has tried assiduously to deny, but with only lim-ited success. Modernity's exaltation of all things rational and empirical, for example, failed to quell the popularity of vampires, whether in Bram Stoker's nineteenth-century *Dracula*, Anne Rice's *Vampire Chronicles*, or television's *Buffy the Vampire Slayer* and *True Blood*.[8] The origins of vampire lore predate these modern versions by centuries, tapping into the persistent queerness of love's entanglement with death.

The resilient fascination with the uncanny, extending even to falling in love with the "undead," reflects a queer though mostly unspoken perplex-ity over death itself. A rather puzzling feature of the Bible only compounds that perplexity as it confounds any attempt to create a consistent theology of death with its texts. Early Israelite texts portrayed death as resting peace-fully with one's ancestors (1 Kings 1:21) while later prophets imagine it as a shroud covering the people that God would one day remove (Isaiah 25:6–8). Paul sometimes describes death as "sleep" (1 Thessalonians 4:14),[9] at other times as the final enemy to overcome (1 Corinthians 15:26), or as a transi-tion to being "at home with the Lord" (2 Corinthians 5:8), or as the "wages

---

8. For more on the philosophical and theological fecundity of vampires, see *Buffy the Vampire Slayer and Philosophy: Fear and Trembling in Sunnydale*, ed. James B. South (Peru, IL: Carus, 2003); more spe-cifically about sex and death, see especially Melissa M. Milavec and Sharon M. Kaye, "Buffy in the Buff: A Slayer's Solution to Aristotle's Love Paradox," 173–84.

9. Paul writes in this verse about those who have "died" (New Revised Standard version) yet the Greek verb he uses commonly refers to being asleep.

of sin" (Romans 6:23). Even these few biblical images resist being assembled coherently into a single, knowable phenomenon called "death." Do we treat death as a welcome transition to another life or something to fight and struggle against as that which Christ will trample under his feet at the end of time? Absent any compelling, much less plausible theology of death in biblical texts, Western society reduces death to the natural rhythms of life. Or rather, some prevailing strands of Western culture naturalized death by demystifying its strange allure and masking its uncanny horror. The modern funeral industry has raised this naturalizing process to a fine art whenever an embalmed corpse appears nearly lifelike, perhaps even as attractive as a perfectly coiffed vampire.[10]

Falling in love and facing death queerly intertwine. Naturalizing death belongs on the flip side of naturalizing love, which likewise eludes consistency in biblical texts and theological traditions. Just like death, love's meaning seems obvious, and Western society has invested a great deal of cultural energy in making love perfectly natural and self-evident. The modern wedding industry capitalizes on that assumption quite successfully. So do Hollywood's romantic comedies, which often leave the impression of trying just a bit too hard to make love naturally fulfilling so that—just like death—it appears safe and domesticated. Little yearning remains to baffle or perplex on the silver screen after boy meets girl and they at last have sex. What could be more natural than that?

Elizabeth Stuart cites Judith Butler's work to name what all these naturalizing processes leave unsaid or ignored or actively repressed: "the unacknowledged grief of impossible love."[11] This peculiar kind of grief lurking throughout the many splendored faces of love makes it imperative for modern Western societies to naturalize death, to remove from view all those uncanny and unresolved bits, those inevitable leftover pieces that continue to puzzle us with dissatisfactions at the very moment of promised fulfillment. By "impossible love," however, Butler does not mean that it ends with death. Rather than grief over its ending, Butler traces the contours of the grief over love that never quite begins. More simply, love and death intertwine in the unbearable weight of regret, in the "should have

---

10. See Paul Fletcher's description of death's naturalization ("Antimarriage," in Loughlin, *Queer Theology*, 264).

11. Elizabeth Stuart, "Queering Death," in Althaus-Reid and Isherwood, *Sexual Theologian*, 60.

done" but didn't, and in the "could have been" but wasn't. The peculiarly gendered world of the modern West, Butler notes, makes love turn first on denial—I must not love *that* gender—and compels a turn only then to what one can desire instead. Love itself rises up from and relies on loss.[12] If death were not removed from view it would force us to confront that unacknowledged and leftover yearning in love. The modern wedding industry thus works perfectly in concert with the modern funeral industry to make both love and death just "natural" parts of life—and fewer people than ever choose to believe it.[13]

Queer home economists see that unbelief etched in the faces of nearly all those who gather for weddings and funerals. Those occasions bring together both regular churchgoers and the "unchurched" alike. Both increasingly find these liturgical rites unbelievable but rarely say so, and queer home economists know why. Modern theological and liturgical sensibilities have acquiesced to modern Western culture by tidying up, demystifying, domesticating, and resolving the messy, mystifying, untamable, and irresolvable moments in human life and relationships, and most especially those moments that punctuate our experiences of love and death. Rituals have historically created space for a shared engagement with both joy and grief; at the same time, ritual can also stylize collective denial and short-circuit the raw edges and ambiguous postures we might otherwise feel compelled to adopt toward these supposedly "natural" events. This impulse to naturalize may help to explain why whole segments of North Atlantic societies today no longer find Christian churches "relevant." For many, the Church simply does not tell the truth. Rather than trying to "make sense" of the uncanny, which fewer and fewer find credible, we might instead adopt a theological and liturgical posture that acknowledges what many people already intuit but which modern institutional Christianity seems to have forgotten: the inherent queerness of both love and death.

Early in the twentieth century J. B. S. Haldane suggested that "the universe is not only queerer than we suppose, but queerer than we *can* suppose."[14] Haldane did not mean to refer to LGBT people or to evoke Christian faith. He was a practicing scientist, in the fields of evolutionary

---

12. See Judith Butler, "Imitation and Gender Insubordination," in *Inside/Out: Lesbian Theories, Gay Theories*, ed. Diana Fuss (New York: Routledge, 1991), 27.

13. See Mark D. Jordan's analysis of these social rites in *Blessing Same-Sex Unions*, 94–97.

14. Quoted in Stuart, "Queering Death," 59.

biology and genetics. For Haldane, the more we learn about the universe and how it works, the queerer it seems. Enlightenment, scientific sensibilities of the modern West, by contrast, find virtually no mystery at all in the cosmos, and more than a few modern Christians agree with that assessment.

Today, however, and even more than Haldane could have anticipated, astro- and quantum-physics bear witness to the truly mysterious and uncanny queerness of the universe. Describing that queerness thwarts common sense at nearly every turn: the interchangeability of matter and energy; subatomic particles showing up in more than one location at a time; those same particles showing up in those locations without apparently traveling through the space in between; the complex relationship between time and space, which are not absolute but relative; and even the malleability of temporality itself in a universe littered with "black holes" where the standard laws of physics no longer apply. Queerly enough, descriptions of quantum realities could reside quite comfortably in gospel accounts of the resurrection.[15]

How peculiar do Christians want our faith to appear and to sound? Can we bear witness to an eschatological faith as queer as the universe itself? These questions make both Protestant liberals and Christian fundamentalists uneasy, especially as both tend to naturalize the queerness of eschatology. Nineteenth-century Protestant liberalism quite helpfully set in motion a cogent critique of the eschatological tendency to denigrate this world in favor of the "world to come." The ecological catastrophes of the twenty-first century only confirm that cautionary note. Keeping one's gaze firmly fixed on heaven or anticipating "Armageddon" can too easily depict earth as disposable.[16] Nonetheless, supposing that apocalyptic fundamentalism exhausts whatever one might say about eschatology leaves unaddressed the trajectory of love's leftover yearning and the inscrutable mystery of death, and especially how these intertwine in truly uncanny ways. Love and death rarely stay put in "nature" and queerly misbehave far more often than either liberals or fundamentalists seem willing to admit.

---

15. For more on these "resonances," and in addition to John Polkinghorne's *The Faith of a Physicist*, see Frank J. Tipler, *The Physics of Christianity* (New York: Doubleday, 2007), especially ch. 8, "The Resurrection of Jesus," 194–225.

16. Catherine Keller cites a particularly egregious illustration from congressional testimony given by James Watt, President Ronald Reagan's first secretary of the interior. In defending the administration's public land-use policy, Watt declared, "I do not know how many generations we can count on before the Lord returns" (*Apocalypse Now and Then: A Feminist Guide to the End of the World* [Boston: Beacon Press, 1996], 4).

Retrieving the queerly unnatural character of ancient Christian texts and practices in the midst of a universe pervaded by more queerness than modern naturalizers can imagine sets a distinctive agenda for Christian witness. Distinctive not least for the courage it requires to embrace faith without certainty. A queer theology for that kind of witness emerges from the intersecting energies of regret and hope without trying to resolve the tension they create. That irresolvable tension thrusts Christian eschatology to the very beginning of the liturgical year where it most properly belongs, on the first Sunday of Advent.

Embracing the eschatological character of Christianity's peculiar faith might well reshape Christian approaches to both weddings and funerals. Queer home economists ponder still broader insights those occasions can so often provoke. Living at the intersection of regret and hope creates the insatiable yearning for unimaginable justice. "Yearning" and "unimaginable" generate all the questions Christian eschatology poses but at its best never finally answers. Christian witness without answers still leaves plenty for Christians to say and especially to do, not least when we grasp the critical connection between the practice of justice and the hope of resurrection.

UNIMAGINABLE JUSTICE

"Jesus is coming; look busy." Seeing those words on a T-shirt in the San Francisco Bay Area rarely raises any eyebrows but likely would if spotted in my Midwestern hometown. Apocalyptic Christianity presents a ripe target for satire, yet its effects, both individual and social, rarely seem funny. Particularly modern forms of eschatological Christian faith have occasionally played a significant role in rather precarious American-style geopolitics. Stephen D. O'Leary, for example, recounts a number of moments during Ronald Reagan's presidency when modern, fundamentalist versions of apocalyptic prophecies inflected the cold war relationship between the United States and the then Soviet Union.[17] Edith Wyschogrod has described these forms of eschatology as perpetuating the great "sorting myths" of Western culture, those grand narratives that divide the saved from the damned, or the sheep from the goats (Matthew 25:32–33). These myths, Wyschogrod argues, have fueled some of the most distressing moments in North Atlantic

---

17. See Stephen D. O'Leary's account of "apocalyptic politics" in *Arguing the Apocalypse*, 172–93.

history, fiercely punctuated by Nazi Germany's concentration camps and gas chambers.[18]

Few if any Christians today would condone genocide, much less suppose Christianity supports such atrocities. Yet how many have recognized yet another and even farther-reaching catastrophe sitting at the doorstep of apocalyptic speculation? I mean the planetary-wide collapse of ecosystems and mass extinctions. Lynn White Jr. tried to sound this alarm as early as 1967 by noting the ecological implications of setting humanity apart from the rest of creation as either superior to it or master over it.[19] That posture is only exacerbated with eschatological logic, the kind that relies by definition on the greatest sorting myth of all, the final division of earth from heaven. The "world to come," in other words, has no room, nor even any need for this "late, great planet Earth," to evoke Hal Lindsey's best-selling title. God will simply dispose of this world for a better one, and without any thought given to recycling.

In the wake of modern science and post-Enlightenment individualism, some Christians tried to present a more credible religious faith by eschewing apocalyptic speculations and turning instead to the immortality of the soul as the essence of Christian eschatology. In the religious milieu of my youth, believing I possessed some indestructible thing called a "soul" seemed perfectly natural if not self-evident. No one told me back then that such a belief relied more on the philosophical dualism of the ancient Greeks than any biblical text.[20] This more moderate expression of eschatology would not of course escape caricature, including kitschy images of harp-playing souls sitting on fluffy clouds. Even "immortality" loses much of its luster in Anne Rice's novel, *The Interview with the Vampire*. Enduring for centuries, watching each year roll tediously by, the immortal creatures in that story long only for death.[21]

Harp-filled heavens and bored vampires aside, a much more potent critique of traditional eschatology appeared in the 1960s and 1970s. Drawing on anthropological studies, some feminist theologians mapped gendered

---

18. Edith Wyschogrod, *Spirit in Ashes: Hegel, Heidegger, and Man-Made Mass Death* (New Haven, CT: Yale University Press, 1985), 36.

19. Lynn White Jr., "The Historical Roots of Our Ecological Crisis," *Science*, March 10, 1967, 1203–7.

20. See, for example, Jürgen Moltmann, *The Coming of God: Christian Eschatology*, trans. Margaret Kohl (Minneapolis: Fortress Press, 1996), 58–71.

21. Anne Rice, *The Interview with the Vampire* (New York: Knopf, 1976).

divisions in human labor to differing conceptions of religion. Regularly confronting death in both hunting and warfare, they suggested, predisposed men to ponder the possibility of an afterlife. Women, by contrast, occupied with childbirth and child rearing, attended more closely to nurturing life on this side of the grave. More severely posed yet historically plausible in this analysis, men worry about their own survival while women worry about their offspring. The critique readily appears: given that men developed eschatological texts and traditions, resurrection and life-after-death have predominated in Christian discourse and, tragically, to the detriment of the web of ecological sustainability in which we now live and move and have our being.[22]

Versions of that analysis still reside in some theological projects today, yet queer theorists would certainly question the dichotomous account of gender on which that kind of analysis relies and also perpetuates. Other questions persist as well, to which Marjorie Suchocki more recently directed her attention. Rejecting eschatological claims entirely, she argued, fails to address the problem of justice, and especially the question of divine justice. Or more pointedly, do Christians worship a faithful, trustworthy God or not? Suchocki addresses that question by recalling several examples of injustice that history cannot correct and focuses on one in particular, the experience of an early modern woman burned at the stake for being a "witch." Thankfully, the Church no longer practices that kind of overt horror. But what about that one woman some five centuries ago, just one woman among so many? Does she have any hope for justice from the divine householder? Suchocki exposes the problem succinctly:

> Five million women living in a world of justice and mutuality make no difference to that one woman's experience of fire, agony and death. She feels no affirmation of her existence and no redress of the crime, no matter how fervently women five centuries later decry patriarchy and its evil of witch burning. Justice for the many is good, but it does not answer the requirement of justice for her. Without the "life of the world to come," her unredeemed experience stands as a finality of injustice, mocking the power even of God's justice. Without resurrection, there is no fullness of justice.[23]

---

22. See Rosemary Radford Ruether, *Sexism and God-Talk: Toward a Feminist Theology* (Boston: Beacon Press, 1983), 235–37.

23. Marjorie Hewitt Suchocki, *God, Christ, Church: A Practical Guide to Process Theology*, new rev. ed. (New York: Crossroad, 1989), 200.

Miroslav Volf adopts a similar posture. "No ultimate fulfillment is possible," Volf writes, "if the past remains unredeemed. . . . Persons cannot be healed without the healing of their specific socially constructed and temporarily structured identities."[24]

Postures like these toward injustice, compelling as they may seem, do little of course to mute the incredulity that Christian eschatology provokes among both Christians and non-Christians alike. Queer home economists know this and they might want to pause there, at the very moment when Christianity's peculiar faith creates incredulous people. Could life itself, perhaps, provoke just as much incredulity? Visit a natural history museum, stargaze at an observatory, watch *Nova* on PBS television, read *National Geographic* magazine—all or any of these display unfathomable mysteries in the intricate complexities of planetary life and cosmic forces. Can Christian faith produce as much jaw-dropping incredulity as the mind-boggling features of the universe? If Christians still want to affirm in some fashion a Creator behind and in the profundities of the cosmos, why would eschatological claims seem and sound less credible? Does the Creator of unimaginable life remain powerless over the tragedies of death? Do resurrection and the life to come belong to a theology just *too* queer to adopt?

Affluent Christians in the North Atlantic will want to ask a more troubling version of those questions. If our lives turn out well on balance, both full and fulfilling, do we dare declare that Christian hope has been realized? Do those who die of "natural causes" at a ripe old age after a meaningful life stand as the only witness to divine justice and faithfulness? What about all those others, the ones whose lives witnessed few if any meaningful moments of fulfillment or whose lives ended before really beginning? Is justice for them not merely unimaginable but actually impossible? Wyschogrod seems to ask a similar question by quoting a German concentration camp survivor: "Be happy, you who torture yourself with metaphysical problems, and . . . you the sick who are being cared for, and you who care for them, and be happy, oh, how happy, you who die a death as normal as life."[25]

---

24. Miroslav Volf, "Enter into Joy! Sin, Death, and the Life of the World to Come," in *The End of the World and the Ends of God*, ed. John Polkinghorne and Michael Welker (Harrisburg, PA: Trinity Press International, 2000), 262.

25. Wyschogrod, *Spirit in Ashes*, 13.

Stephen Webb turns to these eschatological topics from within the doctrine of creation where the quandaries only expand to the whole panoply of nonhuman animals. How does God's household embrace the faithfulness of the Creator whose "intelligent design" apparently runs on the unrelenting pain and suffering of nearly every animal on the planet?[26] Is that the kind of divine householder we can trust? Christopher Southgate posed this very question, a form of what he calls "evolutionary theodicy," in part to reflect the intensification of this problem in the wake of Darwin's theory of how species evolve. The problem stated succinctly from a Darwinian perspective is just this: later forms of life emerge only from the pain of their predecessors. As early as 1888 Anglican theologian J. R. Illingworth took seriously the theological challenge Darwin posed:

> The universality of pain throughout the range of the animal world, reaching back into the distant ages of geology, and involved in the very structure of the animal organism, is without doubt among the most serious problems which the Theist has to face.[27]

Much earlier still, of course, Paul seemed equally vexed as he describes the whole of creation groaning for divine liberation (Romans 8:19–22).

Suchocki, Volf, Webb, and Southgate do not suppose that any of their proposals offers anything like proof for life after death or the resurrection of Jesus or apocalyptic predictions. Rather than a persuasive argument or an explanation or a posture of certainty, Christian eschatology invites the Household of God instead to face the inscrutable leftovers of both love and death and to sit with the intersecting energies of regret and hope they create. Few can sit there easily or comfortably, nor should we. The restless energy catalyzed at that intersection ought to animate a socially transformative witness in a world of broken hearts and homeless spaces. A queer theology for that kind of witness will draw a naturally odd collection of people into its orbit, seduced into perversely Pentecostal communities by a love that is stronger than death. At the heart of this peculiar faith stands the unspeakably divine Word without the assurance of guarantees. That Word nonetheless invites a life of trust, or more precisely, of shared vulnerability.

---

26. Stephen H. Webb, *On God and Dogs: A Christian Theology of Compassion for Animals* (New York: Oxford University Press, 1998), 115–23, 174–80.

27. Quoted in Christopher Southgate, *The Groaning of Creation: God, Evolution, and the Problem of Evil* (Louisville, KY: Westminster John Knox Press, 2008), 1.

Judith Butler proposes to make vulnerability itself the basis for a much wider sense of connectedness, of human community itself. In particular, the vulnerability to loss just might describe something like a universally shared human condition. She explains:

> This means that each of us is constituted politically in part by virtue of the social vulnerability of our bodies—as a site of desire and physical vulnerability, as a site of a publicity at once assertive and exposed. Loss and vulnerability seem to follow from our being socially constituted bodies, attached to others, at risk of losing those attachments, exposed to others, at risk of violence by virtue of that exposure.[28]

Butler's simple yet piercing description of shared vulnerability lends additional poignancy to one of Christianity's central claims: the vulnerability of God. To suppose that God shares with us not only attachments but also the exposure to loss, and still more, to violence, suggests another central feature of Christianity's peculiar faith: a posture of trust. Whether and how Jesus can still lead us to adopt that posture in our lives with each other will shape the dynamics of queer home economics in nearly every respect.

NEVERTHELESS, TRUST

Blurring the line between sincerity and satire inevitably generates religious kitsch. Contemporary popular culture brims over with it, from upturned bathtub grottos in the backyard for the Virgin Mary to glow-in-the dark paintings of DaVinci's Last Supper on black velvet. Discerning the difference between kitsch and piety can prove surprisingly difficult. Displayed prominently in my office, for example, is a Jesus action figure doll, a gift from one of my students. I keep this doll in its package, which is one of its queerest aspects. The front of the package looks like any other action figure in today's pantheon of cartoon superheroes, whether Superman, Batman, or Wonder Woman. It even touts the figure's "pose-able arms" and "gliding action." The back of the package, however, presents a list of biblical texts about Jesus and the helpful explanation that his name means "God saves."

---

28. Judith Butler, *Precarious Life: The Powers of Mourning and Violence* (New York: Verson, 2004), 20.

Do we shelve this toy with all the other artifacts of religious satire, as a kitschy portrayal of Christianity's central figure? Or do we take it as a type of mass-marketing tool for Christian evangelism designed by culturally savvy yet pious entrepreneurs? I suspect we should do both. Appearing as this toy did, during a time when Hollywood had ramped up production of superhero movies, what better way to promote the only divine superhero who saves the day by conquering death itself? Queer home economists might take that action figure as a prompt for pondering divine action and whether Jesus really belongs in a superhero cult. That question sounds new, but it actually shaped the first-century origins of a peculiar faith.

Biblical writers long ago took to heart Dale Martin's proposal to "make Scripture" from textual traditions. The gospel writers themselves illustrate this process as they made Scripture from ancient religious texts (the Hebrew Bible), oral traditions about Jesus, and the experiences of their own communities. Christians today do the same thing with those gospel texts, frequently without realizing it, and often through the theological lenses many of us inherited from an early age. The lenses from my childhood, for example, tend to filter out the political intrigue of the passion narratives and how Jesus stood wrongly accused and executed by the occupying forces of an imperial state. Reading Jesus as a victim of profound injustice poses a troubling question: Could he have prevented those unfolding events? Troubling, because even asking that question begins to unravel the theological necessity of his death for our salvation. Troubling for another reason as well: Jesus himself apparently posed it. Now is my soul troubled, he says (John 12:27), and then prays that he might avoid drinking from the "cup" of suffering, praying with such distress as to sweat drops of blood (Luke 22:44).

The troubled Jesus also prays for a rather long time in a convoluted passage often referred to as the "farewell discourse" (John 13–17). In that highly stylized text Jesus says goodbye to his friends, to the ones he tried to love and to the one he loved in particular. Whenever I read that Johannine passage I think less of superhero action figures and more about Oskar Schindler. In Stephen Spielberg's film portrayal of his life, the final scene depicts Schindler surrounded by dozens of Jews, the ones he helped to escape from Nazi Germany. One of those gathered there thanks Schindler, who wonders whether he could have done more; "I didn't do enough," he says. He begins to weep, realizing how many more he could have saved.[29] As John's Jesus faces his own death, he prays for those he has known and loved and those he has never met and he prays that all of them might be one with him and with God. Jesus *prays* for this; he does not declare it. And in that moment I read more than a little "Schindler" into that text. Even for Jesus, faith sits at the precarious intersection of regret and hope.

Regret redoubles the theological trouble this troubled Jesus presents. Not *our* regret but the possibility of *divine* regret surely complicates our attempts to make meaning in a world of heart-wrenching despair. Some would make that attempt by mitigating the regret, suffering, and injustice of the crucifixion with the certainty of a "happy ending." But assurances of resurrection comprise only part of the strategy for soothing the tragedy of crucifixion. Later theological categorizations of Jesus's identity complete that move. More simply, the unfolding horror of the cross does not rise to the level of the truly tragic for the "Son of God." Important insights hover around that claim yet they do not land easily in the fluidity, ambiguity, and multiplicity of Jesus's identity in the gospel texts themselves. Queer theorists notice this rather quickly in the high-stakes game that unfolds when Jesus stands before the Roman Governor, Pontius Pilate. There, in John's account of the gospel, Pilate interrogates Jesus concerning who he claims to be, what kind of identity he will at last embrace, and how he should finally be categorized. Jesus cannot, in that moment, afford the luxury of theorizing as his own life hangs in the balance. Even so, he refuses to play by those rules, not even to save his own life. Jesus rejects the identity discourse being thrust on him by both his own religious leaders and the representatives of the imperial state (John 18:33–38). Jesus queers that moment and, arguably, it cost him his life.

Encountering and engaging with gospel texts in the light of that Johannine queerness, Christians have good reason to object to Jesus as comic book action figure. Jesus is no superhero of the kind envisioned by Marvel Comics. Rather than to Batman's bat cave or Superman's ice palace, and indeed, rather than the Temple of Zeus or any other Greek god or goddess, the peculiar faith Jesus embodied leads to the unfathomable Abyss. On that brink, no slack-jawed incredulity ensues as if peering over the lip of the Grand Canyon, where awe-inspiring depth seems unimaginable yet

---

29. *Schindler's List*, DVD, directed by Stephen Spielberg, 1993; Los Angeles: Universal Studios, 2004.

nonetheless measurable. The Abyss to which Jesus leads and every mystic
we can name has followed has no depth to measure; there may well be
nothing there, nothing at all.[30] On that brink there remains but one thing:
trust in the utter gratuity of life itself. This trust evacuates comfort from
faith and strips us down to a naked vulnerability, not to mention terror. The
gospel writers portray that moment vividly as God's poignant question in
Eden—"Where are you?"—morphs into the terror of desolation: "My God,
my God, why have you forsaken me?" (Matthew 27:46, Mark 15:34).

American popular culture, in the thrall of action figures, should find
this Jesus and his faith not only peculiar but quite queer indeed. As Albert
Schweitzer noted more than a century ago, this Jesus always comes to us first
as a stranger rather than familiar friend, beckoning each to follow toward
that horizon over which none of us can see.[31] How then to package this
queer Jesus? What kind of mass-marketing tool would make him attractive?
In the end, what do any of us want from him or want him to be? In the first
decade of the twenty-first century as North Atlantic societies faced the worst
economic crisis since the Great Depression, the eschatological "end" takes on
alarming textures. Do we imagine Jesus riding in to save free-market capitalism or at least to rescue homeowners from mortgages they can no longer
afford to pay? For decades the "American dream" turned on the certainty
of ever-increasing real estate values. One's home fit the bill for one's castle,
fending off the uncertainties of market forces with a guaranteed investment.
If Christian hope inspires finding ourselves at home, then the American
dream of universal home ownership would work just as well, or at least that is
what so many willingly believed. In that dreamscape, Jesus emerged in some
circles as the champion of family values tied to an unsustainable economic
system destined for collapse. Tying the Gospel to socioeconomic patterns of
prosperity leads only to crushing disappointment; it always has. Schweitzer's
insight still rings true: the quest of the historical Jesus, he argued, invariably
leads each generation to creating a Jesus in its own image.[32]

If not familiar friend but stubbornly alien stranger, Jesus invites a life
not of security but of risk. Rather than certainty, the faith Jesus inspires turns

---

30. See Robert Neville's moving and disturbingly honest description of the Abyss as humanity's utter
aloneness and loneliness in the cosmos in *Symbols of Jesus*, 221–23.

31. Albert Schweitzer, *The Quest of the Historical Jesus: A Critical Study of Its Progress from Reimarus to
Wrede*, trans. W. Montgomery (London: A & C Black, 1910; New York: Macmillan, 1968), 403.

32. Ibid., 399.

mostly on vulnerability in the face of the unknown. If faith were a play produced on a stage, the spiritually astute director would cast trust and hope in the leading roles, not guarantees or optimism, and its narrative arc would turn mostly on courage. Schweitzer knew that "play" well and lived that courage by embarking on medical missionary work in Africa. Not only his life but also the scholarship that urged him to lead that life makes Schweitzer a model of queerly eschatological faith. For decades, liberal Protestants had searched for the real historical Jesus who could fit in a bit more comfortably with modern Western culture. They could do this, Schweitzer came to see, only be omitting any reference to Jesus as an eschatological prophet, the Jesus who bore witness not to conformity but to transformation, whose teaching turned not on the world's progress but on its ending.[33]

Far more than a few others have seen what Schweitzer saw and followed a similarly courageous path. The queer home economists I keep evoking in this book belong among all those energized by the queerness of Christianity without knowing precisely where that energy will lead. Standing with Jesus on the brink of the Abyss means at the very least finding the courage not to live as a narcissist, the courage to admit plenty of good reasons to live a life of comfortable, consumerist self-interest but nevertheless to live differently. That "nevertheless" marks the life of faith rather than the "therefore" of a logical argument. Queer people of a peculiar faith live with no guarantees; nevertheless, we trust.

That one word could make a bit more Scripture still from overly familiar biblical texts. Who today would choose an obscure nomadic tribe of people, once enslaved by a powerful nation, as God's own people? *Nevertheless*, God did so with ancient Israelites. Few today would take the humiliating public execution of an obscure itinerant preacher as an occasion for life-changing faith. *Nevertheless*, gospel writers did so with the unspeakably divine life of Jesus. Not many would look to a ragtag bunch of uneducated day laborers to turn the world upside down, defy government authorities, create new kinds of community, and generate a worldwide movement of countercultural practices. *Nevertheless*, the perversely Pentecostal Spirit did precisely that with Jesus's followers.

The queerest ones in our midst will bring these biblical touchstones of the great "nevertheless" most vividly to light. In a society where security

---

33. Ibid., 402.

roots itself in marriage and single-family residences, the queerly gendered
and childless among us suggest a radically different locus for the vulnerability of faithful trust. Luke's Gospel/Acts evokes exactly that kind of peculiar
faith. Luke not only inaugurated the ministry of Jesus with Isaiah, but surely
had in mind Isaiah's radical reordering of hope in the story of the Ethiopian
eunuch. Just as the newly inspirited Christian community lurches toward
organization, Philip encounters the queer figure of a eunuch, who just happens to be reading from Isaiah. The eunuch persuades Philip that nothing
prevents him from being baptized (Acts 8:29–39). Nothing, in other words,
will thwart the Spirit's own insistence on expanding the circle of God's
household ever wider.[34] Surely Luke found inspiration for this story in Isaiah's moving vision:

> Do not let the foreigner joined to the Lord say, "The Lord will surely sepa-
> rate me from his people"; and do not let the eunuch say, "I am just a dry
> tree." For thus says the Lord: To the eunuchs who keep my sabbaths, who
> choose the things that please me and hold fast my covenant, I will give, in
> my house and within my walls, a monument and a name better than sons
> and daughters; I will give them an everlasting name that shall not be cut
> off. (Isaiah 56:3–5)

We need look no further, of course, than Jesus and Paul for a radical
reordering of faith, both of whom were unmarried and childless in a society
where security, divine blessing, and the assurance of being at home in the
world all attached to marriage and children. Making Scripture from all these
biblical markers will happen only in the company of others, in a household
committed to transformation. The great "nevertheless" of Christian eschatology can inspire God's household with the courage to live as if all the support
structures typically assumed by North Atlantic society for security and assurance do not in fact matter. To be sure, social security remains important, so
does the movement for universal health care, helping people caught in fore-
closed mortgages, and all the many other governmental programs that can
secure wider and deeper communities of both human and ecological flourishing. Nevertheless, none of these will enable God's household to face the
Abyss with a peculiar faith, with the vulnerability of trust.

---

34. See Sean D. Burke's analysis of the eunuch in Acts and his argument for that story's centrality in
that biblical book in *Queering the Ethiopian Eunuch* (Minneapolis: Fortress Press, 2013).

Many queer people I know have learned to face any number of abyssal realities with a deceptively simple strategy: shared laughter. Elizabeth Stuart has noticed this as well and recommends a queer reading of biblical texts rooted in humor, especially in the style of humor known as "camp." Laughter itself remains difficult to explain, whether psychologically or biologically, and even more so the version of it associated with campy forms of gay culture. Stuart nonetheless finds in biblical and medieval traditions reasons to embrace laughter for both theological and spiritual reasons, a way to appreciate the incongruities of Christianity's peculiar faith as a source of hope. The Feast of Fools, she notes, celebrated throughout Europe on January 1, though mostly in France, "was a feast of outrageous buffoonery in which the lower clergy ridiculed the higher clergy, dressed as animals and women, ran around the churches, brayed like donkeys, and mocked the liturgy."[35] Following on the heels of Christmas, this foolish display, Stuart believes, represents an explosion of incarnational energy. What better way to celebrate the absurdity of God not only in human flesh but the flesh of a peasant woman and born in a stable than to laugh? More peculiar still, the medieval Church found reasons to laugh also at death. In mostly German-speaking locales, celebrations of resurrection included the practice known as the *risus paschalis*, or Easter laughter. Preachers inspired this spiritual discipline by using bawdy humor from the pulpit, and for more than one reason: "relief at the vindication of Christ, joy at the defeat of death, and delight in the transfiguration of the body."[36] Whether for incarnation or resurrection, in other words, laughter marks the absurdity of the unexpected, the overturning of stable categories, and thus carries the potential to "disturb, disorder, and transform."[37]

For all those reasons, Stuart laments the lack of humor in modern Christian circles (and I imagine her doing so while on the verge of telling a good joke). Over the last few centuries, she observes, "laughter-lines were replaced by the paleness of melancholy as the Church simultaneously lost confidence in the reality of the resurrection and bought into modern constructions of gender and sexuality."[38] The melancholia to which she refers harkens back to Butler's description of love as a product of grief, imbued with a sense of

---

35. Stuart, "Camping Around the Canon," 25.

36. Ibid.

37. Ibid., 31.

38. Stuart, "Queering Death," 66.

gendered loss. For Stuart, Christian baptism overturns that loss as gendered constructions die with Christ. The time has come, she argues, for the Church to recover its sense of humor over this theological absurdity and reclaim our "parodic rhythms" as queer people of faith. Stuart understands such a posture as part and parcel of a divine vocation. "The Church is mandated to laugh," she writes, "in the midst of a world misted in melancholia, thereby disrupting it."[39] To disturb the world with God, queer people of a peculiar faith could simply laugh.

Death is no laughing matter; nevertheless it should and shall be. Religion is a terribly serious business; nevertheless it could be much more fun. The Christian Gospel invites careful thinking and studious analysis of matters of ultimate concern; nevertheless, it qualifies as thoroughly queer. I wonder whether this queerness could translate into a good deal more humor at the heart of Christian witness. No one, including Elizabeth Stuart, would imagine a pastor laughing when notified about the death of a parishioner, and a good joke will rarely if ever soothe the tears of grief among that parishioner's family members and friends. And yet, or rather *nevertheless*, Paul encourages the Thessalonians not to grieve over death like others do, the ones who have no hope (1 Thessalonians 4:13). This biblical posture charts with further depth the vocation of religious leadership marked by theological education and ritual formation. Well before the moment of death or planning a funeral (not to mention a wedding), queer home economists need to plant the seeds of a risible faith, the kind of faith that prepares God's household to face eschatological quandaries, not with guarantees nor with despair, but with the energy of hope. More often than we might imagine, that hope will issue in laughter.

Laughing with my friends and colleagues keeps me sane. It certainly keeps me from despair when I try to live well with all the deep perplexities posed by those eschatological moments that eschatology itself never fully resolves. The great "nevertheless" that fuels the possibility of trust recalibrates expectations, not to lower them but to expand and deepen them beyond what would otherwise seem reasonable. More often than not, this peculiar faith inspires us, not to appear rational and sensible but actually quite foolish indeed, as Paul seemed to recommend (1 Corinthians 1:18-27, 3:18). This faithfully foolish "nevertheless" thus shapes Christian witness in those

---

39. Ibid., 67.

irresolvable moments with a quiet and steady confidence, the kind of witness that shares fearlessly in the vulnerability that trust inevitably generates. Living with all these vexations in the company of other equally vexed queer people of faith can teach us over time to laugh eschatologically, to laugh neither with unqualified mirth nor derision, but with absurdly hopeful anticipation.

That kind of laughter might well describe how the peculiar faith of Christianity itself began, more than 2,000 years ago. It began, not with a doctrine, or a creed, or an institution, but with table fellowship. As Diarmuid O'Murchu reminds us, the *kind* of table fellowship Jesus initiated ranks as comically absurd. What one ate, how the food was prepared, and especially with whom one shared that food mattered a great deal in first-century Palestine, both socially and religiously. Food stratified that society just as severely as gender or ethnicity; the sharing of food actually manifested and maintained those divisive hierarchies. Jesus, who apparently loved food and took every opportunity to share food with others, simply swept away those divisions. O'Murchu describes it like this:

> For Jesus, there seems to be no doubt about the fact that the table always had to be open. Nobody, for any reason, was to be excluded. From the highways and byways all are brought in till the banquet hall is full. Prostitutes, sinners, tax-collectors, the outcasts and marginalized of every type were welcome. Not merely were they the beneficiaries of some new bold hospitality, but it seems they were the ones who had the primary right to be at table with Jesus.[40]

Elizabeth Stuart would likely encourage us to read that description while grinning and to imagine Jesus laughing joyfully while inviting the least likely to sit at the head table.

Christian Eucharistic worship, whether ornate or austere, often transpires with a deep solemnity. Queer home economists affirm such propriety while they also dream of crafting Christian liturgies with a bit more of the frivolity that percolates among good friends at a dinner party. Sharing both food and laughter in equal measure invites a disarming posture, a welcoming stance, and a generous embrace. That kind of sharing creates the possibility of sharing something else as well: vulnerability. Attaching ourselves to one another at the table—whether for dinner or Eucharist—exposes us to a

---

40. O'Murchu, *Christianity's Dangerous Memory*, 96.

double risk, the risk of losing ourselves in love and the risk of losing others, the ones we love. Nothing will mitigate either of those risks; and nothing but that double-risk can lead us toward divine encounter.

Queer theology for Christian witness matters most when it gives us reasons to risk the vulnerability of trust, the very essence of Christianity's peculiar faith. Queer home economists will take this theology with them into all those multiform moments when the insatiable yearning for an unimaginable justice tempts God's household to despair. They do this trusting that the queerly good news of the Gospel will transform the Household of God into a glimmering beacon. That shimmering household will beckon, not with a neatly defined or tidy institution but with a community of people who are quite frequently beside themselves—with laughter at times, yes, but most especially with an ecstatic hope.

Queer beyond Belief?

*A*ccording to an old and familiar proverb, home is where the heart is. Jesus said something similar, but more pointedly: "For where your treasure is, there your heart will be also" (Matthew 6:21). I take the first as rather comforting and the second as far more troubling. What I *think* I give my heart to—the original sense of the verb "to believe"—may not be where I store my treasure. I believe my house is a home, especially when it hums with the presence of treasured friends and family members. But the value of my house plummeted in the early years of the twenty-first century, nearly as much as my retirement account. The depth of the anxiety created by those declines speaks volumes about what I actually treasure. Do I want my heart to languish in a brokerage firm? In the vaults of a bank? Tangled up in bundled mortgages? Perhaps Jesus would try to soothe these anxieties with a bit more specificity: If we learn to treasure our own bodies and our relationships with other bodies in our life with God we might then find ourselves at home, regardless of refinancing options for our physical houses. In a world of countless homeless spaces, that should sound hopeful and even something like "good news." For many, it raises more than a few suspicions, especially when Christians say it.

I grew up believing that my house and my church together made a home worthy of whatever treasure I could offer. Like many other LGBT people I soon discovered the fragility of counting on church as any substantive part of a heart-worthy home. Rejecting both our hearts and our treasure, institutional Christianity lost much of its credibility among LGBT people on many more topics than only sexually gendered lives and relationships. Regaining that credulity will take time, a process that has witnessed significant strides forward since the 1980s. Those strides, rather surprisingly, came in part because of the theological and spiritual contributions of LGBT people.

Striding forward, however, does not merely restore what was lost; the process transforms what both home and treasure might actually mean, for *everyone*. Queerly enough, that sounds a bit more like Gospel, enough so to write a book about it.

The list of synonyms for "queer" and its adjectival complements grows with each new essay published, online chat room entered, and Internet blog entry posted. Only a few of those terms have informed my approach to Christianity's peculiar faith in this book: stressing the invitational more than explanatory; preferring the fluid and dynamic over the fixed and static; indulging the fragmentary and experimental at the expense of the systematic and cohesive; hopeful, but not optimistic; convinced, yet without guarantees. All of these queer markers in theological work preclude any attempt to provide summary conclusions, which one typically finds in a book's final chapter. I conclude instead by noting some of the prospects for the theological housework left unfinished in the foregoing chapters; and there is plenty of it.

To highlight some of the more pressing concerns in that work, I have organized three of them around the mantra-like image running throughout the rest of this book, the ever-elusive yet still galvanizing image of "home." I consider first the ongoing need for deliberate and sustained attention to the effects of geopolitics on our efforts to be *at home in our own bodies*. The modern West tends to relegate bodily intimacies to a putative "private" sphere, safely sequestered from the wider public realm of intergovernmental policies. Postcolonial theorists expose a much broader terrain on which theological reflection needs to transpire and with significant implications for sexually gendered bodies, which of course includes everyone.

Similarly, and second, the quest to find fruitful pathways for being *at home among others* increasingly transpires not in physical spaces but virtual ones. The world of online social media presents far more, of course, than convenient modes for networking. Perhaps more precisely, the networking itself has been rapidly redrawing the cultural landscape, and with it, the role played by religious texts and institutions in the evolution of human meaning-making. This world, the virtual one, displays a particularly queer horizon where we might finally say modernity ends. What would this mean for Christian faith, or more pointedly, for *modern* Western Christianity?

Taken together, these first two pieces of leftover housework elicit still further reflection on a third, the ambivalent and often contested posture

Christianity has so often adopted toward physical, material reality. Can we find ourselves *at home with God* here, in the world of God's creation? What about all the other animals of the same Creator? Does God make a home with them as well? These questions may spring from ancient claims about incarnation yet take on the texture of a crisis with every new ominous warning about global climate change.

Each of these prospects for further theological housework evokes the need for an *active* Christian witness: to resist imperial forces of domination; to engage with newly forming, often unrecognizable modes of faith community; and to champion ecological sustainability and flourishing. The depth of that need to act can quite easily eclipse the equally vital practice of theological reflection, perhaps replicating the well-worn dichotomy between theory and practice. For some, that dichotomy calls into question the relevance of theological belief itself in a world that demands actors and not just believers. Christian traditions, however, have always and in various ways affirmed the integral function of believing for the life of faith, which does not necessarily require intellectual acumen or cognitive assent. Some observations about what belief does entail and why it still matters rounds out these concluding prospects and returns us to where this book began, on a road toward a village called Emmaus. That Eucharistic story toward the end of Luke's gospel account prompts more than liturgical piety alone; it depicts the fragility of belief, its irreducibly social character, and *therefore*, its mission-driven focus. Belief itself, including Christian believing, never floats free from a commitment to act. The content of that commitment today will depend in large measure on addressing the theological housework that remains as this book concludes.

SEXUALLY AT HOME IN OUR BODIES

Some readers, perhaps especially LGBT ones, will wonder why sexual intimacy played such a minor role in this book. In my view, sex is both over- and underrated as a source for theological reflection. More than a few books have appeared over the years that extol the pleasures of the body but far fewer explore the theological implications of transgressing socially mandated parameters for experiencing and expressing those pleasures. Queer theory can help tease out those implications for Christian witness more broadly, one approach to which I have tried to outline in these pages.

Giving postcolonial theorizing only a cameo appearance in this approach highlights one of the major areas of theological housework still remaining to address, especially for the sake of finding ourselves sexually at home in our variously gendered bodies.

Western approaches to both sexuality and gender—not to mention to society itself and its relation to religion—present only one facet of the complex human prism through which to view the dynamics of God's household. Not only the theological proposals I have tried to construct here but also the very questions that generated those proposals look and sound different, and sometimes dramatically so, in cultural contexts outside the North Atlantic. We could note the same thing about religious multiplicity on this planet and the increasing opportunities, if not the urgency for deep interreligious conversation and cooperation. Christians have much to learn from other religious traditions, not only about how we might think theologically and spiritually about sexuality and gender, but also about faith itself in relation to emerging postcolonial sensibilities. The quest to be at home in our own bodies, in other words, transpires within and is molded by complex sociopolitical relationships.[1]

More than a few theologians in recent years have been entreating Christians to attend carefully to the perduring mark of empire on that wider social context, not just historically but also today. The composition of the gospel accounts and the emergence of conciliar creeds mark but two among many moments of imperial influence on the shape of Christian faith. Walter Wink read the Christian Testament through that very lens in his attempt to bring the Gospel to bear on the complexities of contemporary geopolitical systems of power. He referred to that kind of imperial power as the "Domination System" and described it like this:

> This overarching network of Powers is . . . characterized by unjust economic relations, oppressive political relations, biased race relations, patriarchal gender relations, hierarchical power relations, and the use of violence to maintain them all, . . . from the ancient Near Eastern states to the Pax Romana, to feudal Europe, to communist state capitalism, to modern market capitalism.

---

1. Michael Sepidoza Campos, for example, offers an insightful analysis of the particular ways gender is mapped to sexual affinities in the Philippines that differ significantly from Western expectations ("The *Baklà*: Gendered Religious Performance in Filipino Cultural Spaces," in Boisvert and Johnson, *Queer Religion*, 167–92).

Notice Wink's insistence on linking all of those modes of dominating power into a single system. Diarmuid O'Murchu noticed this and proposed a way to read the gospel accounts as a sustained critique and dismantling of the entire system for the sake of thriving life for all. O'Murchu included that quotation from Wink to frame his own interpretive approach to modern nationalism and its twin expression, patriotism. O'Murchu depicts the revolutionary posture of Jesus toward such dominating systems as Christianity's "dangerous memory," one that has been obscured by the Church's entanglements with empire.[2]

Postcolonial forms of analysis can shed important light on the parochialism of nation-states, a light that might also shine a bit closer to home. A queer theology for Christian witness will necessarily need to draw from resources well beyond those typically delineated by American or North Atlantic or Western approaches. I have, for example, mostly imagined "queer home economists" as undertaking recognizably Christian forms of ministry. Yet those queerly called to this divine housework appreciate how far the Household of God extends beyond the usual boundaries of self-identified Christian congregations. On a planet that has so dramatically shrunk, not least through telecommunications technologies and the ubiquity of the Internet, clearly delineated national and religious borders belong to a rapidly changing world. Even more, the older world has been mostly left behind entirely by a whole generation of the cyber-savvy denizens of virtual realities who pay no attention whatsoever to the contrivances of modern Western classification schemes to which queer theorists devote so much of their critical gaze. To gain any traction in the forms of Christian ministry they might inspire, the theological proposals I have offered here will necessarily transform notions of God's household with visions of a borderless global village. That too may sound a bit quaint, perhaps even more so than "household."

Breaking free from quaintness does not always rise to the level of theological virtue, but it might in at least one respect. Traditional congregational ministry today still relies not merely on modern sensibilities but medieval ones, even in self-styled "progressive" communities. While some find those traditional patterns comforting, and perhaps a source of critiquing modern cultural dynamics, the so-called "mainline" congregations today tend to suffer from insularity, whether actual or only perceived. In response, those

---

2. O'Murchu, *Christianity's Dangerous Memory*, 6–7.

trying to forge a path for "emergent Christianity" pursue a variety of models for Christian community and often by pointing toward or actually inhabiting the online world of social media. This digital world signals further unfinished theological housework for a number of reasons, not least the challenge to make a better home with others in a world being rendered virtual.

VIRTUALLY AT HOME WITH OTHERS

The roles and responsibilities of ordained clergy in many faith communities today harken back to a time when the local parish church sat at the center of every European village and many New England towns as well; such geographical placement was certainly not accidental. That centralized locale symbolized the role religion played to integrate all the various aspects of personal, social, cultural, and economic life into a single fabric of meaning. What stands at the center of today's global village? Not a church building, but millions of desktop monitors and handheld smartphones. Do digital networks now provide the integrative function that religion once did? If so, what does this mean for Christian witness? Where can queerly good news sneak its way into all the fragmented clamor of cultural noise? How would such a gospel proclamation inspire a homeward hope, the hope of being at home with others?

I remain convinced of the centrality of hope in the peculiar faith of Christians, yet I wonder how many find its energies jaded, or how many can repeat without any irony the line from then presidential candidate Bill Clinton: "I still believe in a place called Hope."[3] The distinction between hope and optimism matters but perhaps less so now in a culture drenched in both satire and irony and populated by quickly crafted online "memes." Consider "The Daily Show with Jon Stewart" on the cable television network Comedy Central. The show presents a humorous parody of mainstream television news media, which it achieves with the satirical tone it adopts toward reporting the day's news. A surprising number of young adults rank the "The Daily Show" among their top sources for news and current events.[4] Turning to a

---

3. Clinton used that phrase at the conclusion of his speech at the Democratic National Convention in 1992 to evoke simultaneously the name of his hometown in Arkansas and his vision for the United States (Bill Clinton, *My Life* [New York: Alfred A. Knopf, 2004], 421).

4. Associated Press, "A New Model for News: Studying the Deep Structure of Young-Adult News Consumption," June 2008 (*http://www.ap.org*).

comedy show for news surely makes mainstream news media seem at least ironic if not actually a satire of itself.

That one television show sits at the tip of a much larger iceberg of irony in contemporary Western society. Both civic and religious institutions now function mostly as props on the stage of public discourse to support ideologies and policies that very few find credible. Those who do pontificate with any gravity rather quickly (often the same day) provide fodder for jest and parody in late-night television talk shows and, even more rapidly, in Facebook posts and Twitter tweets. Whether an archbishop or a prime minister speaks on that stage, one expects at any moment that Toto will pull back the curtain to reveal, not the mighty Wizard of Oz, but a simple con artist. More than a few consider this old news. To speak of "institutional authorities" today sounds old-fashioned if not oxymoronic in a world where brick-and-mortar has crumbled into pixels. Others find this cultural moment alarming and, like Dorothy with Toto at her side, want only to go back home to a simpler world populated with authorities one could trust.

Today, however, whatever else "home" might mean, it usually has the word "page" appended to it. Home can change as easily and quickly as registering a new URL and creating whatever kind of homey website space one wishes. No one needs magical ruby slippers to go home; just click a mouse. What counts and what matters have been rendered virtual, which in the great irony of our day makes them real—accessible, yes, but also malleable, fluid, pliable, and therefore subject to perpetual reconstruction and reconfiguration. All of this flies well under the radar of anything most Christians might still want to call the "institutional church." Even brief visits online to the blogosphere suggests that it will soon make little if any sense to speak of *institutional* Christianity at all. With few exceptions, the only forms of institutionalization left today not riddled with irony are prisons and psychiatric hospitals.

Whatever religion generally or Christianity in particular may mean no longer requires any official imprimatur from anyone claiming to represent it. At best, official texts and institutional pronouncements constitute just one possible source among many for discerning the meaning and import of Christian faith. Increasingly, that source pales in comparison to what people find online, or in the labyrinthine "wikipediazation" of religion and spirituality. Christianity, in other words, now churns through the process of being hyperlinked, multicircuited, networked, and made instantly contestable in a planetary community.[5] French academics started writing modernity's epitaph as early as the 1960s; but they were premature. Today's online cyber-moment signals the end of modern Western culture, which had relied on the printed page for its taxonomic categorization, classification, and commodification of social, cultural, and political interactions, including those in and among religious institutions. Queer home economists face not only a new world but also a smaller, faster, and deeply contested one.

The "end" of modernity, however, need not spell disaster. For two millennia, Christian communities have treated world-ending moments with as much if not more hope than despair. What does this present cyber-induced ending portend? Queerly enough, this shrinking planet has only broadened what it contains, something like the phone-booth of science fiction character Dr. Who, which is bigger on the inside than on the outside. Or perhaps more traditionally like the divine "house" Jesus describes in John's gospel, which contains many "mansions" (John 14:2, KJV). The more we learn about this planet, its many cultures and perspectives, its astonishing ecosystems and intricately interdependent environments—all of which floods directly into our living rooms, classrooms, and coffeehouses through cables, antennae, and satellites—the bigger and more diverse this planetary home becomes. Much of that diversity, of course, has now been irretrievably lost, whether cultures and languages in the mechanisms of Western (neo)colonialism or the biodiversity of species and habitats in the relentless forces of environmental degradation. Nonetheless, only the most resolutely parochial among us can fail to notice the vexing challenges and wildly rich opportunities presented by the socioreligious diversity of the worldwide human family.

"Wherever truth may be found," Augustine insisted, it belongs to God.[6] Few have wanted to believe him or to entertain the implications of his claim. Queer home economists will take that claim as seriously as they can and search for truth wherever it may pop up and however it might appear. That alone marks a good deal of the theological housework still left to address. Christianity's own "backyard" may well brim over with wonderfully and

---

5. As early as 1997, Graham Ward wrote incisively on the revolutionary shifts catalyzed by a cyberworld. That world has greatly expanded and intensified since then, yet his theological analysis of it still proves useful. See his introduction in *The Postmodern God: A Theological Reader*, ed. Graham Ward (Malden, MA: Blackwell Publishers, 1997), xv–xlvii.

6. Augustine, *On Christian Doctrine*, ed. Philip Schaff, Nicene and Post-Nicene Fathers, Series 1, Vol. 2 (Grand Rapids, MI: Christian Classics Ethereal Library), 1230.

wildly queer theological resources for Christian witness, but still more waits beyond our backyard fence in field after field of fruitful religious and spiritual treasures.

Taking Augustine's claim to heart, every queer home economist should expect surprises: divine reality cannot be contained; the risen Jesus disappears before we can grab hold of him; the Spirit blows where it wills; divine eroticism spills over not only the walls of church buildings but also every attempt we make to speak that breach. Queer energy easily dissolves neatly organized systems, synods, and sermons like pinches of salt in a pot of boiling water. Some will fret over those moments; others will see in them the beginning of a delectable stew. In either case, the ephemeral character of digital homemaking might draw our attention to a more ancient quandary still spurring our theological housework today: What difference does the material world make in our quest to be at home with God?

ECOLOGICALLY AT HOME WITH GOD

The word "ecology," just like the word "economy," begins with the Greek word *oikos*, which means "house." In that sense, ecologists and economists alike devote their attention to homemaking, the former with reference to the vast and intricately woven network of ecosystems, and the latter concerning the countless forms of relational exchange, not least of course those dealing with money. Theologians may ponder whether and how God makes a home with us in this material world, but in the meantime humanity more generally seems committed to trashing it, through environmental destruction or market-driven greed or the entanglements of both. The severity of today's ecological/economic crisis ought to sit at the top of any list of unfinished theological housework. After all, even the best strategies for dismantling racism, undoing male privilege, and liberating categorical sexual identities matter little without a habitable planet on which to enjoy the benefits of social transformation. This challenge presents an unprecedented opportunity to discern deeper interconnections among all the concerns that otherwise appear distinct and unrelated, from race and ethnicity to sexuality and gender. Bringing all of those concerns together under the same roof, as it were, likely charts the only sustainable path forward toward an economically flourishing ecosystem for all. Doing so would assuredly qualify as queer in the midst of modernity's still unrelenting penchant for categorical divisions.

The diversity of today's Christian landscape still bears the marks of a broad and painful breach few seem able to bridge. Liberal Protestants, often referred to as "mainline" Christians, continue to locate the primary significance of their faith in social ethics, derived largely from the teachings of the historical Jesus, for the sake of remaking and reshaping society. Christian fundamentalists (and many Evangelicals) continue to stress the significance of personal conversion and the forgiveness of sins for the sake of eternal life with God beyond the grave. In short and more crudely, the breach delineates two broad Christian options from which to choose: a remade earth *or* a new heaven.[7]

Queer home economists reject most binary choices and especially the one marking today's Christian breach. Rather than choosing either earthly or heavenly aspirations, a queer theology for Christian witness unites them in the human body—the body of Jesus, to be sure, and also and because of that, our bodies as well, and even more, the countless bodies of other-than-human creatures of the same God.[8] Theologians throughout Christian history have tried to gesture toward this profound sense of union, this otherwise odd and disruptive insistence on joining earth to heaven. The queerly peculiar character of this claim, however, exerts considerable pressure toward the more familiar and therefore comfortable dichotomies that tend especially to infect modern Western Christianity.

Queer home economists might begin to bridge the breach between earthy materiality and heavenly spirituality with a rather modest practice: embodying compassion toward other-than-human animals. This likely seems far *too* modest given the severity of the breach and the crisis it has spawned, yet it nonetheless can mark a profound beginning as such compassion tends to erode the customary boundaries that separate humanity from the rest of creation. Those boundaries have most often been drawn by appealing to the *imago Dei*, the image of God, in which humans have been made, an image that sets us apart from all other creatures. Theological history, however, exhibits little if any consensus on what exactly that image entails. Potential candidates populate a broad map indeed. Guunlaugur Jonsson's survey

---

7. Brian D. McLaren is among those who have tried to repair that breach yet continues to be classified together with emergent "progressives" (see his *A Generous Orthodoxy* [Grand Rapids, MI: Zondervan, 2004]).

8. This felicitous phrase comes from Andrew Linzey's compelling attempts to develop a more robust theology of creation in *Creatures of the Same God: Explorations in Animal Theology* (Brooklyn, NY: Lantern Books, 2007).

of those possibilities, which he restricted to the period between 1882 and 1982, ranges from "mental endowment" and self-awareness to physical morphology, upright stance, and sexual differentiation.[9] Curiously and rather queerly, that range of possible options continues to shrink. Today, biologists and ethologists alike find many if not most mammals sharing with humans some key components for rational thinking, including problem solving and the use of tools, as well as a previously unimagined affective life replete with experiences of joy, envy, love, grief, companionship, and fear.[10]

Adopting as a *spiritual* practice, this *material* posture of compassion toward other-than-human animals creates a frame for significant theological housework. This frame could, for example, help to illumine not only the conceptual but especially the bodily connections that bring all of our concerns over race, ethnicity, sexuality, and gender together, under one roof, in the one Household of God. The expansive, capacious character of that work in turn deepens what "Church" might still portend and offer in a twenty-first century world, not least its capacity to inspire belief, or perhaps to inspire more simply the desire to believe *in* Church once again.

HOMEMAKING AFTER EMMAUS

The longing to be at home—in our bodies and among others and with God—animates Christianity's peculiar faith even as it seems perpetually beyond our ability to grasp, let alone fulfill. More than a few theologians in Christian history express a similar vexation, not as a thwarting of a homeward hope but as a source of hope's renewal. They do this, as queer home economists realize, to caution against idolatry, or mistaking interim homemaking efforts for what still lies beyond that horizon over which we cannot presently see. More simply, Christian faith demands ongoing conversion, the willingness to relax our grip on what we now possess for the sake of what we have yet to imagine. This will sound rather queer in communities where

---

9. Quoted in Andrew Linzey, *Why Animal Suffering Matters: Philosophy, Theology, and Practical Ethics* (Oxford: Oxford University Press, 2009), 28.

10. Among the many examples, see Temple Grandin, *Animals Make Us Human: Creating the Best Life for Animals* (Boston: Houghton Mifflin Harcourt, 2009); Vilmos Csányi, *If Dogs Could Talk: Exploring the Canine Mind*, trans. Richard E. Quandt (New York: Farrar, Straus and Giroux, 2000); Jeffrey Moussaieff Masson and Susan McCarthy, *When Elephants Weep: The Emotional Lives of Animals* (New York: Delacorte Press, 1995); and, for the results of the first MRI studies of canine brains in conscious dogs, Gregory Berns, *How Dogs Love Us: A Neuroscientist and His Adopted Dog Decode the Canine Brain* (New York: Houghton Mifflin Harcourt, 2013).

conversion entails not a looser but a tighter hold on belief, yet it is precisely the queerly elusive character of belief itself that sits at the heart of Christian spiritual practice.

The believing home I was given and the one I made in a neatly packaged world of Evangelical Christian faith unraveled as an undergraduate. To my surprise, another world rose up from those childhood fragments, a world far richer than I could have imagined at the time. That pattern of death and rebirth shaped Christianity's peculiar faith from the very beginning. I have tried to sketch some of that world's contours in this book with a rather modest hope: that my attempt might inspire others to travel still farther along this queer theological road. We build this road while we travel on it, which Christians have done ever since startled disciples left a village called Emmaus bearing witness to a resilient, irrepressible love, a love stronger than even death (Luke 24:34–35).

In my experience, building and traveling this theological road usually intensifies the vexations of relating academic theory (of any kind, queer or not) to the lived realities of people on the street or in the pew. Some will want to pave the road and map its destination before embarking on it at all. Others grow impatient with the plodding deliberations of theorists and are eager to blaze trails in uncharted terrain. I remain convinced that theorizing shapes every one of the countless decisions all of us make every day. At its best, theory makes trail-blazing more effective. But can "queer theory" help us do that work in Christian faith communities? Can retrieving, speaking, and doing Christianity's inherent queerness make a constructive difference, not only for the institutional church but even more for a world of homeless hearts?

For some, the word "queer" itself suffices to dismiss the theology in these pages as heretical if not destructive to Christian witness; this book is just too queer, it is queer beyond belief. Others will read it and wish that its queerness went much farther still, perhaps beyond belief itself. The time has come to stop worrying about what anyone believes, they might say, and get on with the business of changing the world.

Clergy, seminarians, and lay people alike confront these questions repeatedly in explorations of Christianity's peculiar faith traditions. Even brief exposure to the instability of queer theory and the complexities of Christian history (of which there are many) stirs up a desire to lay hold of something, anything to secure a foundation for this work. I sympathize with that yearning, but neither the Bible nor subsequent theological traditions will deliver that stable "thing." When that realization dawns, some version of this question nearly always arises: Why then try to believe anything at all about God, Jesus, or ourselves if absolutely everything sloshes around in a big vat of ambiguity? That question infuses all the other tasks still remaining on the list of queer theological housework, the question of belief itself. Here I bring this book to a close with my own approach to why believing and belief still matter for our homemaking—why, that is, giving our hearts to a homeward journey matters.

People of course believe all sorts of things, with or without sufficient reason. Some of the things Christians believed eighteen or even two centuries ago seem preposterous to Christians today. Some things that Christians no longer believe today would seem scandalous to Christians in even recent history, let alone the originators of early Christian orthodoxy. Christians have always devoted time and energy to which beliefs among that complex mix they ought properly to adopt, which to discard, and which ones could "imperil one's immortal soul."[11] Few Christians, by contrast, spend much time on what belief entails, why we believe something at all, and how it matters.

In the church of my youth, believing mattered—a lot. What one believed (about God, Jesus, and humanity) made all the difference for one's eternal fate. Needless to say, that can create more than a little anxiety. Am I believing the right things? Do I have enough belief? What if my belief wavers? That kind of scrupulosity can make a lasting impression. Even now, when I no longer believe those things about belief, I still wonder occasionally whether I should. I may no longer assign dictatorial control to belief but I still believe in its constructive power.

Charles Sanders Peirce, the originating force behind American pragmatism in philosophical circles, understood beliefs of any kind, from the mundane to the sublime, as behavioral habits or patterns of conduct.[12] A belief, in other words, is something on which I am willing to act. I believe sufficiently in gravity, for example, to watch my step near a cliff. My belief

---

11. While this concern percolates in a number of different forms in various eras of Christian history, the creedal statement attributed to Athanasius from the fourth century—and included in the "Historical Documents" section of the 1979 Book of Common Prayer—articulates this source of anxiety succinctly: "Whosoever will be saved, before all things it is necessary that he hold the Catholic Faith." Apart from that faith, we "perish everlastingly" (Book of Common Prayer, 864).

12. See John K. Sheriff, *Charles Peirce's Guess at the Riddle: Grounds for Human Significance* (Bloomington: University of Indiana Press, 1994), 48–50.

in the love of a good friend leads me to trust that person with confidential information. I believe capital punishment is morally wrong, which urges me to show up at death penalty protest rallies or write to my elected government officials. In each of those examples the belief in question came from a different kind of source yet Peirce's observation still holds: I believe something to the degree that it shapes my conduct of life.

This approach to belief reorients rather dramatically the kind of theological believing I first learned as a child. Believing matters, but not because God maintains a checklist of correct ideas and monitors our creedal conformity. It matters because what we believe about a whole range of topics, from science, friends, and politics, to the Bible, history, and God will shape how we live, the communities we form, and the actions we take. This account of belief shows up in nearly every story about religious conversion. Changing one's beliefs about the world alters how one lives, whether subtly, dramatically, temporarily, or permanently. The obverse pertains with equal force: how I live, with whom, and to what purpose will shape what I believe, or that to which I deem worthy enough to give my heart. Belief makes a difference.

I believe it matters what people believe about God. The difference between believing in a God who merely tolerates me and the God who desires me like a lover desiring the beloved makes a difference, not only in my own self-perception but also how I treat all those others who are equally beloved creatures of an erotically passionate God. The difference may not appear all at once (I still have to remind myself to see a desired creature when I look in a mirror), but it does make a difference over time.

In the ministries they undertake, queer home economists will pay close attention to Peirce's notion of beliefs as habits. As nearly everyone knows, old habits are hard to break; good ones are difficult to cultivate. That certainly rings true in theological habits of belief, but often with even greater effect. Beliefs about God are not just any kind of belief. They shape entire worldviews, support institutional machinery, give rise to careers with paychecks and pension plans, and more generally "make sense" of countless daily decisions about how people live, work, love, and play. Calling any of those beliefs into question can threaten that whole socioreligious superstructure, right down to its foundation.

I once heard Frank Griswold talk about this very challenge. As the former presiding bishop of the Episcopal Church, during whose tenure the diocese of New Hampshire elected Gene Robinson as their bishop, Griswold found himself trying to address and manage the threats of schism erupting throughout the worldwide Anglican Communion. In the course of many conversations and heated debates, he came to realize that sound biblical exegesis alone will not resolve the issue of "homosexuality." Rather than changing one's mind about biblical interpretation, accepting the election of Gene Robinson would mean for some (and probably quite a few) changing one's entire worldview.

Griswold made no mention of "queer theory" in his observations, but he invoked queer theory's insights. Controversies over "homosexuality" have little if anything to do with whether people love each other. Those controversies instead tap into how all of us organize our perceptions of reality into a meaningful picture, how we categorize and classify both people and things, and especially how deeply we plant the roots of those perceptions into a neatly ordered gendered system. For people of faith, that "system" intertwines with everything we believe about God.

Griswold just happens to be the bishop who ordained me in 1988, when he served as the bishop of the Episcopal diocese of Chicago. During my brief time under his episcopal authority, I heard him say often that the words "conversation" and "conversion" come from the same linguistic root. In saying this, he posed a challenge to everyone, regardless of one's position or opinion on anything. Engaging in genuine conversation leaves one vulnerable to conversion, to changing one's mind and adopting new beliefs or transformed versions of old ones, and with that transformation comes a brand new world. I heard Gene Robinson himself make a similar observation by citing the experience of Chuck Yeager, the first pilot officially to break the sound barrier. As Yeager described it, his jet shook the hardest right before breaking that barrier, exactly what happens to worldviews on the brink of change.

I bring these personal anecdotes and reminiscences into these concluding prospects for a theological reason, just as I also did throughout this book. Marcella Althaus-Reid articulated that reason quite succinctly. Modern institutional Christianity, she wrote, has separated theology from the theologian.[13] Acquiescing to modernity's standards for rational objectivity, the church mostly embraced a disembodied theology, a theology detached from all the quirks and foibles, all the exaltations and triumphs that make

---

13. Althaus-Reid, *Queer God*, 8.

theologians human, not least among them our sexually gendered peculiarities. This detachment, Althaus-Reid firmly believed, leads only to theological disaster for a tradition constructed on claims for divine incarnation. Those claims invite us to see and hear this: when God chooses to speak, God does so with bodies. Restoring that ancient insight to contemporary Christian witness can begin both modestly and profoundly with what Althaus-Reid urged theologians to do: write and speak autobiographically.[14] Christian Wiman expressed the same thing but with more urgency for the sake of our beliefs:

> There is no clean intellectual coherence, no abstract ultimate meaning to be found, and if this is not recognized, then the compulsion to find such certainty becomes its own punishment. This realization is not the end of theology, but the beginning of it: trust no theory, no religious history or creed, in which the author's personal faith is not actively at risk.[15]

Under the tutelage of both Althaus-Reid and Wiman, I bring Frank Griswold into these concluding prospects, not only for his insights into the dynamics of conversion, but even more for how his Chicago episcopacy intersected with what became my own most insightful location for Christian witness: holy orders to preside at the Eucharistic table. Frank ordained me as a priest knowing full well—because I told him—that he was ordaining a gay man. This matters not only for LGBT inclusion, but also and even more for why belief itself matters.

I can stand at the Eucharistic table and dare to speak words attributed to Jesus and hallowed by centuries of Christian tradition for one singularly important reason: others believe I can. This defines not only the inner logic of ordination but also of belief itself. Left on my own at that table, my belief would falter; surrounded by other equally hungry people eager to find a home in their own bodies, among others, and with God, I believe anew. I believe not merely in God abstractly at that table, but the particular God who desires communion with us, and indeed with the whole creation. This also helps to explain the ancient ecclesial prohibition against celebrating at that table alone; a "valid" Eucharist requires at least two people, and "valid" I take to mean in any way meaningful and intelligible.

---

14. Ibid.

15. Wiman, *My Bright Abyss*, 75.

To be clear, standing at the table with others does not make Christianity's peculiar faith more comfortable. To the contrary, seeing myself as desired and beloved in the company of other desirable beloveds makes me profoundly *un*comfortable. The deeper that belief nestles into my bones and muscles, and indeed my heart, the more I feel compelled to change how I live. At the very least, I cannot live for myself alone—and "cannot" does not mean "may not" here. It means more than ethical obligation. It means, theologically and spiritually, that all the countless decisions I make every day about how I live derive from what I believe at that table and about that table.

A queer theology for Christian witness does indeed pose a threat to tightly constructed worldviews; it shakes the institutional church on the edge of breaking a divine sound barrier. But this is not new, nor should it come as a surprise. I cannot imagine first-century evangelists bothering to write anything at all if they had not believed that Jesus had unraveled their social and religious worlds. Why would the earliest Christian communities risk turning the world upside down with dangerous economics and peculiar households if the Spirit had not overturned their own world first? Were all the martyrs of the first three centuries of Christian traditions mentally ill? Were medieval mystics merely suffering from deeply ingrained psychoses? Perhaps, but they might have had a life-changing encounter with the fathomless mystery of God, an encounter that reordered their worlds. That would surely suffice to drive anyone mad or at least to appear terribly queer. It drove some of them into the deserts of simplicity, others into erotic ecstasies, and still others into risky postures that challenged prevailing institutional authorities. What does their witness to Christianity's peculiar faith contribute to my own? Or rather, what does it contribute to the faith I share with others gathered around the table?

That ancient witness means at least this much: Christians still live our faith "after Emmaus." Recalling Luke's iconic story, Christians believe we encounter the risen Christ in a shared meal, no matter how tantalizingly glorious or teasingly brief that encounter might be. That moment of real presence then sends us out, as Michelangelo might describe it, to "live and love in God's peculiar light."[16] That moment inspires us to "set the world

---

16. Bliss Carman, et al., eds., *The World's Best Poetry*, Vol. II (Philadelphia: John D. Morris & Co., 1904), 329.

on fire," as Catherine of Siena imagined we would just by being the peculiar people God calls us to be.[17] That moment at the table sets us on fire with the light of love, sufficiently aflame to turn the world upside down. We set out from the table to transform a world full of homeless hearts living in so many homeless spaces. And we do all this, just as the first disciples did, without any blueprints or roadmaps, without any carefully designed strategies or meticulously crafted flowcharts. They did all this, as Luke tried to show, even without the physical presence of the one who first inspired them. What we do have, also like those first disciples, is the Holy Spirit.

The Holy Spirit queerly calls naturally odd people of a wildly creative God and knits them together into perversely Pentecostal communities. There we encounter the erotically social character of God in a ritually aroused life of communion, a life that points continually to an eternally queer horizon over which we cannot presently see but because of which we find the courage to share in the vulnerability of trust. This is the peculiar faith of Christians, which I could not believe apart from all the others who find themselves strangely drawn to the Table. The uncanny and ineluctable desire that draws us together is the same desire sufficient to turn even the modern Western world upside down. Responding to that desire, in all the myriad forms that response can take, bears witness to its source. In the end as in the beginning, that witness shimmers with an enduring hope: God's own desire shall draw the whole creation home.

---

17. Quoted in Thomas Dubay, *Deep Conversion / Deep Prayer* (San Francisco, CA: Ignatius Press, 2006), 63.

Reading from Here to Queer

"*Q*ueer" rarely appears on anyone's list of aesthetically pleasing words. I made that understated observation in the preface to this book to acknowledge the disruptive and disturbing character of the word "queer." More than a few lesbian, gay, bisexual, and transgender people find that word troubling. Many more Christians (LGBT-identified or not) would object to associating that word with theology and perhaps consider it scandalous to do so; I find it insightful and invigorating. My aim with this book has been to suggest and illustrate how Christian faith itself qualifies as queer—odd, strange, unusual, and thoroughly peculiar—and further, how this faith calls Christians themselves to live as peculiar people in the world.

LGBT-related sensibilities spark this approach to Christian theology, but it certainly does not belong to LGBT-identified people alone. I am convinced that the queerness of Christianity carries the potential to renew the whole Church and refresh Christian witness to the Gospel in socially transformative ways. I am also aware that many if not most Christian communities will find this kind of theological reflection unsettling, yet I do hope it will spark lively and prayerful conversation. Theology of any kind, queer or not, ought to serve the spiritual formation of a faith community rather than remaining only in a book. Indeed, the most compelling and effective theology emerges from ongoing communal engagement.

To facilitate and nurture shared theological reflection, this appendix provides a brief, annotated list of books for both individuals and groups interested in reading from "here to queer." I mean, ways to read, think, and converse beyond the generally expected approaches to Christian faith and theology that one typically encounters in today's churches. I do *not* mean that everything about those common theological patterns (signified by "here") ought to be rejected in favor of the new or startling (signified by "queer"). I would invite instead a movement from one to the other, from here to queer and back again, as a way to enrich and deepen our exploration of Christianity's peculiar faith. This process of *re*reading matters for many reasons, not least my conviction that some of the queerest aspects of Christian theology are actually the oldest, not the newest, and that some of today's most familiar theological rhythms are modern innovations.

This reading list is clearly not comprehensive. The books annotated here are written by some of the theologians I have consulted the most in my own work or who have played a particularly important role in the development of this book. I also find their work to be suitable for a broad audience of both specialist and novice alike. I organized the books into groups based broadly on topic, whether Bible, theology, church, or LGBT-related issues. In queer fashion, of course, these categorical classifications tend to blur and dissolve, but they may help to focus reflection and conversation toward particular areas of passionate interest. Overall, I hope these books, and indeed *this* book, will inspire or renew hope itself and become occasions for a shared encounter with the infinite mystery of God, which theology has always sought to catalyze.

FROM BIBLE TO SCRIPTURE

Fewer topics have occupied and exercised Christian faith communities in the United States more than the Bible. From the institution of slavery and women's rights in the nineteenth century, to economics, race relations, and sexual ethics in the twentieth, the Bible has been used and interpreted in countless and often contradictory ways. Why and how do we read those ancient and sacred texts today? Could we adopt a more proactive engagement with those texts and "make Scripture" from them?

- Dale Martin's collection of essays in *Sex and the Single Savior: Gender and Sexuality in Biblical Interpretation* (2006) offers a way to read the Bible well beyond questions of gender and sexuality. His introductory and concluding essays, from which the notion of "making Scripture" comes, would certainly generate a lively conversation in faith communities about multiple meanings for the same biblical text. His shorter book, *Pedagogy of the Bible: An Analysis and Proposal* (2008) focuses on biblical studies in seminaries but is quite useful for faith communities more generally, especially for his illustrations of the historically varied approaches to interpreting the Bible.

- *Take Back the Word: A Queer Reading of the Bible* (2000, edited by Robert E. Goss and Mona West) is a collection of essays by scholars and pastors who read biblical texts through their own sexually gendered contexts, and in ways that help to open the interpretive possibilities for "making Scripture" from those texts today. These essays move well beyond "apologetic" approaches to the Bible and illustrate a far more proactive appropriation of those texts for our lives of faith.

- The most common approaches to biblical interpretation in the modern West would have seemed quite strange to our ancestors in faith, whether just three or eighteen centuries ago. Pondering how they read the Bible can shed new light on our own strategies for reading, and John L. Thornton can guide us in that work with *Reading the Bible with Dead People: What You Can Learn from the History of Exegesis That You Can't Learn from Exegesis Alone* (2007).

- Every North Atlantic Christian should read Musa Dube's *Postcolonial Feminist Interpretation of the Bible* (2000). She presents an accessible and useful introduction to postcolonial theorizing and then illustrates that method in her reading of Matthew's account of the gospel. She does this to expose the neocolonial and imperial forces at work in her own African context, including in Christian churches, and with implications for how all of us read the Bible in our particular locations.

FROM CREEDS TO THEOLOGY

Like many other Christians, I grew up with an understanding of Christian faith as involving two key elements: personal conversion and agreeing with doctrines, usually expressed in creeds. I still turn to Christianity's historic creeds for indispensable insight and broad guidelines, but I also worry how often they can eclipse a more active engagement with theological reflection. Creedal statements are of course a form of theological speech, but focusing on them alone is something like abstracting a single frame from a feature-length film. Theology generally exhibits a much more dynamic character and invites our own active engagement and participation. What kind of theology would our historical traditions invite each of us to write today?

- Scott Cowdell encourages a personally transformative approach to theological reflection in *Abiding Faith: Christianity Beyond Certainty, Anxiety, and Violence* (2009). He does this in part by reading theological traditions in the light of some of modern Western society's most troubling aspects, whether in terms of consumerism or an ever-deepening sense of isolated individualism. His work contributed to my image of "home" and "homemaking" in this book and could spark provocative conversations about the relationship between church and culture.

- Mark D. Jordan's book *Telling Truths in Church: Scandal, Flesh, and Christian Speech* (2003) began as a series of lectures that addressed the unfolding sex abuse scandal in the Roman Catholic Church at the beginning of this century. This published edition can prompt approaches to theological reflection well beyond that sense of ecclesial crisis, including ways to think about embodiment, the importance of apophatic traditions in Christian history, and how we can bring our own bodily experiences into our theological speaking and living.

- My first book offers an introduction to doing theology that is rooted in creedal claims while also aiming toward a constructive appropriation of those traditions for today. I wrote *Dancing with God: Anglican Christianity and the Practice of Hope* (2005) especially for, but not by any means limited to Anglicans.

- Proactive engagements with theology for Christians in the North Atlantic need to turn frequently to non-Western sources and especially those deriving from postcolonial sensibilities. Kwok Pui-Lan presents an accessible and inspiring overview of postcolonial approaches and the breadth of options they spark, including conceptions of sexuality and gender, in *Postcolonial Imagination and Feminist Theology* (2005).

FROM INSTITUTION TO COMMUNITY

The word "church" can refer to a number of different things, whether an individual congregation, a broader collection of ecclesial bodies, or even the mystical body of Christ. Today, however, "church" usually provokes all the objections about "organized religion" that lead people to purse "spirituality" instead. Some do this without any explicit reference to Christian traditions while others are trying to remake the institutional church into a more vibrant spiritual community. The somewhat odd collection of books in this section all point toward that rich sense of community, or the kind of communion that often fuels the desire for spiritual practice apart from institutional bureaucracies. Where do we find or how do we create the kind of communal commitment to faith we seek?

- Phyllis Tickle has catalogued in numerous ways the "emergent Christianity" phenomenon, which draws from a number of mainline and Evangelical traditions. She is especially keen to analyze the various sociopolitical and cultural aspects of the modern West that have contributed to this "Great Emergence" from traditional institutional structures and toward varied forms of communal practice. Any of these would energize a book club: *The Great Emergence: How Christianity Is Changing and Why* (2008); *Emergence Christianity: What It Is, Where It Is Going, and Why It Matters* (2012); and *Embracing Emergence Christianity* (2011), a DVD with a six-session educational program.

- John D. Zizioulas writes critically and constructively about the history, theology, and liturgical practice of Eucharist in *The Eucharistic Communion and the World* (2011). He writes from an Eastern Orthodox perspective, and that alone can prompt unexpected insights for Christians steeped in Western traditions. More than this, Zizioulas draws our attention to the formation of ecclesial persons in community at the Eucharistic table as a form of countercultural witness, regardless of the particular culture in which one lives.

- The table fellowship of Jesus created community, not least among the particular twelve called as disciples. The *kind* of fellowship he initiated also matters as it shapes the character of the witness offered by those who share that meal together. Rather than institutional hierarchies, Gospel table fellowship creates what Diarmuid O'Murchu calls the "companionship of empowerment." In *Christianity's Dangerous Memory: A Rediscovery of the Revolutionary Jesus* (2011), O'Murchu traces the implications of that communal character through topics ranging from gender and economics to race and neocolonialism.

- Twenty-first-century ecological crises now demand a significant expansion of human community to include all the other-than-human creatures who share this planet with us. Andrew Linzey has devoted his entire career to the role of animals, or its lack, in Christian theology and has published numerous books and articles on the topic. *Creatures of the*

Same God: Explorations in Animal Theology (2007) is a good place to begin as he responds to the critics of his work, presents biblical rationales for a robust theological approach to animals, and outlines practical steps for Christians to take who seek to expand their sense of community to include the wider world of all of God's creatures.

FROM LGBT TO Q

What began as sodomy morphed into "homosexuality" and later emerged as lesbian, gay, and bisexual, with a still later addition of transgender phenomena. All of this continues to vex both politicians and religious leaders alike. How to think theologically and spiritually about the diversity of human sexuality and gender remains a vital concern for Christian churches today but not only for discerning the moral status of differently gendered sexual practices. Addressing this topic evokes a much wider constellation of concerns for Christian faith communities, which "queer" can help to signal in some cases. The first two books in this section provide an overview of "queer theory" and the remaining books represent some of the ways theologians have reflected that kind of theorizing in their work.

- Annamarie Jagose published one of the first introductory overviews of queer theorizing in *Queer Theory: An Introduction* (1997), which helps to situate culturally the vexing questions about sexual identity. Nikki Sullivan's *A Critical Introduction to Queer Theory* (2003) is a bit more challenging but covers a broader range of topics, including connections to race and ethnicity and the role played by economics and pop culture in constructing sexually gendered identifications.

- Martti Nissinen's *Homoeroticism in the Biblical World* (1998) belongs in this section for the accessible and engaging way she describes and analyzes how sexuality and gender were perceived in ancient Mediterranean societies. The significant and often dramatic differences between those ancient perspectives and our own lends additional texture to the critiques queer theorists make of supposedly stable identities organized around sexuality and gender. Nissinen's work also contributes key insights and strategies for biblical interpretation more broadly, especially as it helps to highlight the severity of the historical and cultural gap between the world of the biblical writers and today's global village.

- The evolution of theological thinking about gendered sexuality over the last thirty years appears in Elizabeth Stuart's *Gay and Lesbian Theologies: Repetitions with Critical Difference* (2003). She outlines the variety of approaches taken in lesbian and gay theological projects and then proposes why and how the Church now stands in need of "queering" those projects. She means to extrapolate from modes of inclusion for a select few to a clarion call for transformation for all, which she believes the inherent queerness of Christian faith can do. This book reoriented my own theological work in some important ways and offers an accessible, useful guide for congregational study.

- A growing number of theologians engaged with queer theory recognize the imperative of dealing with the complex intersections of sexuality, gender, race, ethnicity, and economics. Kelly Brown Douglas has pioneered approaches to those intersections in, for, and among African-American communities, which can and should prompt significant reassessments of Christian traditions in white communities. I would encourage reading both of these in this sequence: *Sexuality and the Black Church* (1999) and *What's Faith Got to Do with It? Black Bodies/Christian Souls* (2005).

- Patrick S. Cheng organized a helpful overview of varying approaches to LGBTQ theologizing and also proposed his own constructive approach in *Radical Love: An Introduction to Queer Theology* (2011). He also helpfully weaves critical observations concerning race and ethnicity into his analysis of sexuality and gender. More specifically, he does this with reference to Asian-American sensibilities, a truly pioneering move and an important conversation partner for the work of Kelly Brown Douglas noted above.

- Precious little consensus has appeared concerning what queer theory actually entails or how it contributes to Christian faith and theology. Susannah Cornwall outlines various approaches and raises critical questions in *Controversies in Queer Theology* (2011). Her line of questioning also applies more generally and broadly to how Christians read biblical texts and think theologically. She digs deeply into some complex academic theories yet presents the results of her research in an inviting and accessible way. This book alone would animate extended and energetic conversations in most faith communities.

When reading and discussing any of the books on this list (including the Bible!), I recommend recalling this Buddhist aphorism: "the finger is not the moon." Theology itself (including the texts of the Bible) can never fully capture but can only point toward Divine Reality, like someone on a dark and starry night pointing toward the full moon. Theologians point like that with the hope of facilitating, inspiring, or provoking an encounter with Infinite Mystery. For these reasons, among others, theology always remains imperfect and unfinished. The many loose ends and open spaces in theological projects invite the participation of those who read and engage with them, offering their own histories and perspectives to the perpetually unfolding endeavor of trying to bear transformative witness to the Source of life itself.

Given those goals and aims, I further recommend reading and discussing theological books *prayerfully*. In John's account of the Gospel, Jesus encourages his disciples to seek the guidance of the Holy Spirit for things that they cannot yet understand (John 16:13). We, too, need that guidance when we read, not only for understanding texts but also for how to navigate the complexities of a twenty-first-century world with faith, hope, and especially with love (1 Corinthians 13:13).

That textual crescendo in Paul's first letter to the Christians in Corinth could well stand as the most peculiar thing about Christian faith. After all is read, said, and done, what matters most, and really *all* that matters, is God's love, for us and for the whole creation. Reading and discussing books on theology can help us encounter that divine love; bearing witness to it can change the world.